Take Nothing for Granted in Baseball

The Harry Pulliam Story

Mark Peavey

Dead Ball Books
2018

Chapters

1. The Poor Colonels 1
2. Better off in Jail 17
3. A Big German with Enormous Hands 36
4. Too Many Mascots in Louisville 54
5. Swan Song 81
6. The Smoky City 100
7. The Baseball Wars 119
8. Anywhere but Louisville 134
9. The Quest for Peace 148
10. Nothing Comes Easy in New York City 168
11. A Little Closet under the Grandstand 179
12. I had an Audience with the Pope 191
13. I Think Mr. Pulliam has it Dead Right 201
14. A Fateful Day in September 209
15. That Man was Poor Harry Pulliam 227

Harry Pulliam

Chapter One

The Poor Colonels

*"The cold wind doth blow
And we shall have snow
Oh, what will Bill Hertz do then?
By the stove he will ponder
And sit there and wonder
If the Colonels will win in the spring,
Poor things."*

The Louisville Colonels had not always been losers; in 1891 they won the American Association League championship. But in 1892, the jump to the National League had been too much for them, and for the next few seasons, they finished twelfth in the twelve-team League. Still, the fans supported them, cheered for them, and hoped that better times lay ahead. They were a patient lot, the cranks of Louisville. It was, after all, their duty as citizens to show up for games, drink beer and yell at the umpire, just like the cranks in the eleven other cities.

The city of Louisville was named after King Louis XVI of France for his support of the Americans during the Revolutionary War. In 1890, the citizenry had been devastated by what became known as the Great Louisville Tornado, which had descended near downtown Main Street and swept all the way to the outskirts of town, destroying nearly eight hundred buildings and killing more than one hundred people. Owing to the migration of the 1850's, the populace had a high concentration of Germans and Irishmen, who worked hard to rebuild after the storm. But, as far as major league baseball was concerned, Louisville had one major problem. It may have been the largest city in Kentucky, but it was the smallest town in the National League.

The Colonels played their home games in a cozy ball park on the south side of town. Known as League Park, it had one of the smallest grandstands in the League, and when large crowds turned out to watch the Colonels play, the overflow of spectators often had to stand in the far reaches of the outfield to attend the game. League Park was, like every other ball park of the day, made almost entirely of wood, and therefore was susceptible to fire at any moment. In fact, the team's previous home, Eclipse Park, named after a semi-pro team from the 1880's, had suffered such a fate in 1892, just a few blocks away.

Prior to 1895, the greatest player in Louisville baseball history had been Pete Browning. Known affectionately to the locals as "The Gladiator," he was also sometimes called "The Louisville Slugger," a tribute not only to Browning, but also the Hillerich Bat Company, the baseball bat manufacturer located in Louisville to this day. Browning had been one of the greatest batsmen of the early years of the game, occasionally breaking the finger of a rival defender who tried to catch one of his line drives in the days before gloves and mitts were commonly used. But by 1895 the Gladiator had grown old and retired, leaving the Colonels with no superstar to build a team around.

The owners of the Louisville Base Ball Club, as they called themselves, were not particularly good judges of baseball talent. In fact, most of them were not really all that fond of the game, being more intrigued by the opportunity to make a profit than winning games. In 1891, they had signed a red-headed freckle-faced youngster to a contract. He was only eighteen-years-old, and so small the team did not have a uniform that came close to fitting him. A tailor was not in the budget, so he took the field in a jersey that looked about three sizes too big, drawing hoots of derision from the cranks.

Even so, the kid had a decent year in 1891, but slumped badly in 1892 and 1893. Eventually, the club gave up on him and traded him to the Baltimore organization. As an Oriole he found his way, and Hugh Jennings was the best player in the National League from 1894 to 1896, before injuries slowed him. Who did the Colonels get in return? They got Tim O'Rourke and Harry Taylor, two players who would no longer be in the League one year later.

Barney Dreyfuss

One of those owners, though, was different from the rest. Bernhard Dreyfuss – he preferred to be called Barney – had immigrated to the United States in the early 1880's as a teenager. Born in Freiberg, Germany, he had left the country to avoid conscription, having heard one too many frightful stories about how Jewish soldiers were treated in the German army. Arriving in Paducah, Kentucky, he found employment as a laborer in a distillery owned by his cousins. They were impressed by his intelligence and his work ethic, and soon Dreyfuss was promoted to bookkeeper. At night, he studied English, and soon mastered the language. In 1888, the distillery moved its operations to Louisville.

While suffering an illness, a physician advised Dreyfuss that he needed more fresh air and exercise. He recommended playing baseball as a means of achieving both. Soon, he was playing second base for a local amateur team. He learned to love the game, and quickly found himself organizing leagues, creating teams and scouting players to recruit.

Eventually, Dreyfuss sought to buy stock in the Louisville Base Ball Club, but the stockholders would only allow him to purchase one share. That was all he needed. One share was enough to sit in on shareholder meetings, and before long, the other owners were so impressed with his dedication and knowledge of the game that he was allowed to increase his holdings. Barney Dreyfuss had become a baseball magnate.

However, being one of the owners of the Louisville Colonels was not necessarily a lucrative endeavor. The team lost most of its games every year, causing fans to lose interest, leading to a decline in revenue from ticket sales. Declining revenue meant the club had less money to scout and sign good players, which meant more losses, more apathy, and less revenue still. It was a vicious downward spiral. In January of 1895, Dreyfuss recommended the team hire Harry Pulliam.

Harry Pulliam was a reporter and city editor for the Louisville Commercial. He was a native Kentuckian, born in the small town of Scottsville. Before being promoted to the position of city editor, he had been a sports reporter, assigned to cover the Louisville Colonels baseball team. He was a talented writer, praised for his knowledge of the game. His job required that he work long hours, which was fine, because Harry Pulliam was a workaholic.

Harry was quite popular with the locals and made friends easily. He had a calm and reassuring manner in conversation, but at the same time was energetic, and had something of a nervous nature about him, which seemed to further endear him to people. He was also well-dressed, in a very colorful way, and everything about him was in place at all times. He was easy to like, and almost everyone who knew him did like him.

Dreyfuss and Pulliam had met through their mutual interest in baseball in general, and more specifically, through their shared association with the Louisville Colonels. The two had become friends, and Dreyfuss had noticed in Harry an ability to bring people together in pursuit of a common goal in his job as city editor of the Louisville Commercial newspaper. He was organized, focused, and had the ability to prioritize and multi-task. To Dreyfuss, Harry was just the sort of man the Colonels needed.

On the evening of January 24, 1895, in a meeting held at the City Brewery, the Board of Directors voted to offer the position of financial manager of the Louisville Colonels to Harry Pulliam. He accepted and took a six month leave from his job at the newspaper.

To the Directors, one of Harry's most endearing traits was that he knew baseball inside and out. They were already familiar with him through his sports column in The Commercial. "Mr. Pulliam knew the game by heart. The umpires dreaded to have him present at the game on this account, but Mr. Pulliam could not help this, and for two years his accurate and humorous reports of the game delighted the cranks."

Harry immediately went to work. First, he began organizing the trip south to Galveston for "spring practice," as spring training was referred to at the time, scheduling exhibition games, and making plans for the opening game of the championship season. Once again, the schedule makers had not been kind to the Colonels, with only two Sunday home dates, and none on the Fourth of July. But it was no use to complain, as the League was dominated by the Eastern teams, and they looked out for themselves first and foremost. The same woes were being felt by all the Western clubs.

The Colonels arrived in Galveston the second week of March, led by Manager 'Honest John" McCloskey, a Kentucky native, born and raised in Louisville. He immediately put the team on a modest and predictable training schedule. A reporter for the Louisville Courier-Journal was in attendance:

"The Louisville players did some hard work last week. The park is four miles from the city. A game is played every afternoon between the regular team and a team composed of the remaining players. After the game Manager McCloskey starts the men ahead of him on the run, and the twenty-two men run the four miles over the track of the Houston Central railroad to the city. When they arrive at the hotel the players are taken charge of by a corps of rubbers and they are well rubbed down. Manager McCloskey says all are rapidly getting into perfect condition."

On March 10, the Colonels played their first exhibition game, an 11-9 victory over Cap Anson's Chicago Colts. 3,500 locals attended, more than the Colonels would usually draw for a home game in Louisville. Still the most influential player in the National League, Anson was nearing the end of his playing career, but planned to continue as manager of the Chicago club. His players affectionately called him "Pop." When he retired years later, the newspaper men stopped calling them the Colts and began referring to the Chicago team as the Orphans. The name stuck.

As usual, the Louisville Courier-Journal expressed optimism about the upcoming season, even as it acknowledged that the players were a bunch of no names – especially the pitchers. "If anyone imagines that McCloskey's combination of ball-tossing Colonels are doomed to tail-end honors in the National League pennant race of 1895 they are destined to run up against an able-bodied surprise."

But the Chicago Tribune, and most of the other newspapers as well, were predicting another last place finish. The only player of note, they mentioned, was Fred Pfeffer, and he was determined to get out of town as fast as he could.

Two weeks later, Harry left for Houston to meet with Manager McCloskey. They discussed the outlook for 1895, which players might and might not make the trip north for the start of the season, and ways the team could improve from the previous campaign, which had ended in last place by a large margin. Afterward, they traveled to Galveston to watch an 18-14 loss to the Colts.

A writer for The Sporting Life, though, could not help but notice that the Colts had an advantage. "McCloskey's training grounds at Houston are five miles out, and he makes the boys take shank's mare both ways over railroad ties. The Colts have it decidedly easy. Their park gate is only one hundred feet from the hotel on the beach." It wasn't fun being the worst team in the League.

Pop Anson seemed to be impressed with the Colonels nonetheless. "It won't do to underrate the Colonels," he said. "They strike me as being a lot of dashing youngsters, who may create trouble in the League ranks, and they have a vigorous and energetic manager."

When he returned to Louisville several days later, Harry opened a new business office for the club in room 810 of the

Columbia Building. It was to serve as the club's headquarters, so he arranged to have it nicely furnished and comfortable. Having settled in, he began working on preparations for the opening game at home, to be played on April 18. He wrote personal letters of invitation to the most prominent citizens of Kentucky, and many wrote back to accept. Henry S. Tyler, the mayor of Louisville and a former member of the old Louisville Red Stockings, was recruited to throw out the first ball. The city council voted to attend on opening day as a group in order to support the team.

"Extensive preparations have been made for the opening this year, and it is likely that all previous efforts will be eclipsed," reported The Sporting Life magazine. "The mayors of Louisville, New Albany and Jeffersonville will receive special invitations, as well as the governor and his staff. There will be a big parade, five bands, and Mayor Tyler of Louisville will be asked to first toss the ball over the plate at the beginning of the game."

The Pirates of Pittsburgh had reached Louisville by train the night before the opener, and were more than ready to finally play ball. "Manager Mack, of the Pittsburghs, is a tall, spare-built young man, and he is smart. He sat in the Louisville Hotel last night with a satisfied smile on his face – a smile of pleasant anticipation. 'What we will do to you people to-morrow will be a plenty,' he said to a Louisville man."

But the local fans were excited and bullish about their chances. "To-day I watched the pigeons flying about the tower over there. That's always a sign of good luck. One and then another would alight on the railing and fly off again. Whenever they do that, it's good luck for the town. I watched 'em for hours. We couldn't lose if we tried," one boasted.

When opening day finally arrived, Mayor Tyler and other city officials were escorted to the park by an electric train consisting of three cars. The parade through town may have been the biggest in the history of the city to date. The procession met at noon in front of the Louisville Hotel, where the Pirates had spent the night. A band led the way, followed by both teams riding in carriages. From the hotel, the ensemble marched down Main Street to Thirteenth, from Thirteenth to Market, then Market to First, First to Jefferson, down Jefferson to Eighth, from Eighth to Walnut, then Walnut to Fourth, on to the Gait House, and finally to League Park. At every turn crowds cheered them along the way.

The fans were so excited for the return of baseball that the grandstand was full two hours before the game was to start. When the gates opened they had rushed the field to get the best seats. But the ticket seller continued to sell tickets, and soon, the good citizens of Louisville were pushing and shoving each other in the bleachers and the grandstand, trying to establish a suitable view of the grounds. Some perched on the guard rails, and on the fences surrounding the park. Many were attending a game for the first time, and were shocked to witness the battle for seats. Harry witnessed the unfortunate scene, and took note.

Two hours later, everyone except the Pirates went home happy, having watched the home team run up the score in an 11-2 victory. Pittsburgh bounced back and won the next two, leaving town with a win of the three-game series. But the Colonels were playing good baseball, and ten days into the season they were one of eight teams tied for second place, with three wins and three losses.

By the middle of May, though, the Colonels were losing games, and losing lots of them. They started the month by losing three in a row, dropping to tenth place in the twelve-team League, on their way to Chicago to lose to the Colts in their new South Side Park. Veteran infielder Fred Pfeffer, having been caught in the off-season recruiting National League players to start a new league, left the team in disgust and announced his retirement. The punishment for his indiscretion had been an assignment to join the losers of Louisville, and he simply couldn't take it anymore. No one was sorry to see him go.

Meanwhile, some of the local amateur teams were having a much better go of it. In town ball, the Louisville Coffin Company Stars defeated the Sausage club 32-10. The star player for the Coffin Stars was one-armed pitcher Will Miller, who held the Sausages to four hits and was perfect at the plate.

The Colonels' probably could have used Will Miller. The team's Board of Directors, noting the obvious lack of quality pitching on the team, instructed Harry to find and sign the best pitchers he could, no matter the cost. Harry went on a scouting trip, but finding good pitchers was much easier said than done, and so was paying for them. He returned without any new pitchers, but he did acquire outfielder James Collins from the Boston Beaneaters in a cash deal, and he turned out to be a steal. Unfortunately, Collins was only a rental, a favor to help prop up a losing team and assist them at the gate. The Boston club retained the right to take Collins back any time they pleased.

Doubleheaders were played throughout the National League on May 30, in observance of Decoration Day. In the morning game at Union Park in Baltimore, the Colonels were thrashed by the Orioles, 18-11. After fans and players all broke for lunch, the Orioles completed the sweep with an 8-4 victory in the afternoon. After the debacle in game one, holding the Birds to eight runs in game two must have seemed like something of a moral victory to the struggling Colonels.

In 1895, the Baltimore Orioles were the best team in all of baseball. They had Hughey Jennings, the talented shortstop who had once been a Colonel, but the undisputed leader of the team was one John J. McGraw, the greatest "kicker" of them all. The term "kicking," in the 1890's, referred to players who would assault an umpire, usually verbally but often physically as well, to gain an advantage in a game. The Baltimore team was full of kickers, including stars Joe Kelley, Wilbert Robinson, and Jennings. McGraw would often start the kicking, and the others joined in, outnumbering the umpire, and in almost all cases overwhelming and intimidating him. McGraw's reputation preceded him, and the umpires, who almost always worked alone, were half whipped before the game even began.

"We hear much of the glories and durability of the old Orioles, but the truth about this team seldom has been told," wrote future National League president John Heydler years later. "They were mean, vicious, ready at any time to maim a rival player or an umpire, if it helped their cause. The things they would say to an umpire were unbelievably vile, and they broke the spirits of some fine men."

McGraw had been kicking since his first year in the League. The newspapers in the various cities around the League regularly ran stories about his mistreatment of umpires. The following appeared in the Pittsburgh Dispatch on July 5, 1892, McGraw's rookie season:

"The visitors had the nerve to blame the umpire for robbing them of the game. The fact is they didn't know what they were kicking about, because some of them were arguing for one thing and others were arguing in quite an opposite direction. McGraw used some very offensive language and was ordered out of the game, but the umpire allowed him to stay in. McGraw and (Jocko) Halligan were each fined, but the former should certainly have been sent to the bench."

In a 2-0 loss to Pittsburgh that same week, Umpire Tom McLaughlin threw McGraw out of the game in the fourth inning for back talking and intentionally interfering with first baseman Jake Beckley on a throw to first base. He also fined McGraw $35 for his efforts.

The following year, McGraw was still at it. In July of 1893, a Baltimore newspaper detailed yet another incident:

"In the fifth inning McGraw threw down his cap and bat and began to dance around the plate because (Pop) Snyder would not let him take his base when he was hit by a pitched ball. Snyder said McGraw made an effort to strike at the ball, and after warning the young short stop, the umpire fined him five dollars. This made McGraw angry, and Snyder fined him twenty dollars more and ordered him out of the game."

Predictably, "Muggsy" McGraw, as the newsmen liked to call him, had another eventful July in 1894. In a 19-9 loss to Pittsburgh on July 10, McGraw was "fined for hitting the umpire with a ball which had been returned from over the fence. McGraw claimed that it was accidental and apologized, but Mr. Lynch refused to accept the apology."

McGraw despised the moniker "Muggsy," and threatened to fight anyone who called him that to his face. Few ever did. Several years later, John McGraw and Harry Pulliam would be engaged in an epic confrontation that neither of them could scarcely have imagined in 1895.

John McGraw

While the Orioles continued to win, and McGraw continued to kick, the situation grew desperate for the Louisville Colonels. No one seemed to remember the last time they had actually won a game. The local paper, the Courier-Journal, had taken to calling them the Louisville Amateurs. The pitchers were not pitching well, the hitters were not hitting, and the fielders were committing an ungodly number of errors.

On the first of July, the weary Colonels returned home from a long road trip on the Louisville & Nashville Railroad. McCloskey immediately set out for his home on Oak Street, but Harry, ever the optimist, lingered to address the newspaper men:

"We have been playing the greatest ball in the country since we arrived at Cleveland last week. The people of Cleveland and Cincinnati say they cannot understand how it is that Louisville stands so low in the race. The team is now made up, and is in perfect working order. The Louisville public will not recognize the old Louisvilles when they see the team positioned this afternoon. They have the signs down all right, and will surprise the people. Louisville has at present the best team it ever had, and this will be proved when the people see it. The pitchers are doing the best work of any in the League circuit. We lost thirteen games by one run, and one in ten innings. The umpires have been very bad to us while we were on the Eastern trip, giving nearly every decision in favor of the Eastern clubs. The boys are all happy and enthusiastic, and, mark my words, the Louisville Club will not be in last place within ten days."

To the surprise of everyone, probably including Harry, the team did get hot and went on a winning streak, playing an entire week without a loss. Outfielder Collins, who was turning into a terrific player, led the way. This was both good news and bad, as the Boston club still held the rights to Collins for 1896, and he was already being considered as a replacement for fading Beaneater shortstop Herman Long.

Collins, however, was not shy about expressing his desire to remain a Colonel.

Yet despite the improvement on the field, the Colonels were still nine games below eleventh place St. Louis. In short order, the losing would resume, and everything would be business as usual. On July 14, they were bombed by the Brooklyn Bridegrooms, 16-3. The Courier-Journal, ever optimistic, chose to blame it on the umpire. "A man named Murray umpired the game. If (National League) President (Nick) Young has any more like him, he should keep them at home to tend to the children."

Still, they persevered, despite having to face some of the best pitchers in the League – Cy Young, Billy Rhines and Cuppy Gardner – and having to deal with a series of nagging injuries. Harry continued making road trips, looking for players other teams had missed, hoping to land championship caliber men. And, despite disappointments at the gate, the team was not losing money. In fact, it was possible they might break even or, heaven forbid, realize a small profit. Harry was watching the bottom line closely, cutting costs where he could, while trying to build a winning team in a town that wasn't large enough to support it. It was a tall task indeed.

During a break in the schedule, Louisville played exhibition games in the Illinois towns of Murphysboro and Cairo. Scheduling such games was helpful for Harry as he tried to balance the books, but it wasn't easy on the players. The various injuries needed time and rest to heal. They had no choice but to play on.

"Manager McCloskey has now the largest hospital in the League," wrote a Courier-Journal reporter. "McDermott seems to be all out of sorts. Inks is not in shape. McCreery's arm is bad; Spies is crippled; Trost is ill; Hassamaer's arm is stiff; Gettinger cannot wear a shoe; Meakim was left at Philadelphia sick, and Shugart is in bad shape. It would be justice to Shugart to let him rest, but there is no one to fill the gap in the field."

In September, the Beaneaters requested the return of Jimmy Collins. He was told to report to Boston, but refused to leave Louisville. Collins enjoyed the town, and the people of Louisville had treated him well. President Arthur Soden of Boston sent a telegram to Stucky, asking why Collins had not reported. Stucky replied that Collins had been released, and there was nothing more they could do.

After holding his frustrations in check all season, McCloskey let off some steam in the local paper. "Once started down the hill it cannot stop. It is indeed a true saying, 'a winning club can't lose, and a losing club can't win.' No mercy is shown to the poor tail-enders, and they are taught in a hundred ways that they have no right to live. They are jumped on by opposing players, they get the worst of every close decision in the umpire's stock, and the bleachers guy them gleefully both at home and abroad. The newspapers chime in, and funny paragraphs are sprung the country over."

When the season mercifully came to an end, once again, the Colonels had finished in last place, with a record even worse than the year before. Even so, thanks largely to the efforts of Harry Pulliam, the club turned a profit for the first time in six years. The last game of the season was a 13-8 win over Cleveland. The men were given the balance of their pay due for the season, fifteen days' worth. Then the Louisville Colonels disbanded for the season, bound in various directions, on various trains, to their homes in distant cities in faraway parts of the country.

"Notwithstanding all rumors to the contrary, Mr. Harry Pulliam has not been made a Colonel, and will not likely be so commissioned unless Gov. Bradley sees himself under obligations to him. Should Gov. Bradley consider that Mr. Pulliam deserves such a title, Mr. Pulliam will ask that it be conferred in another way. He will ask that every member of the Louisville Base-ball Club be commissioned a Colonel, including the financial manager, and thus he will heap vengeance upon those decriers who last season accused the Louisville players of not being Colonels, but said they were mere privates." -Louisville Courier-Journal.

In December, the annual meeting of stockholders was held at the Galt House. Perhaps just a bit too accustomed to losing, the Directors remained positive and optimistic about the future. An offer of $21,000 from an undisclosed team for several of the players was refused by vote of the Board. In preparation for 1896, it was announced that the grounds were being resodded and the grandstand painted. The Directors boasted that Louisville would have one of the top ball parks in the League when the gates opened for the first game in the spring.

At the end of the year, Harry and Barney Dreyfuss made a trip to Chicago on a Saturday night. It was suspected they intended to make a trade with Cap Anson to acquire outfielder Bill "Little Eva" Lange. President Stucky denied the rumor.

Prior to leaving, Harry had told friends he was simply going to see Anson perform on stage in "A Runaway Colt." If indeed he did attend the show, he might not have appreciated Anson's most memorable line, offered to one of his players while he was trying to avoid a woman with amorous intentions. "Don't leave me alone with her!" he shouted, "or I'll expel you from the League. Worse, I'll sell you to Louisville!"

Chapter Two

Better off in Jail

At a meeting of the Board of Directors on the evening of January 3, new business was discussed. Much of it evolved around the decision to train in the South again in the spring of 1896, with the two most likely destinations being Houston, Texas and St. Augustine, Florida. Hashed out in detail was the issue of season tickets, but not the price, rather, how large they should be. Patrons had complained that last year's version was too large and did not fit in a vest pocket. It was decided to reduce the size for the 1896 season. The Board also voted to increase the size of the bleachers, despite the fact the park had rarely been filled to capacity in 1895. Harry was in attendance, received praise and admiration for his handling of the club's financial matters, and was given charge of selling advertisements and creating scorecards.

Third baseman Collins never had reported to Boston, and in consideration of this, the Colonels were trying to make a deal to keep him longer, perhaps permanently. He insisted that he would "drive a pair of street-car mules before he will play ball in that city." The Beaneaters asked for pitcher Mike McDermott in exchange, but also wanted Louisville to throw in several thousand dollars cash. An extra several thousand dollars was something the Colonels definitely did not have. They were struggling just to have enough baseballs on hand for the games.

The next day, Collins changed his mind and signed with Boston.

Other players were trying to get out of town as well. According to a report in the Courier-Journal, Tom

McCreery, Louisville's best pitcher, had met with Pittsburgh manager Connie Mack, formerly of Milwaukee, in St. Louis, telling him he wanted to leave the Louisville team and play for the Pirates. Mack became angry, replying, "I must decline to discuss the matter with you, as you are under contract with the Louisville club."

On February 24, Pulliam, President Stucky and Vice-President Charles Dreher attended the annual League meeting in New York. The big question of the day was whether "kicking" players would be fined or removed from games. Cap Anson argued in favor of fines. "The public pays to see Duffy, Tebeau, McGraw, Doyle and others," he said, "and the spectators are the ones who suffer." Others favored suspension. The magnates were hopelessly split on the issue, so they took the easy way out and did nothing.

New rule proposals were also on the agenda. Henry Chadwick supported an amendment to the rules governing pitchers. In 1895, pitchers threw from a box outlined on the ground, with a rubber slab in the middle. There was no pitcher's mound. Noting that pitchers routinely cheated by not keeping one foot in contact with the rubber, as required, he suggested a 24-inch square frame that a pitcher must keep one foot within. This would make it easier for the umpire to spot violations that gave pitchers an unwarranted advantage. His idea made no headway.

As the season of 1896 approached, there was also much concern about how to deal with rowdyism in baseball. Rowdyism differed from kicking in that it did not involve umpires. Rowdyism included, but was not limited to, players hitting other players, calling them offensive names, intentionally spiking them and other forms of intimidation. Umpires were routinely fining players and throwing them out of games for offensive language and poor behavior. Rowdyism was on the increase, and was even spreading to the fans, who often joined in.

As always, Harry put his best effort into designing the scorecard. "The Louisville Club will issue the handsomest score cards this season that have ever been printed," he announced to the press. "Each copy will be a book of some twenty-five pages, neatly bound, with handsome lithograph cover. Besides the score card proper, on the inside, there will be half-tone pictures of all the members and officers of the club, a picture of the grand stand and park, the schedule for the season, and all the new rules."

Meanwhile, in Cincinnati, Manager Frank Bancroft of the Reds had stated a refusal to play spring practice games against Louisville, citing his belief that his team would "wallop the Colonels so badly that there would be no attendance at the Cincinnati ball park when the Louisvilles played there." When Harry heard of this he laughed out loud, noting that his Colonels had "badly licked the Pork Eaters" the previous season. The rivalry between the two clubs had been intense for years. Louisville sportswriters often referred to the Reds as the "Pork Eaters."

In early February, Harry received a letter from left fielder Fred Clarke, who wintered at his home in Kansas, boasting that the outfielders were all in fine condition, "having sawed wood and worked on the farm and hunted all winter." Thus, began his annual ritual of hosting players at his ranch so they would not grow fat over the layoff. The free labor was a side benefit.

The headline of the Courier-Journal the morning of February 27 revealed Montgomery, Alabama as the host city for spring workouts for the Colonels. According to the paper, the club was to depart on March 7 to begin the trip. Manager McCloskey had visited the site, and had declared it his personal choice.

Harry arrived back in town the afternoon of February 28, and having seen the new schedule, enthusiastically endorsed it. In a letter to vice-president Dreher he wrote, "Get out a band wagon and a band; we've got the earth." Harry was in such good spirits that, in continuing the banter with the Cincinnati club, he offered an even bet of $300 that the Colonels would finish ahead of the Reds in the season series between the two. To some extent, the Eastern teams had addressed the complaints of the Western teams, and several more favorable home dates were on the slate.

By then he had heard from all the players under contract. Most sent him letters indicating their intention to arrive in Louisville by early March. The players were to be housed at the Eckert Hotel until they departed for Montgomery and spring practice. As they slowly trickled in to town, Harry was busy working on other matters. There was a dead week between the end of spring training and the start of the regular season. This presented an opportunity to make money, so he was contacting local college teams, trying to arrange a series of exhibition games.

Fred Clarke arrived in Louisville the evening of March 2. He expressed great optimism for the coming season, particularly due to the addition of Fog Horn Miller, who, while playing for St. Louis the previous season, had very much been a thorn in the Colonels' side. Clarke then set about playfully boxing and wrestling with Ducky Holmes, his good friend, and the team's centerfielder. The Courier-Journal took notice. "Fred Clarke, for whose release President Freedman, of the New York club, offered $10,000, arrived in the city at 6 o'clock last evening, as brown as chocolate and as lively as a well-fed kitten."

Two days later came McCreery, one of the last to arrive. He denied the reported meeting with Connie Mack. "Please say that all that was a lie. I've always wanted to play in Louisville. Why, they treated me like a lord last year, and I did not have any kick coming."

The trip to Montgomery was postponed for one day, from Saturday to Sunday, to allow the working class the opportunity to watch the Colonels play an exhibition game before they left. The team departed from Union Station on the Louisville & Nashville Sunday morning. A large crowd was there to see them off. Most of the players had taken care of themselves over the winter and were in fine condition, but

Fred Clarke

others, not so much. In Montgomery, the men in good shape were allowed to ride to the practice field in street cars, but those needing to lose weight were required to use leg power to make the journey.

"The other day, while the running crowd were on their way to the park, they encountered a farmer who was going in the same direction. He sat in a log wagon, to which was hitched a small mule and an old ox. With one accord the gang jumped on the wagon just as the team was starting up one of the long hills. The wheels sank down in the sand six inches, and the team came to a dead stop. The farmer used the whip and his voice collectively and individually, but to no purpose. The strangely mated pair refused to move. The players all got off the wagon and tried to push it up the hill, but the team had balked and refused to be pushed. The matter ended by the Colonels carrying the wagon up the hill. It was good practice." - Louisville Courier -Journal.

Back home in Louisville, fifty men were hard at work getting the grounds ready for opening day. The field was being rolled and drained daily, and the grandstand was being painted. The groundskeeper, Mr. Conrad, and his crew, were working hard to smooth out the ruts in the outfield that had caused many a player to stumble at an unfortunate moment in games the previous summer. Harry had plans to make this the grandest opening the town had ever seen.

The ongoing rivalry between Louisville and Cincinnati had flared up again, this time helped along by the schedule makers, who had the Colonels playing their first Sunday game of the new season in the Queen City. Thinking ahead, with the game more than a month down the road, Harry made an effort to maximize the gate by chartering a train to haul cranks from Kentucky and Ohio to the game and home again. He negotiated special rates to make it more affordable for the working men. Newspaper reporters in both cities were already claiming victory.

March 10 was a lost day at the training camp, a downpour blanketing the city for the entire day. The players whiled away the hours in the hotel lobby playing cards, telling jokes and talking ball. McCloskey regretted the weather. He needed all the practice time he could get, mostly because he had a large number of new players on the club, and they were quite young. The next day was a washout as well, with cold temperatures to boot.

When the weather cleared, and practice resumed, centerfielder Ducky Holmes broke his collarbone close to his neck during an exhibition game. While chasing down a fly ball he tripped and fell forward, landing on his head. Holmes returned to the hotel, and the broken bone was set by a surgeon. McCloskey decided to send him back to Louisville, where he might rest more easily, and would be watched over by Dr. Stucky, one of the team owners, who was also a physician. Holmes was expected to miss several weeks of play. Several other players were injured as well, including catcher Eddie Boyle, who was not even able to walk, having two sprained ankles. There were so many injuries the team had trouble fielding a full lineup for exhibition games.

Despite the crippled and wounded, optimism for the summer of 1896 remained high. "I'm willing to stake whatever reputation I have that, barring accidents, we have one of the best teams in the League," said Clarke. "This is no 'jolly' nor is it said to get my name in the paper, for if it turned out bad I would get the 'horse laugh' all over the country. The team is 100% stronger than it was last year. I am willing to bet $100 that we finish better than eighth. I think we will be the greatest surprise that ever happened in baseball, not even excepting the Baltimores."

While Harry was happy and impressed by the prospects, he made it known that he believed they were being hyped beyond reason, and thought people might have unrealistic expectations. In an interview, he simply confirmed that they were at least healthy. "The twenty-three men whom Mr. McCloskey has employed to represent Louisville in the National League and American Association of Baseball Clubs this year, have been tutored and fed, run, walked, trotted and rubbed down, dieted and looked after with as much care as a thoroughbred, and now they are coming home fit"

McCloskey issued an order that all players who had moustaches must be rid of them before the team returned to Louisville, stating that, "We don't want to go back home looking like a lot of Yanigans." But one player, Fred Clausen, was reluctant to do so, and was avoiding the manager to delay the inevitable. Apparently, vanity was the cause of the delay. "Now, if there is one thing above all else that Clausen prides himself on, it is his good looks, and the soft, silky, brown curl on his upper lip is the prettiest feature of his general appearances, and he knows it," wrote a reporter. To protect his prettiest feature, the clever Clausen feigned sickness, but to no avail, as one of his teammates sold him out to McCloskey.

The Colonels arrived home on April 2 at 12:27 aboard the L & N from Montgomery. A large crowd met them at the train depot. "Capt. Neal and his organized 'rooters' were there and extended to all a hearty hand-clasp and gave three cheers."

The players reported to the ballpark at 3:00 p.m. There was a light practice and they were assigned lockers. The next day a series of exhibition games would begin, leading up to the regular championship series. Chic Fraser was to be the pitcher in the first practice game, against the Detroit club from the Western League. That evening, players from both teams enjoyed a performance of "Buried Alive" at the McDonald Opera House. "During the last act, when Miss Laura Alberta was doomed to die in the vault, Miller wept copiously on the shoulder of Still Bill Hill, who was also weeping." Bill Hill was considered one of the toughest players on the club, but apparently, he had a soft side as well.

Harry, meanwhile, was working late hours, finalizing plans for opening day ceremonies to be held prior to the game against Chicago on April 16. At noon, the players, in uniform, were to gather at the Louisville Hotel. Preceded by a band, they would then ride carriages in a parade through the town and arrive at the ballpark a half hour prior to the game. Club officials and baseball reporters were also to ride carriages in the parade. Between innings of the game, an "open-air" concert was to play for the crowd.

Harry announced on April 3 that season tickets had been printed and were available for purchase. The cost was $33, and they were vest pocket size. By April 6, he had managed to schedule exhibition games with two local colleges, but citing a large number of players with wounds, he decided to cancel them and allow the injured players time to heal before opening day. "If we play these people Clarke will break his neck sure," he said, "or some other accident will happen to the team. We will try and keep them all in glass cages from now until Thursday, when we play Columbus." The injured included Frank Eustace, who slid head first into the spikes of a second baseman and ripped open three fingers, Pete Cassidy with a strained wrist, and Charlie Dexter, who managed to hurt himself simply by catching a fly ball. Holmes was still nursing his broken collar bone.

As opening day neared, to help sell tickets, Harry was sounding more optimistic about the teams' prospects. But it really wasn't necessary. League Park, with the new bleachers now in place, could hold as many as 15,000 spectators, and an opening day sellout was anticipated. Still, he was constantly being harassed by citizens wanting free tickets, as the team had so often done in the past to fill the park. Harry suddenly had more friends than he ever thought possible.

His spirits high, He shared with the newspaper men a letter he had recently received:

"'Dear Harry, I want to go to the opening game. Send us two tickets. Your old sweetheart.' Now, if that don't take the rag off the bush I don't want a cent. I never heard of that woman before. A man who is worth more than a million dollars has been after me for four days to get a season ticket, which costs $33. Oh my! Oh my!"

"Business Manager Pulliam sold a number of season tickets yesterday," noted a reporter. "The little books are of vest-pocket size and convenient to carry. Last season they were as big as family Bibles." He was also distributing complimentary tickets for opening day to dignitaries.

The day before the first game, injured centerfielder Ducky Holmes said it would take a whole platoon of police to keep him from playing in the game, as a broken collar bone was no excuse to sit out. Manager McCloskey thought otherwise, and told him he could collect tickets in the grandstand instead. But the bad news was tempered by the good; the new uniforms had arrived.

"The new uniforms of the Colonels arrived yesterday and will be worn this afternoon for the first time. The bodies of the uniforms are white flannel, with dark blue collars, cuffs, belts, stockings and caps. The word 'Louisville' is printed in large letters of blue across the front of the shirts. The players are so eager to get them on that they can hardly wait for 1:00 o'clock this afternoon, when they meet at the Louisville Hotel to take part in the parade."

The Colonels lost the season opener to Chicago 4-2. Despite the apparent great interest in the game, the attendance of 10,000 was second lowest in the League. Only Washington had a smaller opening day crowd. Even so, to support the team, the Courier-Journal embellished just a bit.

"Never before in the history of the game had such a crowd witnessed a ball game in this city. There was one unbroken, endless stream of people, moving like grain into a funnel, as they swarmed into the gates from the outside. The grand stand was a black and white mass of humanity. Just back of the screens fans fluttered in the hands of the most beautiful women in the world."

Harry was praised by all for pulling off a perfect spectacle of an opening day. There was only one glitch; the start of the parade had been delayed thirty minutes while Anson went to Hillerich Brothers to pick up the bats he had forgotten. While the Colts were in town, the question of Anson's retirement was heavy in the air. Finally tiring of the subject, he said, "Let us go and drink something. I am awful dry." He had shaved his famous moustache.

The train chartered by Harry to transport the fans to Cincinnati left Louisville at 7:35 a.m. on April 19. The players rode with them, and altogether 572 men and women, "not counting Ernest, the colored assistant park-keeper," arrived in downtown Cincinnati at 11:00.

"Throughout the 110 miles the train was gazed upon by an open-mouthed, straw-hatted, wondering population. Only three stops were made. The members of the team, Director Casper Hammer, Barney Dreyfuss and Charlie Dreher and Capt. William Neal, with dozens of his 'rooters' occupied the Pullman sleeper, 'Carlsbad', which was attached to the rear of the train. On either side of the car was hung a long streamer bearing the words 'Colonels' and Rooters' Special.' Every platform was crowded with enthusiastic people as the train sped by. It seemed as if all the people in the little towns had heard that the Colonels were on the train and wanted to urge them on to victory by their cheers." – Louisville Courier-Journal.

Several minutes before the start of the game, the Colonels were presented before a deputy of the court, and each signed a bond agreeing to appear in court the next morning, charged with breaking the Sabbath. This was done at all Cincinnati home games played on Sunday as a matter of form. Sunday baseball was still illegal in the Queen City. As usual, no charges were pressed the next day.

The team might have been better off going to jail; they were trounced by the Reds, 13-3. 16,500 were in attendance to watch the game. The train was somewhat less jovial on the trip home. The morning paper the next day showed the Colonels in last place, all by themselves. Another long season appeared to be in the works. When April mercifully came to a close, the Colonels had one win and eleven losses. However, as a small measure of consolation, they were not in last place alone. The Giants had the same record.

The team would get a shot at redemption on May 3, when they were scheduled to play their first Sunday game in League Park, against the hated Reds. Harry planned to use this opportunity against their arch rivals to bring in a big crowd, chartering trains on the C., O. & S. W. Railroad to Elizabethtown and Owensboro for citizens to ride to the big game. The Baltimore and Ohio Rail would bring fans from Indianapolis as well. He once again hoped to set a new attendance record. Eventually, ten "excursions" from neighboring towns were in the loop. Police officers were to be on hand to make sure the crowd didn't get out of control, but in the opinion of the Courier-Journal, this most likely would not be an issue. "For Cincinnati-Louisville crowds, while they are as warm competitors as the teams themselves, are jolly and good-natured. They borrow each other's tobacco, eat from the same peanut bags, and use the same expressions when errors are made, and altogether form a pretty congenial assemblage."

Perhaps because they were looking ahead to the game against the Reds, or perhaps just because they were a bad baseball team, the Colonels lost the Saturday game to the Pirates, 14-0. The game wasn't, as they say, as close at the final score indicated.

The weather was warm and the ball park full of energy for the Sunday game with the Reds. It was a nail biter, back and forth, but errors at key moments by Eustace and Fraser, and the failure to get timely hits with men on base did the Colonels in. They were on the losing end of a 5-3 score. The crowd was rowdy and loud, but Harry was disappointed that there were only 8,000 in the stands. It was nowhere close to a new record. The optimism of spring had begun to fade by May Day.

When the Colonels' record fell to 2-13, the latest embarrassment a 17-1 "comedy of errors" against Boston, rumors began circulating that McCloskey was going to be removed as manager and replaced by William McGunnigle. Considered a strict disciplinarian, McGunnigle was a former player and manager who had not been involved with baseball for several years. He arrived in town in early May for an interview with the Board of Directors. Also in consideration for the job was John Montgomery Ward, the former great player who doubled as an attorney.

President Stucky preferred Ward, but the post went to McGunnigle, who took over on May 10. Stucky, who had previously threatened to fine players for excessive errors, backed off from the idea, noting that "with the team in its present condition, there may be no limit to errors." If implemented, he surmised, most of the players would soon be penniless.

"Next to a few old Leaguers, what the Louisvilles seem to need most is discipline and instruction in team work. I began on both today," McGunnigle told a reporter. "We arranged an entirely new code of signals and will perfect them as rapidly as possible. The men seem to be eager to be led, and I see no reason why we should not have a winning team."

He also told his players in no uncertain terms that there was to be no kicking by the Louisville team, with the exception of George Miller, who was the captain, and "will say all the mean things to the umpire." In his opinion, kicking would only make matters worse for the team that kicks, perhaps by removing a key player, and therefore benefits the opponent.

His first game in charge was an encounter with Brooklyn at League Park. He changed the batting order just prior to the game, and since the score cards had the incorrect batting order printed on them, Harry would not allow any to be sold. Although a small matter, this decision revealed an important trait in Harry's value system. Although the team was always pinching pennies by necessity, and took a small hit on the cost of printing the score cards, Harry stuck to his principles and did what was right for the fans.

Shortly after McGunnigle signed on, the club began a modest winning streak of three games. In an 11-5 win over the Phillies, Clarke and McCreery both hit home runs that rolled all the way to the outfield fence, both astonishing and delighting the faithful. Suddenly, the new man was the toast of the town.

"When a ball team plays successful base ball, the manager is lauded to the skies. When a team loses continually the manager is called mean, rotten, a slob and every other name known to the inventive mind of the ball fan. Just at present Manager McGunnigle is a peach, a bird, a daisy, out of sight, a corker, a wonder and all the other things which stand for a successful base ball manager." – Louisville Courier-Journal.

But the winning ways were short lived. On May 24, the club left for an 18-game road trip against the Eastern teams. They left with a record of 7 wins and 22 losses. When they returned home on June 14, their record stood at 10 wins and 35 losses. And if that wasn't bad enough, The Sporting News was reporting internal dissent. "There are cliques on the Louisville team. Knocking is going merrily on. There is the (John) O'Brien clique and the Miller clique. Miller replaced O'Brien as captain, and that's the cause of it. Verily, there are more jealousy and hammers in a base-ball team than in a soubrette show."

While the team was away, the lingering question of how to let the citizens know if a game was to be played on a given day had been solved by Harry and announced to the public. On game days, a blue flag with white stripes, the team colors, was to fly from the flag pole atop the Courier-Journal building. This would be particularly helpful on rainy days.

It had been Harry's intention to raise a large ball in the center of town to signal game days. He settled for the flag.

Meanwhile, the writers at the local papers were having a heyday mocking the team:

"There were no details to yesterday's game. It was a conglomeration of disgusting plays, with an odor about them that rivaled that from the distillery across the car tracks."

"The infielders thought nothing of throwing the ball into the stand. It seemed the proper thing to do."

"'I've got it! I've got it!' was his (first baseman George Treadway) favorite expression, as a little fly would go up into his territory. Of course, he dropped it, every time, and even staid old Mr. Sheridan, the umpire, laughed."

Treadwell was released the next day.

Near the end of a 9-2 loss to Cincinnati on June 30, President Stucky looked around the park, sighed, and said, "There are about a thousand more people here than ought to be." There were barely 1,000 people in the stands.

Throughout another long summer of lopsided losses, Harry continued to keep the team afloat by keeping a close eye on the bottom line, cutting expenses where he could, finding discount rail rates for the team to travel to road games, booking the cheapest hotels, and perhaps most significantly, remaining optimistic about the team, insisting to anyone who would listen that they were better than people thought, and just needed a few breaks to turn the corner and start winning. But the fans could see with their own eyes, and they didn't like much of what they were seeing.

And as the only team official who really knew anything about baseball, or maybe even cared, it was left to Harry to scout for better players and sign them to contracts, subject to the approval of ownership. Most players, though, didn't want to play for the Colonels, or weren't really major league players, and those who were worth signing were offered better salaries by more financially secure clubs. Harry was caught in a classic catch 22; he couldn't win without better players, and he couldn't get better players without winning.

On July 19, the Colonels lost two games to the Cleveland Spiders before a crowd of 13,500 at League Park, many who were from Cleveland, as the Spiders were in a fight for first place with Baltimore and Cincinnati. Harry finally broke the attendance record; it was believed to be largest crowd ever to see a game in the city of Louisville to that date. After the first game, there was a longer break than the customary thirty minutes. Harry had received a telegram from the Dexter Club, an assembly of 103 cranks who wanted to attend the game to honor Colonel's catcher Charlie Dexter, and were delayed traveling by rail.

"Marengo, Ind., H.C. Pulliam – Had a hot box. For Heaven's sake hold second game until we get there. Will be at the park by 4 o'clock."

When the train arrived, it carried ten coach loads in all.

"They arrived at 4 o'clock shouting, yelling and blowing their horns. The members of the Dexter Club wore big orange-colored silk badges, on which the word "Dexter" was printed in large black letters. As this crowd filed in and took charge of the private boxes the crowd arose and cheered itself hoarse. It was the proudest moment of Dexter's life. He was as happy as a small boy carrying water to an elephant. The noise was so great that the game was delayed for fifteen minutes."

The endless losing frustrated the Colonels, particularly Clarke, a fiercely competitive man, who seemed to be turning into the club's leader. Clarke was a kicker. In a close loss to the Reds in August, he was arrested for assaulting an umpire. He attempted to score from third on a batted ball and was called out at the plate by Umpire Bud Lally. Clarke became angry, rushed the umpire, but did not strike him, according to published reports. Lally took a swing at Clarke, and the two men engaged in a fist fight. Players from both teams intervened, and both were arrested before the end of the game. Harry hired attorneys to represent Clarke in court the next day. A large crowd attended the proceedings, where the case was quickly dismissed.

The low point of the season came on September 7. On that date, the Colonels lost a tripleheader to John McGraw and the Orioles in Baltimore by the scores of 4-3, 9-1 and 12-1. The first game was a morning affair, the second and third contested in the afternoon. Game one drew a paltry crowd of 1,120. The afternoon games fared much better, with 11,788 in attendance. McGraw was ejected in the eighth inning of game one by Umpire Lally. The umpire insisted McGraw leave the grounds, but he refused to do so, finally settling in on the steps to the team bench under the grandstand. Lally later explained that McGraw was thrown out for abusive language.

When the club left for a tour of the Eastern cities in mid September, they were mired in last place in the National League, with no hope of catching any of the teams ranked higher. They had 34 wins and 88 losses. McGunnigle and his men fought gamely the rest of the way, but lost five of the remaining nine games. When the season ended, the players returned to Louisville, collected the balance of pay due them, and headed home.

Before the team returned from the East, a curious article appeared in the Courier-Journal.

"While Business Manager Pulliam was on the Eastern circuit with the team someone called at his boarding-house and said that he was Mr. Pulliam's warm friend and that he wanted to borrow his overcoat: that Mr. Pulliam had said that it was all right. The servant gave the man the garment. The day before the team returned the man carried the coat back to Mr. Pulliam's house. Mr. Pulliam says he is glad the man returned it. He has no idea who his cold friend is."

In November, Harry attended the League meetings in Chicago. When he returned to Louisville he was suffering a fever, and was admitted for medical care at the Norton

Infirmary. Dr. Stucky served as his physician while he recovered. Over the next several years, Harry would often require medical attention, much attributed to nerves, stress and his heavy work load.

During the off-season, pitchers throughout the League were greatly alarmed by the invention of what was called a "baseball cannon." It was the brainchild of a Professor Hinton of Princeton, and some had proposed replacing human pitchers with the new machinery during professional ball games, including the National League. The Courier-Journal saw merit to the idea, citing in an article that the baseball cannon would never get drunk, would always be in condition, would never get injured, would never argue with an umpire and, best of all, it would never "cuss the manager, or make his life a misery."

While first developing and testing his cannon, Professor Hinton aimed at a barn. His aim was true, but the ball smashed through both sides of the barn, a cottage, an outhouse and a wooden fence before landing in a river. However, according to reports, he refined the weapon to the point where it had adjustable speed, with a maximum speed that would not impale a batter. Thankfully, the baseball cannon was never used in an actual game.

Prior to the annual Board of Directors meeting on December 20, President Stucky resigned as president, citing poor health and lack of time to focus on his practice. It was speculated that Harry might be offered the position, but he had let it be known that he "will not accept unless he is given full control and is allowed to run the entire club as suits his fancy."

In Louisville, there was considerable public support for the idea of making Harry Pulliam president of the baseball team. He was well liked and respected in the community, he knew the game of baseball inside and out, and he had already become an integral part of the organization. Harry wanted the job. But he knew all too well that the key to building a championship team was the acquisition of championship quality players.

Soon enough, help would be on its way.

Chapter Three

A Big German with Enormous Hands

At the meeting of club Directors on January 6, 1897, Harry Pulliam was named president of the Louisville Colonels Baseball Club. The decision had been made several days earlier, but the owners wanted to make sure Harry would accept before making any public declaration. They saw in him the same traits the fans saw, no doubt, but in fact, a change had to be made, and Harry was clearly the only viable option. He was already doing much of the work a president normally did anyway, and there was a level of trust in him that no other employee enjoyed. Harry had gotten what he wanted – complete control of the team. Barney Dreyfuss was chosen to serve as the new secretary and treasurer, and the newly named field manager was James Rogers, who had played first base for the Colonels in 1896. McGunnigle had been let go, it was noted, for criticizing the team after the season ended, and also for drinking in the company of his players.

In accepting the promotion, Harry embraced the challenge, and promised to build a team the city could be proud of. His plan was to immediately begin recruiting the best players possible. As a gesture of good faith, he was given $10,000 cash to secure them. It was also expected that Harry would perform many of the duties that field managers usually did.

The new man, Rogers, was only 27 years old, but had managed four teams in the New England League previously and won four pennants. He was to be one of ten player managers in the twelve-team National League in the coming season.

Harry spent the next day in his room at the Louisville Hotel, welcoming visitors wanting to shake his hand and wish him well and receiving telegrams from baseball officials all over the country, and the editors of the major newspapers as well. Even John T. "Svengali" Brush, owner of the Cincinnati club, sent a congratulatory note. "Accept my hearty congratulations upon your advancement to the position of magnate, and I also wish to congratulate the citizens of Louisville and the Louisville club upon securing so good a man. Best wishes for you and success to the Louisville club." - J.T. Brush.

"Mr. Pulliam is a very young man at the business of being president, but he has learned a lesson by the acts of the army of past managers who have managed the Louisville club," opined the Courier-Journal. "He says first and foremost that he is not going to brag about what he is going to do; that he will do his best and if he fails he expects the people to 'roast him,' which will surely be done if he does not give Louisville a winning ball team."

Harry started by re-evaluating the current team. The greatest needs were the positions of catcher, second base and third base. Rumors soon spread that Harry was working a deal to bring catcher Jack Clements, a twelve-year veteran who had played his entire career with the Philadelphia club, and third baseman Lave Cross to Louisville. Clements was considered a good mentor for young pitchers. Harry had great trade bait in hurler Chic Fraser, who was highly regarded throughout the League. He offered Fraser to Philadelphia for Cross and Clements, and also offered $1500 to Anson of Chicago for second baseman Jim Connor. Chicago, he felt, had a surplus of infielders, and could easily spare him. The outfield was already set with Clarke, Oliver Pickering and McCreery, and Ducky Holmes in reserve. Joe Dolan was to be the shortstop. Completing these two deals would round out the regulars.

"If the Louisville management will close these two deals at once all will be forgiven," wrote a local reporter, "and the Colonels of 1897 will be fairly well started on the greased scale, whether it prove a toboggan or a hill-climber."

But it wasn't going to be quite that easy. The deals were never completed. And barely a week into his new job, Harry had a new headache to deal with, specifically, the contract demands of his star right fielder, Tom McCreery, who was threatening to not sign unless he received the League maximum of $2,400 for the year. Clarke and Fraser had already made similar demands. They were all probably worth the money, but the Colonels simply could not afford to pay such high salaries.

"The Louisville Club last week voted $10,000 with which to strengthen its team. Next day one of the local banks closed its doors. It doesn't take much these days to start a panic" –O.P. Taylor.

Harry tried to keep his negotiations with other teams quiet, despite the best efforts of the papers to find him out. On January 24 in Chicago, he met with manager W.H. Watkins of the Indianapolis club, most likely to propose a trade, with Dreher and Dreyfuss also in attendance. The press was unable to learn any details of the proceedings. According to Harry, it was simply a social call and nothing more. Nobody believed him. Returning to Louisville emptyhanded, he met with Clarke and Fraser. Fraser relented and signed. Clarke did not.

A week later, Harry spent two hours in the Equitable Building, where team headquarters were now located, talking with Dan McGann, formerly of Boston, who had been recently released. He had been interested in McGann for a while and intended to try to sign him now that he was available. Harry envisioned him as a possible second baseman, and though he was somewhat slow afoot, he was considered a good batter. After the meeting, Harry took him on a tour of the town. McGann asked for $2,100 for his services during the upcoming season; Harry offered $1,600. No deal was struck.

But not all the news was bad; shortstop Dolan, who impressed while with the club the second half of the previous season, arrived in town from Omaha at the Tenth Street station, jumped on a trolley, and immediately proceeded to the offices of President Pulliam. "I just got tired of loafing out there in Omaha," he said to Harry and several teammates. "I feel like a winner. In fact, I never felt better in my life. I'm as hard as nails and eager to get on the diamond."

As Clarke and McCreery remained unsigned and unseen, with the spring trip drawing near, Harry considered using the money offered them to buy a second baseman, and in fact tried to do so. Furthermore, he stated that if $5,000 won't buy that particular player (unknown), then he had another second baseman in mind as well. "If a fine, hard-hitting second baseman is signed, bought, traded for or stolen – any old way – the Louisville fans will be satisfied, for that is certainly the weakest spot on the team," said Harry.

At a meeting of the Board of Directors on February 25, it was revealed that former manager Bill McGunnigle was threatening legal action, claiming the team still owed him $2,700 for services rendered. The owners saw it differently; they considered McGunnigle the debtor, for an amount of $72. Furthermore, according to some accounts, Dr. Stucky asked for McGunnigle to be reinstated as manager. He had never approved of Rogers, and considered him not qualified for the job. The original issue on the agenda, a plan to lower the cost of tickets in order to improve attendance, was not even discussed. Afterward, Harry sent a telegram to the press.

"Have this day signed Rogers to manage and captain the Louisville Club for the season of 1897. I am in perfect accord with Dr. Stucky, who assures me the reports referred to have been garbled and are not his views. Mr. Rogers is here and while not sanguine or enthusiastic, he hopes to give

Louisville a good team whose work will be more noted for its conscientious and earnest endeavor than for its brilliancy." Harry C. Pulliam, President, Louisville Club.

As February came to a close, Harry and Stucky returned from the annual League meeting with no new players, and a check for $10,000 still in hand. None of the deals proposed by the magnates made sense to Harry; indeed, he felt, and correctly so, that they were trying to take advantage of his inexperience by pawning off old talent for promising youngsters. In the end, the Colonels still had Perry Werden for first, and either Rogers or Abbie Johnson could play second. Fraser, Art Herman and Bill Hill would be the key pitchers.

"The Louisville Club will stand pat as it is," Harry said to a Courier-Journal correspondent. "I have brought a fine bottle of old Kentucky Bourbon for (Orioles) Manager Hanlon. It is as old as I am. I have already given him two bottles, and I will give him one every time he wins the pennant."

Groundskeeper Conrad visited Harry at team headquarters a week into March to report on the condition of the field and other work being done. "Several dry wells have been sunk in the crawfishy spot in center field," he said, "and the entire outfield has been given a thick coating of loam." He assured Harry that the field was in good condition and they were ahead of schedule on improvements. Many of the bleachers were rotted and broken, in need of replacement. A second tier of bleachers was to be added, and the entire grandstand moved fifty feet closer to the field.

As players began arriving in town, Harry's office became a crowded and busy place. Many of them asked him for advance money, other sought details of the upcoming trip. Harry had received almost one hundred letters from citizens offering advice on how to improve the team, and they continue to arrive in the mail daily. Ever dutiful, he responded thoughtfully to as many as he could manage.

But a higher priority was to send letters to the players, including Clarke and McCreery, instructing them to report no later than March 22 to begin training for the season. In his correspondence, he reminded them it was their responsibility to bring sweaters and running shoes with them upon arrival. Clarke asked Harry to travel to Chicago to discuss his contract, but Harry declined, citing his belief there was nothing to negotiate. He was playing hard ball.

With the roster set and players notified, he turned his attention to spring practice. "Rogers will be here with his wife next Monday, and then all the details of the preliminary practice will be arranged," reported the Courier-Journal. "The measures of the players for their new uniforms will be taken as soon as the men arrive. The home uniforms will be white, with trimming of dark blue. The visiting uniforms will be gray with blue trimmings. The last year's uniforms will be used in the preliminary exhibition games. Instead of the word 'Louisville' on the shirts there will be a fancy 'L'."

In mid-March, Harry decided to turn up the pressure on Clarke. Having grown weary of his stubborn salary demands, Harry announced that Clarke would not play for the Colonels in 1897. He also stated that at this point, should Clarke concede, he would join the team as a substitute and would not get regular playing time. Ducky Holmes was named as the new leftfielder, and McCreery had signed to continue in right. Harry issued a written statement explaining his position:

"The negotiations carried on by the Louisville Club since last October to induce Fred Clarke to sign a contract for $2,100 are at an end, and if Mr. Clarke plays ball this season with the Louisville Club it will have to be through his own solicitation for a place on the team. Whether Clarke reports or not or plays ball rests solely with him. We have made all preparations to fill his place, and from now on will not count on him to play left field. This place has been assigned to Holmes. Clarke has stated that he can make more than the salary offered him in the rice business. If this is true, the Louisville Club wishes him every success in the rice business."

For once, the reserve clause worked in Louisville's favor; Clarke would not ever have the option of playing for another team without Harry's consent.

Harry arranged for the team, consisting of sixteen players, to leave aboard the Monan Railroad on March 24 for preliminary training in West Baden, Indiana. Although they only inhabited West Baden Springs for ten days, an elaborate training program was implemented.

"This will consist of hand-ball, and plenty of it; running on the covered bicycle track at the springs, boxing, riding bicycles, throwing balls, gymnasium work and other forms of indoor exercise. The men who are overweight will be worked the hardest." –Louisville Courier-Journal.

To Harry, the most significant benefit was found in the mineral springs water itself. "Now don't let anybody entertain the idea for a moment," he said, "that there are any drunkards on the team, for there are not, but I find that the mineral water at West Baden is good for this evil as well as to put a man in good fix to receive hard work. There are no waters so favorably known for the cure of alcoholism. The most hardened 'toper' who has used the water for a few days is astonished to discover that his appetite for liquor has disappeared, leaving him with a repugnance for his former favorite tipple."

In late March, while in West Baden to check in on the team, Harry was awakened suddenly by a loud knock on his hotel room door. Thinking it a drunk or a robber, he told the intruder to go away, but the knocking persisted. Then there was a strong kick, prompting Harry to pull out his revolver, throw the door open, and confront the man. "If you don't go away from there something will happen around here," he shouted. The man only laughed, and then Harry's eyes cleared enough to identify the 'criminal.' It was none other than Fred Clarke. Five minutes later he had signed the contract that Harry had been carrying around in his hip pocket – just in case. Clarke then proceeded to run down the hotel hallway shouting, waking all the players, and sparking a splendid celebration. The great leftfielder had returned.

Fearing his players were in danger of contacting malaria, Harry decided to leave West Baden early, on March 31.

As the new team president, Harry chose to leave the design of the new score card to someone else. He selected a local designer and gathered the score cards of all twelve teams from the previous year for him to choose the best features to incorporate in the new design. He informed the manager prior to the start of the season that once the daily score card was printed, he was not allowed to make changes to the lineup, unless a player was injured.

Harry addressed the issue of giveaway tickets in a statement released by the club: "The Louisville Club this season will be conducted on a strictly business basis. A number of people who have attended the games on passes for several seasons need not be surprised if they wake up and find their passes missing. This is no little policy, but we simply cannot afford it. Last season the club lost $7,000."

The players were dealing with financial issues as well. Manager Rogers has ordered them to pay for car-fare to and from the park twice a day for training, but many claimed not to have the cash to pay for it. Harry, though, wasn't buying it. "When we got back from West Baden I gave the players three dollars apiece, $57 for nineteen men, for car fare. Some of them have been smoking ten-cent cigars." In the end he conceded, giving salary advances to those who needed it.

In early April, in New York City, the magnates attended a secret meeting that had been hastily arranged by owner John T. Brush of the Cincinnati team. Brush was trying to orchestrate the transfer of the Cleveland team to Indianapolis. Harry left for New York in a rush to attend, not bothering to notify anyone of his destination, and certainly not of the business at hand. Cleveland owner Frank de Hass Robison wanted to transfer his team to Indianapolis because Sunday baseball was banned in Cleveland, thus denying him the large gate Sunday games always attracted. Since such a transfer would require the approval of all club owners, its approval was uncertain. The city of Detroit had also applied for a franchise. Brush was highly recognized as the most powerful of the owners and had the unquestioned support of several franchises in all matters. Still, despite his efforts, no action was taken.

Twelve thousand people turned out for the season opener on April 22, and witnessed the Colonels' hard fought 3-1 victory over the Cleveland Spiders, runners-up to Baltimore in the Temple Cup series of the previous year. Chic Fraser outpitched Cy Young. The Spiders were once again expected to be an excellent team, making the win that much more gratifying.

The opener was also notable as the major league debut of Penobscot Indian Louis Sockalexis for the Cleveland team. "This young man is the purest American of all those who are to take part in this, America's greatest game," reported the Courier-Journal. "He is Sockalexis, the Indian. He belongs to the Penobscot tribe, and the home of his ancestors was in the forests of Maine. He stands there as straight as an arrow. His face is dark and swarthy, like that of a Greek or a Hindoo. But his cheek bones are high, his hair is straight and black, and he looks as hard as a nail. There is nothing about him which suggests that he is highly educated – a graduate of Holy Cross College. He is tall and graceful, and certainly not affected by the throng of people."

Sockalexis went 0 for 3.

It was only one game, but for the first time in years, the Colonels were in first place.

The glee of the faithful was so great that Harry felt the need to soften expectations. "We don't think we are the only peach in the orchard simply because we played fine ball and won the first game. Some of the teams are bound to lose, or there would be no base-ball, and Louisville will not kick at her share." Still, Harry could hardly contain himself; he bought 500 copies of the Courier-Journal to distribute throughout the League. Then he went back to work.

In yet another effort to shore up the pitching, Harry attempted to secure Sadie McMahon, who had won 35 and 36 games in previous years, from Baltimore, offering him a salary increase of $600, but McMahon rejected the offer, claiming the Louisville cranks were "a gang of knockers" who were quick to criticize their own team when things went wrong, and were strangely silent when the team excelled. Harry was offended, but there was validity to the accusation, as noted in the Courier-Journal:

"During the early part of yesterdays' game, the Chicagos made two hits off (George) Hemming. Then some unspeakable 'knocker' on the bleachers set up a howl of 'Take him out!' 'He's rotten!', and other choice selections. Then a half dozen city police who happened to be near the bleachers tried to locate the man, but failed." - Courier-Journal.

In response, Harry arranged for police to dress undercover and scatter themselves among the crowd to identify the knockers and remove them from the park. "We do not want those people here," he announced, "and we are not going to have them. We can get along splendidly without them." It was a fruitless attempt, but then knockers were commonplace throughout the League, as they are still today.

In Baltimore, knockers were few in number, because the Orioles usually played well and won. But kicking was always in style. On May 7, the Baltimore Sun reported that in a game the previous day against the Phillies, "McGraw got into an argument with Umpire Tom Lynch and was ordered from the field and was threatened with a fine. McGraw's offence, it is said, was a suggestion to Mr. Lynch that as Thompson was not playing he might perhaps borrow Thompson's eyeglasses, whereat Mr. Lynch took dire offense."

Ten days later, the Colonels lost a tight game on the road, 7-6 to the Reds, before a crowd of 20,000. On the trip home after the game, they shared a train with the Philadelphia team, on their way to Louisville. The next day the following commentary appeared in the Courier-Journal:

"Among those who accompanied the Colonels here today was Ernest, the colored park tender. He was assigned to the compartment in the first car set apart for colored people, but had hardly got settled when the entire Philadelphia team entered and took possession. President Pulliam worked his way to Ernest and told him that white people had no right to ride in the car for colored passengers and he put Ernest up to making a 'kick' to the conductor. The Colonels' colored bat tender did 'kick' long and loud. He told his woes to the conductor and to the brake man, but those worthies refused to make the Philadelphia players move."

At the end of May, following a loss to the Senators, the team left on a lengthy road trip to play the Eastern teams. The quick start had faded, and they had become a .500 team – 14 wins and 14 losses. Six games into the trip they had fallen to 14 wins and 20 losses. The losing continued, and before the club returned home, Harry had relieved Rogers as field manager. Fred Clarke took his place. But the change in leadership did not stop the misery. The Colonels seemed to hit rock bottom on June 30 when they were humiliated by the Chicago Colts 36-7, establishing a major league record for runs allowed by one team in a single game.

The more charitable cranks blamed the situation on injuries, and indeed, there were many. The following were noted: "Catcher Wilson – broken finger, Catcher Dexter – lame, Second Baseman Johnson – seriously injured, Shortstop Dolan – throwing arm gone, Third Baseman Clingman – right hand badly hurt, Pitcher Hill – tendon in arm strained, President Pulliam – sick at heart, Fred Clarke – feelings hurt, but playing baseball." Harry's team seemed to literally be falling apart.

"The cripples are scheduled to reach Louisville at 6:51 o'clock this morning from Chicago. They will be met at the depot by a brass band, a black hearse and the City Hospital ambulance, besides, twenty-five loyal members of the Rooters' club. This is no joke. Siebert's brass band was engaged last night, and the finest and largest hearse of the Undertaker Pearson was hired, and the hospital ambulance was promised." - Louisville Courier-Journal.

Harry needed to find some new talent, but the archaic rules of the day hindered his efforts tremendously. Under the reserve rule as it stood in 1897, each team was allowed to hold in reserve as many as 32 players, even though the teams only carried sixteen to twenty players on their roster at one time. The wealthier teams flush with cash had the means to stockpile talent simply for the purpose of denying good players to rival teams. And for the most part, they were not willing to make those players available to the Louisville Colonels. Harry had no other option but to seek out raw talent others had missed. He quietly left town, refusing to give any details regarding his purpose or destination, to scout prospects that might be able to help the team.

A fight nearly broke out between the Colonels and the Orioles in a game at Baltimore on July 9. Dexter stole third, sliding in at McGraw's feet and spiking him in the ankle badly enough to force him out of the game. Later, seeking revenge, Jake Stenzel of the Orioles tried to spike Dexter at the plate, ripping open his shoe, but not injuring him. The two engaged in a heated argument, and a fight seemed imminent. The spectators egged them on, hoping to see battle, as they crowded toward the fence separating them from the field. Police quickly restored order, both off the field and on, and the fight was averted.

A week later, more shenanigans from the Orioles in a game the Birds won over the Colts.

"Again, the angelic Jennings, the innocent Stenzel, the lamb-like McGraw and that Sunday-school youth Jacky Doyle fired their broadsides of incendiary repartee into Umpire (Michael) McDermott and fought and rowed and wrangled until they finally won. Their exhibition of high kicking would have caused Captain Chapman to raid the park had it been made in New York."

The next day, McGraw had a new trick up his sleeve in the bottom of the eighth inning. "McGraw came forward with determination printed on every line of his innocent countenance and took his stand with his toes planted on the edge of the plate, clear outside of the batter's box. (Clark) Griffith shot up a fast ball, which brushed against the knee of the little batter, and the crowd roared with disappointment when (Jim) McDonald called one ball. The next ball was against the legs of the batsman, yet over the plate, but McDonald gave the second decision as a ball. Then came a wrangle of a moment, and McGraw was ordered back into the batter's position.

"Again, the ball shot straight across the plate, and Muggsy, by quickly shoving out his knee, was hit, while the crowd roared its rage. McDonald had seen the intent of the batter, and while Kelley, Jennings, McGraw, and Stenzel hurled into his ears volleys of their choicest profanity he ordered the batsman back to bat. Again, Griffith pitched, and again McGraw stepped out and allowed the ball to hit him. The crowd rose and became frantic with indignation. McDonald, despite the fierce protests of the Orioles, sent McGraw back to bat. Three more balls were pitched, each low and straight over the plate, and McGraw was struck out. The stands turned loose a frantic scream of joy."

Six weeks earlier, while traveling with the team in New York, Harry was away on a scouting trip when a Louisville native named Claude McFarlan called on him. McFarlan was a minor league pitcher for the Norfolk team. Since Harry was unavailable, McFarlan met with Fred Clarke instead. He told Clarke about a third baseman playing for Paterson, New Jersey, a team in the Atlantic League. McFarlan raved about him, and Clarke was impressed enough to pass along word to Harry when he returned. Harry went to see the young prospect the next day, and again two days later accompanied by Clarke and Dreyfuss. After a second look, Harry was sold, but Clarke and Dreyfuss were uncertain. Clarke thought him too slow, but Harry persisted, even though the asking price to secure his release was an outrageous $2,500. He was able to negotiate it down to $2,100, and Hans Wagner became a Louisville Colonel.

One writer described the prospect "Hans" Wagner as "a big, raw-boned German, with enormous hands and in the Atlantic League has batted like a fiend." He was pegged immediately as the new regular third baseman for the Colonels. Wagner made his major league debut in a home game against Washington, making one base hit, reaching on a walk, and laying down a key sacrifice bunt. The Colonels won the game, but more significantly, the home folk left the park satisfied that the new player was the real deal.

In late July, the Colonels trailed the Colts by one run in the last of the sixth with a steady rain falling. Clarke singled and was sacrificed to second by McCreery. As Clarke hit second base, the bag came loose in the mud. Thinking quickly, he picked it up and ran to third base, the bag still in his grasp as he slid. When Clarke was tagged before he reached third, Umpire O'Day called him out. Clarke, protested, pointing out that he had never lost contact with a base, but to no avail. The attempted trick failed twice, as Wagner followed with a single that certainly would have scored Clarke from second. The rain continued to fall, and the game was called after seven innings, a 1-0 Chicago win. Clarke accepted the blame for the outcome. "Yes, we lost it and I was responsible," he admitted. "It was my own foolishness."

As July turned to August, the Beaneaters and the Orioles were in a tight race for first place. The much-improved Colonels were the number nine team, with a record of 36 wins and 48 losses, a significant gain from the previous season. They were becoming more confident and capable with experience, and the addition of Wagner had sparked the team.

"His batting is like that of Lajoie, a whipping, cracking snap onto the ball," one newspaper man wrote of Wagner. The rookie had an incredible arm for making magnificent throws, could play several different positions in the field more than capably, and despite his barrel-chested physique, could run like the wind. He was a wonder to behold, and soon, fans in every city were more than willing to pay to do so.

In the city of Boston, on August 10, the kicking of the Orioles turned to rowdyism, and then to something much, much worse:

"At the close of the eighth inning today between the Boston and Baltimore Clubs, Umpire (Tom) Lynch, enraged at the frequent tongue lashing Doyle had inflicted upon him, kept piling up fines until $300 was marked. Then, losing his temper, Lynch planted a powerful blow on Doyle's jaw. The ground in front of the grand stand became a scene of fierce conflict. Players on both sides swarmed around the combatants, and the mob from the bleachers surged along, ready for fight. The police came on the double quick and ran for the mob. Joe Corbett staggered out of the melee with his arm hooked around Lynch's neck. The Baltimore players shook their fists, swore and threatened Lynch with bodily abuse. Blows were struck freely in the crowd, and it took the police ten minutes to secure order so the game might proceed with Doyle out. As the tally-ho drove from the grounds with the Baltimore team a mob followed, throwing mud and stones. McGraw jumped from the top, base-ball club in hand, and the mob fled before his sturdy blows." – Louisville Courier-Journal.

The standings of the clubs in the morning paper on August 14 showed the Colonels had moved up to seventh place, and were within striking distance of the first division. Not since the long-lost championship days in the American Association had the team held such a lofty position so late in the year. Clarke and Wagner were the stars, but the whole team was playing at a high level of competence.

In September, the Colonels played the Orioles in Union Park, losing a well-played game, 5-1. It was a relatively calm affair, with little kicking. Manager Clarke debuted a new battery for the game, catcher Ozzie Schreckengost and pitcher George Waddell. The new hurler, Harry's most recent signee, a lefty, got off to a rough start, but soon settled down, and impressed all in attendance, mostly with the breathtaking speed of his fastball. "Waddell was complete master of the field and try as they would, the Orioles could not connect with another run." Unfortunately, though, the debut of Rube Waddell was one of very few highlights for the team on its western trip. They limped home having won six and lost seventeen, falling to eleventh place in the League, only ahead of the lowly St. Louis team. Clearly, Harry still had much work to do.

The last game of the season was a 9-7 loss to Cincinnati at League Park. 5,000 loyal fans attended. When Manager Clarke came to bat in the first inning, the game was stopped, and he was presented with a diamond ring, courtesy of the home team fans, in appreciation of his work. "Clarke was very proud of his ring. He was as happy as a school-boy eating green apples." After the game it was announced that he would return as manager in 1898.

On September 28, a notice in the Courier-Journal formally announced Harry's nomination for the Kentucky state assembly. "Mr. Harry Pulliam, President of the

Louisville Base-Ball Club and nominee for the Legislature in the district composed of the Ninth and Tenth wards, will begin an active canvass of his district at the close of the baseball season, October 1." He had always been interested in politics, and his unsolicited nomination came from admirers and friends. He was elected to a two-year term in November.

Hans Wagner

As the season ended, Harry expressed concern for the future of the game. Kicking and rowdyism were more prevalent than ever, and nobody seemed able, or even interested, in doing anything to stop it. It had always been easy and convenient to blame the problem on poor umpiring, and most people seemed willing to let it go at that. In 1897, the League had collected more than $1,355 in fines from players for kicking and other offenses. The most penalized team was New York – not Baltimore – with a total of $390. The Orioles were fined $245. Louisville's total for the season was a mere $90. The money was used to fund the owners' end of the year banquet.

During the off-season, despite his best efforts, Harry was unable to make any deals to improve the club. The other teams wanted to trade second class men for first class men. Harry asked for a reconsideration of the reserve clause, arguing passionately and correctly that improving the second division teams would be good for the overall health of the National League. His request was ignored. It was a frustrating end to 1897.

Chapter Four

Too Many Mascots in Louisville

In January of 1898, Harry Clay Pulliam found himself in the state capital of Frankfort, representing the people of Kentucky, or at least those who lived in districts nine and ten. That month, he introduced bill No. 110 in the state assembly, calling for a repeal of the law prohibiting the caging of red-birds. Harry hoped to save the endangered birds from extinction. The bill was referred to the Committee on Warehouses and Granaries for consideration.

The hunters had devised a clever means of hunting the redbirds. A cage was set in the habitat of the red-bird, with a tame bird inside. The hunter left and waited. When the tame bird began to sing, it would arouse the curiosity of a wild redbird. The redbird would arrive to investigate and when it did, the hunter would shoot it. Other hunters were capturing them to sell abroad.

"In Louisville, I saw in an apple orchard a man catching southern red birds in a trap. He skinned them alive before my eyes. He was paid fifty cents apiece for their skins. Five hundred thousand skins of this species alone have been used this fall." - The Lenoir (North Carolina) Times.

The business of building a baseball team did not pause, though, even for important government affairs, and Harry was determined to juggle the two as best he could. In a cost cutting move, the owners had decided to carry only sixteen players for the 1898 season, making the challenge of creating a competitive club that much more difficult. Among those not selected to go south for spring practice was pitcher George "Rube" Waddell. The team already had 28 players under contract, so Harry, along with Clarke, had a lot of decisions to make, and Rube didn't make the cut.

With spring practice still more than two months away, the starting lineup, as envisioned by Harry, included Scoops Carey at first base, Heinie Smith at second, Billy Clingman at third, Pat Dillard the shortstop, and Clarke, Wagner and Doc Nance the outfielders. In an attempt to improve the team's catching, Harry had drafted three catchers, paying each of their minor league teams $500 to get them. They included Arthur Twineham from St. Paul of the Western League, Henry Dixon from Providence of the Eastern League and Fuller from Cedar Rapids of the Western Association. Only one of the three, if any, would make the club, and Harry anticipated a spirited competition among them. A fourth player was also drafted, pitcher Lou Mahaffy, also from Cedar Rapids. Harry continued searching for an outfielder as well. In one final deal, he found the two players he needed to complete the roster, trading pitcher Still Bill Hill to the Reds of Cincinnati in exchange for outfielder Billy Hoy, shortstop Claude Ritchey, and pitcher Phil Ehret to boot.
    By January 23, the club Directors had decided not to take a trip for spring practice, but rather, the team would stay in Louisville as a matter of convenience, a side benefit being that the locals could watch them train. Although they tried their best to downplay the fact, this was obviously another way to save money for the financially strapped team. It was a disappointment for the players, who considered the annual spring trip an opportunity to escape the cold weather and bond as a team.
    Working double duty was taking a toll on Harry's health. He considered taking a few days rest in Florida, at the recommendation of his physician, but there was simply too much work to do. The rest would have to wait.
    He attended the National League meeting held in late February in the city of St. Louis. For the sixth straight year, the issue of kicking and rowdy ball was discussed, and once again it appeared nothing would be done to stop it. They

were, however, in favor of taking steps to curb the use of foul language, either by a short suspension, or blacklisting in extreme cases, the preferred method of John T. Brush, who had proposed a code of conduct that came to be known as the Brush rules. The fact of the matter was that many fans enjoyed kicking and rowdyism, and may not have been inclined to attend games if they were eliminated, which would lead to lower attendance, and therefore, lower profits for the magnates. But that didn't make it any easier for the umpires.

As one umpire explained, "It was plain then to me that unless I stopped offending the magnates by disciplining their unruly players, I would be deprived of a means of livelihood, and, as I had no other way of making a living I let the players kick as much as they pleased. But that made more trouble, for the home clubs found fault with me for letting the visitors kick without being restrained, and all roasted me for not giving all of the close decisions to them. So I shifted my tactics and became what is known as a 'home umpire.' The visiting clubs protested me repeatedly then, but as the home clubs backed me up just as vehemently I was retained on the staff. I'd much prefer, though, to give decisions as I see them, and put a stop to kicking by enforcing the rules."

"President Nick Young talked to-night as if he would favor the Brush blacklist rule," wrote a reporter for the Courier-Journal. "He said he was sick and tired of the rowdy actions of players, and that the public was even more tired, and demanded clean base-ball. However, many of the other magnates will fight such an arbitrary measure to the bitter end. Some of them laughed to-night about it as if it were some very funny joke. They believe that rowdyism should be suppressed, but take the stand that to blacklist a player for objecting vigorously to an umpire's decision would be rank foolishness."

President Frank de Haas Robison of Cleveland led the opposition to blacklisting, claiming the owners were most at fault for encouraging it in the first place, and to punish a player for doing so would be hypocrisy. He was, though, willing to support a thirty-day suspension for a first offense, pointing out that this approach punished both the player and the owner alike. Furthermore, he added that,' I believe the rule placing so much power in the umpire's hands is extremely dangerous. They are just as apt to go off the handle as a player and vent their spite on the players they do not like.'"

On March 1, the vote on the Brush resolution was taken. The resolution passed 11-1, with Harry casting the lone dissenting vote. He was upset that the discussion of the resolution was to have taken place in executive session, and this had not happened. When the roll call was taken, and his name was called, Harry, perhaps overcome with frustration and anger that had been building for some time, made the most of his opportunity. He spoke for several minutes, expressing his belief that the League had always mistreated his club, and he was sure they would find some fine way to make Fred Clarke the first blacklisted player, making an example of him for all other players. He talked about how the teams from large cities were given the advantage in every instance, and how he was certain they would continue to do so. Having spoken his mind, Harry later changed his vote, thinking it in the best interests of the League to have unanimity on the matter. The Brush resolution was affectively adopted for the 1898 season.

Harry's outburst may have gained him some sympathy when the magnates next turned to the issue of the schedule for 1898. The Colonels were given nine Sunday home games, an increase from years past. Equally important and financially beneficial, the new schedule had them playing in Cincinnati on Independence Day, and in Philadelphia for Decoration Day, which would allow them to share in two of the League's largest gates of the season. Had they played home games on the holidays, their share of the gate would have been much smaller. Harry was pleased with the schedule. Cincinnati typically drew in the neighborhood of 25,000 fans on the Fourth of July, as did the Phillies on Decoration Day. Two big paydays could be counted on.

Less than a week beforehand, Clarke had changed his mind and decided not to attend the meeting, citing a need to tend to his rice business in Chicago. Stucky and Dreher were busy celebrating Mardi Gras in New Orleans, so Harry had been left to travel to St. Louis by himself. Besides the schedule, also of importance to the Louisville club was the issue of the National League ten-year agreement expiring after the 1901 season, and the possibility of realignment that threatened the team's membership in the League. Some magnates had already spoken of their desire to reduce the number of teams by four, and Louisville had been mentioned as one of the teams that might not survive. The St. Louis franchise, which was already on the verge of bankruptcy, was also considered to be in jeopardy.

Harry put his political hat back on when he returned to Louisville. Supporters of the red-bird bill were quite concerned that Harry seemed to be giving up on it. "I cannot help it," he responded. "The fact is I have found out that there are very few red-birds in Louisville, and no great harm will be done if the bill does not pass."

A few days later, he seemed to have soured on the whole topic of politics. "I don't think I want to go to the legislature again, although, on the whole, I have had a very pleasant time this winter in Frankfort. I think, though, it is easier to manage a baseball team than try to legislate for the people. At times it is too trying on one's nerves to listen to the proceedings of the house. My red-bird bill, you know, died in the hands of the Committee on Banking and Commerce."

In Baltimore, John McGraw's reaction to the passage of the Brush rules portended dire consequences for the owners. "The trouble brought about last year was largely the fault of spectators, prejudiced against visiting players, and the newspaper writers, who exaggerate every scene," he claimed. "The umpire is as much to blame and has used as much foul language as any player who ever walked. I have been trying to play ball for all there was in me, to help my club win games. This I will continue to do and will try to do it in the way laid down. Should my temper get the better of me, the only thing left will be to abandon the profession entirely. I believe the new rules are required to be signed by the players. Well, I'll sign them if ordered to do so as a condition of my contract, no matter what they are, and continue to try to make my salary well earned. One thing is certain, though: in a year or two there will be an organization of players to perfect their own interests. It is bound to come."

Clarke arrived in town on March 14, preceded by most of his players, with the balance expected within the next two days. He overruled plans for spring practice in Louisville and made arrangements for ten days of work in West Baden Springs. In the meantime, the men who had already arrived took advantage of the good weather to get some light throwing and running in. Before leaving for West Baden, Clarke took time to inspect the facilities at League Park, declared that he liked what he saw, and requested a stove and hot water fixture installed for the players to have a warm bath after practices. The next day, a boiler with a capacity of 400 gallons was ordered for the clubhouse.

The addition of Billy Hoy to the team convinced Clarke to move Wagner back to the infield, and he was penciled in to start the season at second base. He had ended up playing much of 1897 in the outfield. Although he had only been with the Colonels for half a season, by this time Clarke had complete confidence in Wagner to play any position the team needed. His versatility had already been proven.

Around the League, talk of a player rebellion against the owners was spreading. According to the Courier-Journal, an unnamed Baltimore player recently complained that "Cattle, that's what we are. We are ordered to do this and we are driven here; we are forced to play any number of games they choose to fix, and if we don't like anything they say we can get out of the business. The reserve clause must be abolished, or the players will break up the game before long." The major bone of contention was the proposed increase in number of games played from 132 games in 1897 to 154 games in 1898 with no concurrent increase in salary. It was believed that Hugh Jennings, who in addition to playing ball was also an attorney, would lead the rebellion.

Hugh Jennings

When the team arrived in West Baden, they were greeted by rain, which continued heavy for a week. Most of the training was therefore limited to the indoors, until Clarke could stand it no more. "After dinner, he told the boys to get on all the old clothes they had, and he took the entire team on a jaunt of twenty miles in the worst sort of mud. The start was made shortly after dinner, and it was 8 o'clock to-night when they got back to the hotel a sorry party and very muddy. The route lay toward North Vernon, and when seven miles from the springs the Colonels got lost and wandered around in a circle from four o'clock until past six before they got their bearings. They then walked the seven miles in the dark and through the mud. When they arrived here to-night nearly every one of the boys took a Turkish bath and said they wished cross-country runs had never been invented. It is probable that the boys will not take many more such trips. – Louisville Courier-Journal.

Following the excursion, Clarke decided to cut the trip short, and made plans to return to Louisville two days later. He took the players to the bat factory on First Street when they returned. Each man was allowed to pick two bats of his choice. Then they returned to the Gait House, where the bats were scraped, and the rest of the afternoon was dedicated to patching old uniforms and repairing gloves. That evening, most of the men attended a performance at Macauley's Theater.

On a cold, windy and snowy day in late March, the team opted to stay indoors, and during the afternoon they were treated to a class "in the language of the deaf and dumb" led by center fielder Billy "Dummy" Hoy. Contrary to popular belief, Hoy had the ability to say a limited number of words and was a fairly proficient lip reader as well. He could hit a bit, too.

Harry and Clarke met in early April to discuss the team's financial situation. An unexpectedly strong gate at a recent exhibition game had bolstered the ledger, and the decision was made to use the extra funds to add another player or two, upping the roster from sixteen to eighteen. Even so, Clarke still needed to cut five, as there were still 23 under contract. Those cut would be farmed out to minor league teams, perhaps Connie Mack's Milwaukee team, where Waddell had already been sent. Mack was no longer the manager of the Pirates.

The opening game was scheduled for April 15 in Detroit, and the last game of the season set for October 15, making the race six months and one-day long. As expected, Clarke farmed out five, including Lou Mahaffey, Shorty Fuller, Dillard, Dolan and Newton, to set the roster at eighteen. As usual, a parade with all the trimmings was planned, and expectations for the new season soared.

"The Courier-Journal hopes with thousands of 'fans' that the team will prove a success, and cordially gives Mr. Pulliam credit for gathering together a husky team of young, active, intelligent and hustling ball players. And with Fred Clarke in front, leading the crowd and directing the way, there is no reason why they should disappoint their friends."

After a long month of anticipation, and equal amounts of rain, opening day arrived with fair skies and warmer weather. The day before, Clarke had read the Brush amendment to the players, and they all signed it voluntarily, in contrast to many players on other clubs, who had refused to sign in large numbers. The opening day lineup for the game against the Pirates was:

1. Billy Hoy (CF)
2. Claude Ritchey (SS)
3. Fred Clarke (LF)
4. Hans Wagner (2B)
5. Doc Nance (RF)
6. Scoops Carey (1B)
7. Bill Wilson (C)
8. Billy Clingman (3B)

9. Bert Cunningham (P).

As Mayor Weaver prepared to throw the ceremonial first pitch, with Clarke as the ceremonial batter, Dreher, who was standing beside him, warned, "Look out. If he bats that way, he is liable to wound one or both of us." "That's true," agreed the mayor. "Here, Manager Clarke," shouted Weaver. "You can't hit that way at the balls I pitch; get over on the other side." Clarke switched sides, and the crowd howled with laughter. The mayor threw the pitch, a lucky cutter that touched the outside corner of the plate. Clarke swung hard but missed. The crowd chuckled and applauded good-naturedly.

When the fanfare ended, and the game began, Clarke's swing improved. The Colonels attacked early, holding an 8-2 lead after three innings, and never looked back. Ritchey, Clarke and Nance each scored two runs, and Clarke led the way with three big hits. When it ended, the 10,000 cranks in attendance cheered mightily and celebrated the 10-3 victory for the home team.

The Colonels were in first place again, if only for a day. They lost the second and third games of the opening series, each by one run. Game three, played on a Sunday afternoon, drew a crowd of 13,000 at League Park.

Despite the Brush resolutions, things got ugly on the first day of the season at the Polo Grounds in New York. Giants' second baseman Kid Gleason, angry at several calls made by Pop Snyder, was removed from the game for kicking. The spectators objected loudly, one hurling epithets at the umpire. When Snyder approached the stands to identify the foul-mouthed fan he was met with cries of "Lynch him!" and "Kill him!" Cushions were also thrown at Snyder, causing a delay in the game. When it ended in a 4-2 loss for the home team, Snyder was given a police escort out of the park to ensure his safety.

The Orioles weren't behaving either. According to one of the Boston players, "There is apparently no notice taken by the Orioles of the Brush rules. The players there, and especially catcher Clark, 'egg on' the crowd as they formerly did. Why, last Saturday, McGraw ran out to the base line, although not coaching, and stood there and yelled as hard as he could at Nichols. The umpire took no notice of this, although McGraw's actions were clearly illegal."

With the Colonels off to a bad start, losing eight of their first ten games, the old stories about Anson being on his way to replace Clarke were revived. Even the Courier-Journal correspondent in Chicago participated, sending a telegram to the paper. "Chicago, April 26 – (special) - It is reported here that Anson will manage the Louisville club. He was seen tonight and at first denied the story, but later said that nothing definite had been arranged." Clarke, Dehler and Dr. Stucky all denied it, with Dehler and Stucky expressing solid support for Clarke. By the middle of May, following a 4-3 loss to Pittsburgh, the Colonels were back in a familiar position - last place. Their record stood at five wins and seventeen losses.

"President Pulliam arrived in the city last night," stated the Courier-Journal. "At the Louisville Hotel he registered 'from Hardluckville.' He says the club has been losing simply on account of bad luck; that they have played good ball, but could not win."

Clarke had his own explanation for the losing streak. "All of us have been hitting like old women."

Just when the clouds overhead seemed darkest, the spirits of the Louisville men were heartened by the appearance of a new mascot, named Dewey by the players, who wandered into the ball park the day after the team returned from a May game in Cleveland. Some wanted to run him off, but pitcher Dad Clarke insisted that he stay, and would help the team win games. Dad won out.

"To be plain," reported a correspondent, "Dewey is a goat, of the William variety, who has already shown an appetite for tin cans, linen, woolen uniforms and rocks as well as the grass which grows in the outfield. None of the Louisville players took much stock in Dewey's hoodoo powers until the Colonels captured the first game from Brooklyn. The gates are tightly locked each night and during the day Dewey feeds on the rank grass which abounds in center field.

"Besides winning the game from Brooklyn, Dewey has healed the fingers of Clarke and Wagner and 'Dummy' Hoy's thumb. He has given 'Chic' Fraser and Billy Magee control and has found Fred Clarke's batting eye for him. No wonder Dewey is popular with the Louisville players."

On May 25, with Chic Fraser in the box, the Colonels outscored Amos Rusie and the Giants, 8-4, finally defeating an old nemesis in League Park. "Rusie began the game with a smile of supreme confidence. In the third inning a double, a triple and a home run by Clarke's men turned the smile into a sickly grin, and in the eighth, when three singles, a double and a couple of chump plays by (Bill) Joyce came in a bunch, it developed into a dark scowl with trimmings of perspiration." As usual, Clarke, Hoy and Wagner led the way with their bats. A perceptive, if not biased, writer for the local paper noted that Clarke was three time as fast as most runners. "Clarke's great sprinting ability enabled him to stretch his hit into a three-bagger. On an ordinary runner it would have been good only for a single."

The month of May ended with a twin bill loss in Philadelphia on Decoration Day, both games ending with a score of 6-1 in favor of the Phillies, paced by their trio of great hitters, Elmer Flick, Ed Delahanty and Napoleon Lajoie. The Colonels were victimized by a bad call in game one, but true to their pledge on opening day, did not kick. Harry did not get his anticipated large holiday gate; bad weather kept many of the cranks at home, with only 10,000 at the park. The doubleheader loss turned into a four-game sweep two days later, the Colonels scoring a meager total of four runs in the four games, one in each game, wasting strong pitching and excellent work in the field. Next came a 12-4 drubbing at the hands of the Senators. Although they weren't there yet, last place seemed to be their ultimate destination.

Billy Hoy

In June, as his Cincinnati team made an Eastern tour, owner John T. Brush accompanied them, watching to see how the umpires were enforcing the new rules that bore his name. While in New York, he spoke with a reporter from the New York Sun. "As far as I have been able to observe, nearly all of the League clubs are trying to obey the rules which we drew up at St. Louis. But I want to say that the umpires are chiefly to blame for any disorderly behavior on the part of the players, if they fail to eject the offenders immediately from the game." Many magnates were already asking for the dismissal of umpires for incompetence as a way to protect their players. Some were even beginning to seriously consider the two-umpire system.

Two months into the season, many reporters were complaining that the Brush rules were unnecessarily inhibiting the men who played the grand old game. "Baltimore's new way of registering a kick is pretty neat. Instead of, as in the old days, the entire team taking a run for the plate, somebody makes a sign to Kelley and he stops the play and waltzes up to Lynch meekly, and suggests, that the pitcher has an irregular way about him and is dancing on the slab when he should keep his rear foot tied to the ground. When Lynch renders his decision, Kelley heaves a delicate sigh, thanks the gentleman and retires."

So was John McGraw. "I have complied with the League's new rule, and intend to do so," he said. "If I am sorely tempted I may adopt Walter Brodie's plan. He was called out on strikes recently in Pittsburg and walked away from the plate without even looking at the umpire. He rolled up his handkerchief like a gag, and, stuffing it in his mouth, walked to the bench and sat down."

But Earl Wagner, president of the Senators' team, had a different opinion. "The base-ball season of '98 will be entered into the chronicles of the game as the year of reformation. Some . . . insist that the Brush blacklistment and suspension laws and the increased power vested in the umpire are affecting the game, just as chloroform operates on an expiring Thomas cat; that is, the games are becoming as tame as pink teas or bean-bag parties. I will admit that there are fewer bouts at words between umpire and player, but that's a welcome improvement, as any genuine, sport-loving patron of the game will gladly admit."

But the naysayers, to support their claim, pointed out that attendance throughout the League was down significantly. And they were right. Some blamed it on the war with Spain, but others said the game was becoming dull. Either way, Harry was having more difficulty than ever balancing the books, as fewer and fewer fans bought tickets to games. Predictably, calls for contraction, from twelve teams to eight, were revived. The smaller market cities were dragging down the large ones with their small gates and poor play. If four teams were dropped from the League, Louisville would definitely be one of them.

Halfway through the season, Harry threatened to sue the Boston Herald after it ran a story about the Louisville club being on the verge of insolvency. "To tell the truth, we are now ahead," he insisted. "We may lose money on the year, for thus far we are $4,900 behind last year's receipts. Only $1,200 of this is on the home grounds." Many other small market teams were suffering as well.

On June 23, Harry sent the following telegraph to the editor of The Sporting Life:

"Story in your last issue alleging financial distress of Louisville Base Ball Co. absolutely false. The Boston Herald has issued complete retraction. Unless you right the gross libel, will place the matter in the hands of our lawyer."

The Sporting Life responded in kind in print:

"Now, Harry, dear, do please call off the dogs of war – law, we mean. What's the use of burning up money in legal squabbles even though the Louisville club be fairly rolling in wealth? We shudder at the prospective waste. Better use the superfluous cash in still further strengthening the

Louisville ball team, which is cutting such a swath in the League race – at the wrong end."

Nothing seemed to be going right for the Colonels. The team had a crying need for a new catcher, and had been looking for several months to no avail, causing much anxiety among the fans. The three catchers signed in January had long since been dismissed. Attendance began to fall, even on Sundays, even when the weather was pleasant. And the losing continued. Despite the troubles, Fred Clarke managed to stay optimistic and upbeat. Like everyone else, he blamed the umpires, but also took responsibility himself, reporting that the owners had instructed him to improve the team at all costs, but so far, he had been unable to do so.

Harry, however, was frustrated, and it showed. According to Clarke, he had deserted the team in Baltimore.

"'Here they are; take 'em,' Harry said to me," Clarke said. "Do what you can with them."

"Where are you going?" I asked.

"Oh, I don't know," he replied. "It don't make much difference just so I get away from this gang."

On the last day of June, the Colonels moved into a tie with St. Louis with a 9-1 win over the Orioles in League Park. It was a tie for eleventh place. In the third inning, following a collision at home plate, which allowed a second run to cross, the livid Orioles "swarmed around Umpire Hank O'Day like vultures around carrion. They beat on his shoulders with their fingers and said unprintable things." McGraw and his vile cursing were removed from the game, escorted by two policemen. This roused McGraw's anger to a higher level, and as he passed the stand receiving the torment of the local cranks, he responded by calling them "the vilest name which one man can call another. The postal regulations and regard for decency prevent the printing of even the mildest of the words he used."

At that point, however, exactly halfway through the season of reason, only two players had been suspended and none presented before the Board of Discipline. Of the two men, neither was named McGraw. There was indeed much kicking around the League, but for the most part the umpires were choosing to ignore it.

Clarke took advantage of a day off in the schedule to get married on July 5. A gift of a silver table service was received from the Directors of the team, and the players presented the couple with a silver ice cream service. Clarke gave his bride a set of diamond earrings. The honeymoon would be a tour of the League cities as they joined the team in Pittsburgh.

In an effort to increase revenue, the Cleveland team, now generally referred to as the Indians, started moving their home games to cities that drew more spectators. It was announced in the press that the Cleveland- Baltimore game of July 30, originally scheduled to be played in Cleveland, would be played in, of all places, Philadelphia. The wisecrackers in the press started calling them the Cleveland Wanderers.

"What will become of the Cleveland franchise next season is a topic that is being discussed by the Cleveland papers and National League magnates at present," wrote one reporter. "Frank De Haas Robison will not play any more games in Cleveland this year than he will have to. He has transferred a number of games already, and will transfer every one from Cleveland to some other city if it is possible to do so."

In the larger cities, like Philadelphia, the newspaper men were more to the point:

"If Baltimore, Cleveland and Louisville do not want to support major league clubs, why not drop these three dead teams and take in their places some live cities like Buffalo, Minneapolis and St. Paul." -Horace Fogel, Philadelphia Daily Ledger.

And then there were the skeptics:

"The fans in Cleveland are very blasé this season. During a close-score game they sit in the grand stand and bleachers reading war extras. The majority of the war extra cranks in Cleveland who mistake our ball park for a reading room, ought to register a complaint with Mr. Robison. To judge from their actions, they are not disturbed when the other team is in the lead." - Oliver Tebeau.

But attendance was down in the large cities as well. Recent games in Brooklyn and at the Polo Grounds had drawn meager crowds of 500 and 1,000, respectively. On July 19, the Colonels, in the midst of another long Eastern trip, lost 2-1 in a contest in New York shortened by rain. Only 250 die-hards attended. The next day only 400 showed up in Brooklyn, where the Colonels completed a four-game sweep of the Bridegrooms to end the trip. Still, they were in eleventh place, outpacing only the Browns.

Disappointed with the performance of the many young prospects he had signed, Harry made a conscientious decision to change tactics and only pursue players with proven track records. He picked up lefthanded pitcher Nick Altrock, a veteran of the Grand Rapids team. The move paid immediate dividends; in his major league debut, Altrock defeated the Bridegrooms, 7-4.

The losing continued, though, and more and more, with no other scapegoat in sight, the citizens of Louisville were blaming Harry. In a letter to the editor of the paper, a fan wrote, "with due respect and kindness for him, it can be said that a large majority of them have decided that the fault lies with the management – Mr. Pulliam. Even Mr. Pulliam's friends, and lots of them, for he is exceedingly popular, are now persuaded that he made a mistake when he accepted the position of President of the Colonels. The truth is Mr. Pulliam does not know the game of baseball. He has a penchant for signing whole bundles of youngsters, and then dispersing them."

As the 1898 season wore on, observers were beginning to wonder if the entire system of organized baseball was on the verge of collapse. The Western League, long one of the most successful of the minor leagues, was in financial shambles, as was the Interstate League. New York, Brooklyn, and Washington, three of the National League pillars, all had experienced a run of sub-1,000 attendance games. The Cleveland team had all but dissolved. Baltimore was not far behind, and Louisville was in dire straits. The usual suspects were named - the Brush rules and the war – but others sounded a more ominous note. Perhaps the people had simply grown tired of the game.

In a seemingly unimportant contest between the Orioles and the Giants, on July 26, an incident took place that would alter the history of the National League. It happened at the Polo Grounds, home of the Giants, at the midway point of the fourth inning. Former Colonel and current Oriole Ducky Holmes, who for a time had played for Andrew Freedman's Giants, had struck out and was on his way back to the bench, when he was verbally ridiculed by a New York fan.

"Oh, Holmes, you lobster. You're no good. That's why you had to leave the Giants."

"Well, it's a good thing for me that I'm not working for a Sheeney anymore," Holmes shouted back, Sheeney being a common derogatory term for Jewish people at the time. He was referring to Freedman, who was Jewish. Freedman was attending the game, heard the slight, became incensed, and quickly made his way down to the field. He found a policeman, and demanded that Umpire Lynch remove Holmes from the game. Lynch chose not to, claiming he had not heard the remark, ordered the officer to leave the field, and called for the game to resume. Now completely enraged, Freedman ordered his manager to refuse to continue with Holmes in the game, and again attempted to have the policeman remove Holmes, to no avail. When the New

Yorkers held their ground, still refusing to play, Lynch forfeited the game to Baltimore.

Next it was the crowd's turn to become angry. Having been denied the completion of their afternoon's leisure activity, they turned on Freedman, conjuring up insults of their own while demanding their money back. The words "lynch" and "tar and feather" were shouted.

"Freedman mounted the clubhouse steps and addressed the angry populace. His remarks were unheeded, and fearing a riot, he at last offered to return the admission money. This was greeted with cheers, and the crowd lined up in orderly fashion, and each rooter received his half dollar."

But as far as Andrew Freedman was concerned, the matter was far from settled.

"Freeman treated me like a dog when I was a member of his team and I cannot say that I'm sorry he has made a monkey of himself," remarked Holmes after the game. The next day, Freedman informed Orioles manager Hanlon that Holmes would not be permitted in the park at the Polo Grounds the next time the Orioles played in New York. Additionally, he refused to pay the Orioles their share of the gate from the game, citing the fact that much of the gate had been returned to the patrons. Freedman, though, faced a $1,000 fine per the Brush rules, as established prior to the season, for contributing to the melee. He refused to pay.

Two weeks later, meeting behind closed doors, the Board of Directors voted to suspend Ducky Holmes for the remainder of the season, and to uphold the $1,000 fine imposed upon Freedman. The forfeiture of the game to Baltimore was also upheld. The fine to be paid by Freedman was awarded to the Orioles club, on the condition of following through on the suspension of Holmes. In response, Holmes hired a lawyer and threatened to sue, the damage being the denial of his right to earn a living by playing ball.

It was clear to all, from day one, that the sentiments of the fans, newspaper editors and even some of the magnates were on the side of Holmes, over the unpopular Freedman. "Holmes is receiving letters of sympathy from all over the country. Vigorous language is used to condemn the action of the Board of Directors of the League. The Boston players have adopted resolutions condemning the Directors and asking that fair treatment be accorded Holmes. Freedman is roasted to a turn." - Louisville Courier-Journal.

In a stunning move, On August 26, by a vote of 9-1, the Board of Directors revoked the suspension of Holmes. The representatives from Boston, Brooklyn, Chicago, Cincinnati, Cleveland, Philadelphia, Pittsburgh, St. Louis and Washington all favored lifting the suspension. The teams involved, Baltimore and New York, were not allowed to vote. The lone vote to maintain the suspension was cast by the Louisville representative, Harry Pulliam.

Asked to explain his vote, Harry issued a statement:

"Last Monday night at Philadelphia, the Board met, and after five hours' discussion decided unanimously to suspend Holmes for the remainder of the season. The matter was carefully weighed, and each member of the Board signed the findings voluntarily."

Later, when asked, Harry felt the need to further clarify his position:

"I am not taking a stand with Mr. Freedman against Holmes, as a good many of the papers are trying to make believe. I have not voted with Mr. Freedman since I have been in the National League. The vote of the Louisville club has always been cast against the Brush faction."

The $1,000 fine imposed on Freedman was again upheld. When informed of the actions of the Board, Freedman became uncontrollably enraged. In due time, the rest of the League would pay.

In late July, the Colonels went on a surprising eight-game winning streak, capped with a 6-4 victory over Amos Rusie and the Giants. The big hit was a home run by Hans Wagner with the bases full that rolled all the way to the center field fence. The term "grand slam" was not commonly used in 1898. Despite the streak, the club was still mired in eleventh place, but closing in on Washington for tenth. They were playing outstanding baseball, so when the Colonels headed east in August, the newspaper men in the Eastern cities had to find other ways to insult them.

"They have too many mascots in Louisville. Each player owns a dog and the club house is a perfect kennel. That isn't the worst of it, for the pack is turned loose on the field during games and runs over across the diamond while the game is in play. One of them will someday 'queer' a play, and, as the rules don't specify any interference by dogs in their verbose technicalities, there'll be no end of a row."

As the pennant race heated up, the Colonels were one of several teams vying for the services of pitching phenom Charles Phillippe, who was being shopped around by the Minneapolis team in the Western League. The Colonels were well out of the chase, but somehow Harry won the competition for Phillippe. It was a major coup. A few weeks later, he bought the release of third baseman Tommy Leach from the Auburn team of the New York State League. Harry was definitely on a roll. Phillippe and Leach would be stars in the National League for a decade and more.

Meanwhile, feeling insulted and embarrassed by the Holmes incident, Andrew Freedman began dismantling his Giants team. Having a strong team in the League's flagship city of New York had always been considered vital to the health of the League. This was to be Freedman's revenge. The fans became angry and frustrated, and attendance plummeted.

"President Andrew Freedman, who returned from Europe last night, witnessed this afternoon's baseball game. So did sixty-nine other people, none of whom was unfortunate enough to own a ball club. The attendance up at Coogan's

Hollow is gradually decreasing, and near the zero mark." - Louisville Courier-Journal.

In mid-September the Colonels were the hottest team in the National League, having won 16 of their last 23. They were in ninth place, a high-water mark for that late in the year, and the fans were noticing. To some, it felt like the old days in the American Association, when the team had won a championship in the early 1890's. When they returned from the road after a three-game sweep of the Colts, the Colonels were the talk of the town. They were greeted at the train station by a large group of fans who cheered like never before. Both Harry and Fred addressed the adoring crowd, expressing confidence the club could still catch Pittsburgh for eighth position in the League, and hinting that the team would be even better next year. The afternoon game that followed was watched by 3,800 spectators, and featured the first appearance of Tommy Leach as a Colonel. 800 women were at the park for Ladies Day, and a band played during the game.

When the season dwindled to a precious few dates, Harry decided to have a benefit game for the players the day after the last game. He announced it to the press, had tickets printed, and arranged for them to be sold at various business around town. Along with the game, there was to be foot races, a sixteen-pound hammer throw, and contests of baseball skills. Clarke was expected to win the 100-yard dash, although Hoy and Leach could give him a run for his money. All expected Wagner to break the world's record for long distance throwing.

The Pirates arrived in town on October 6, with Louisville now in position to pass them for eighth place in the standings. The cranks at League Park were up for it. "Throughout most of the afternoon the spectators jeered and hissed, stormed and raved, threatened to fight and showered the most abusive expletives on Umpire (Jim) McDonald."

But it wasn't enough; Pirates 4, Louisville 2. The gap between the teams grew to five games.

The final game with Pittsburgh featured a tight pitching duel between Billy Magee and Sam Leever of the Pirates. After eleven innings it was declared a tie at 2-2 due to darkness, and the fact that the Pirates had a train to catch. All hope of passing Pittsburgh for eighth place was now gone. Yet hopes for 1899 were already soaring. Phillippe and Leach had been added to an already strong team, and Harry had re-acquired Rube Waddell for a second try with the Colonels. There were lots of reasons to be optimistic.

At the benefit game, Wagner did indeed break the record for long distance throwing, Clarke tied the record for circling the bases, and the entire team participated in a greased pig race, to the delight of the 4,000 in the stands.

A banquet for the team was held that evening at the Gait House, where many speeches were made, too much food consumed, and goodbyes said for the winter. The players divided the $1,200 raised from the game, each man receiving $60.40. Then each man went home – Clarke to Kansas, Wagner to Pittsburgh, Hoy on a honeymoon with his new bride, Pete Dowling to his zinc mine in the Ozark Mountains of Missouri, others elsewhere.

"Cincinnati, O., Oct. 26 – (Special) -In the chapel of the Children's Home, on West Ninth Street, William Hoy, the well-known ball player, who was with the Cincinnati team for several seasons and is now center fielder of the Louisville Club, was married to Miss Anna M. Lowery tonight. The contracting parties are deaf mutes, and the ceremony was conducted in the sign language. Rev. Holt, a Baptist minister, officiated. A reception and luncheon followed the wedding. The groom's gift to the bride consists of $5,000 in government bonds."

In December, the optimism turned to angst. Speculation was rampant around the circuit that a deal was in the works to transfer the Louisville team to Detroit. Having waited patiently for many years, and now having a team they could brag about, the good people of Louisville were in imminent danger of losing it.

"Van Derbeck, or anybody else who sends a $50,000 certified check to Barney Dreyfuss of Louisville, Ky., after Van's option expires on Monday next, can obtain a quick claim deed of the entire team of Colonels, and a franchise in the National League that has three years of life," wrote a reporter in the Detroit Journal. The 'three years' referred to the amount of time left before the ten-year agreement would expire, and membership for Louisville no longer ensured.

One week later everything had seemingly changed, though the outcome would be just as grim. According to a report in the Chicago Tribune, a major shakeup of organized baseball was in the works. The paper reported that the Baltimore and Brooklyn franchises would be consolidated, and Cleveland and Washington would be dropped from the National League. The Cleveland players would be reassigned to the St. Louis franchise. A buyout of the Louisville team, much to the dismay of the locals, was also part of the grand plan. Louisville, it was believed, would join a reconstructed eight team American Association. The new American Association, as planned, would consist of franchises from Baltimore, Washington, Cleveland, Buffalo, Detroit, Kansas City, Milwaukee and Louisville.

Pulliam, Dreyfuss and Dreher were participating in the negotiations in New York. The situation seemed hopeless. They had given up on trying to save Louisville's membership in the National League and were trying to secure the best terms of sale for the stockholders.

"Our sole object is to sell out," Harry told reporters. "We need that $50,000, and I think we will get it. Will we go into a minor league, formed on the plan of the old American Association? Well that depends. If we should become a party to any such project, we will not spend any of the money obtained by the sale of our League franchise in the purchase of new players. It would be an excellent plan for the New York club to buy us out, should the League fail to do so. The Giants would then have Clarke, Dexter and Cunningham, to say nothing of other valuable players, besides the franchise."

Deacon Phillippe

The headlines in newspapers across the country the next day shook the foundation of the League. It was announced that all the best players from the great Baltimore team were being transferred to the Brooklyn franchise. Ned Hanlon, it was announced, was to be the manager of the newly constructed Bridegrooms. Andrew Freedman had declined an offer to purchase the Louisville franchise for $50,000, claiming that his team was already good enough to compete. It clearly wasn't. The Louisville club had not been sold, and the League had not contracted. The only business they were able to conduct was the sale of pitcher Chic Fraser to Philadelphia for an unknown sum.

A bitter Harry Pulliam, having failed to sell the floundering franchise to both Detroit and New York, was reflective after the dust had settled. "I have learned a whole lot in base-ball. The majority of these fellows they call magnates are good things as long as they can use you. After that you are like the advertising card in a euchre deck. But I have learned a whole lot; yes, heaps and heaps of things have I learned; but they can't keep it up any longer. My eye teeth have been cut way below the gum. We will show you how to run a team next summer."

Chapter Five

Swan Song

Two weeks later, as 1899 began, everything had changed again. Barney Dreyfuss had returned from his journey east with details of a new plan to reduce the League to eight teams. Louisville was not expected to be one of those teams, and several offers had been received for their better players, including an offer of $16,000 for Fred Clarke.

With the future of the franchise very much in question, the stockholders planned a Friday night meeting at Seelbach's Hotel. The magnates of the Louisville team had been conferencing amongst themselves. Although the ten-year agreement was not due to expire for another three years, it was believed by many that all would benefit by settling the issue of shrinking the League sooner rather than later. Baltimore and Brooklyn were nearly bankrupt. The ownership of the Browns was up in the air, and Louisville was right there with them. Treasurer Dreher's financial report showed a major loss for the season. Declining attendance throughout the League was the main reason.

Fred Clarke had arrived in town from Chicago the day before, with plans to attend the Friday night meeting and find out for himself what was going on. Failed attempts to gain information prior to the meeting were fruitless and frustrated him. "The owners seem to be as badly at sea as I am, and I have not been here," he lamented. He returned to Chicago.

In the end, the meeting settled nothing. The Directors made several bold statements to the papers, including a reassurance that the team would remain in Louisville for at least three more years, per the ten-year agreement, and also assurances that no player would be sold. But everyone knew the plan for reduction of the League was still alive, and in reality, the Directors of the Louisville team had little say in the matter.

The next League meeting was scheduled for February 28, with reduction to be decided, hopefully, once and for all. Or, at least for another year. One major factor could not be denied; New York and Brooklyn, in the largest city in the League, had poor teams that needed to be propped up with better players. And Baltimore, Cleveland and Louisville had some awfully good players.

But February 28 was a long way away, and the business of running a baseball team could not wait. In a plan to raise capital, the Directors began an ambitious effort to sell stock at $100 a share to citizens who wanted to demonstrate their support of the Colonels. A total of $34,000 of stock was to be sold, and in early January they reported that more than $2,000 worth had already been spoken for.

Meanwhile, in a show of good faith, Clarke and his wife moved to Louisville to begin preparations for the coming season. After settling, he traveled to several cities in the South, looking for a new location for spring practice, the drenching downpours of West Baden still fresh in his memory. The Southern trip, it was announced, would begin on March 18. Opening day would be April 15.

Dreyfuss, now serving as treasurer, mailed contracts to nineteen players, two more than originally planned, including pitching phenom Walter Woods, newly secured from the Chicago Colts. The players, aware of the precarious financial situation of the League, were expected not to cause difficulties by holding out for more money, and they didn't.

One week later, the initial optimism of the sale of stock was beginning to fade. "I worked hard to-day and disposed of but two shares of stock, and Mr. Pulliam sold but one," complained Dreyfuss. "It is true that we have had very bad weather in which to solicit subscriptions, but for the time we have been at it, very little has been accomplished."

Harry filed paperwork to run for re-election to the Kentucky assembly, then headed to his hometown of Scottsville to visit relatives. He was feeling the stress of the uncertainty of the franchise and needed rest to calm his nerves. Later, he expressed second thoughts about running for re-election, claiming his business interests left him little time to represent his constituents properly.

On February 16, Dreyfuss was named to replace Harry as president of the team. Harry was to return to his old position of secretary, which suited him fine, as he had expressed a desire to retire from the presidency, citing concerns about his health. The club finally gave up the sale of stock as a failure, and all offers collected thus far were to be returned. Harry and Dreyfuss were chosen to attend the important League scheduling meeting scheduled for February 28 in New York.

Harry made a statement to the press:

"I have handled the club for two years, and I think it speaks for itself. I think I have gathered together a team that will stand comparison with any in the League. The Directors have just passed me a vote of thanks upon retiring. In my new position I will work just as hard for the club's interests as I did before. The most harmonious feeling prevails amongst us all."

As Harry and Dreyfuss left for New York, Clarke arrived to begin preparations for the coming season. The players had been told to report on March 16, but it was anticipated that several would arrive early, beginning any day now. Clarke had selected Thomasville, Georgia, as the location for spring training, citing reduced rates at hotels and discounts from the railroads. He had recently visited the town and was convinced it would be a perfect location for the players to focus on getting in shape and polishing their skills. On February 16, he received a package from a supporter back home in Kansas:

Dear Sir;

Let the enclosed be your club's mascot for the season; never leave it behind you. It is said to be the right hind foot of a blind jack rabbit and killed in a graveyard after dark by a big black coon. I would have had it mounted and fixed up, but there is no one in this place could do the job. I send it with best wishes for the Colonels' success in the coming season.

Robert W. Matthis, Parsons, Kansas

A proposed rule change for 1899 would increase the distance necessary for a home run to be hit over the fence from 235 feet to 285 feet. According to Edward Hanlon, "The Boston Club has had a big advantage over other clubs for years in that short left-field fence. I know that we have lost game after game just because of that fence. People little realize what a big advantage it is. The Boston players practice hundreds of hours every season trying to put balls over that short fence, and they have the trick down fine. In a number of close games I have seen them drop flies over that fence with several men on bases that won the game then and there, when on any other grounds in the League the fly would have been an easy out for any good left fielder."

On the eve of the League scheduling meeting, Dreyfuss issued a statement that set the tone. "The Louisville club is in the National League to stay. I will not sell my franchise now for any price. There was a time when I was anxious to sell, and would have done so, but now things are entirely different. I have made arrangements to take a long vacation, and will give my personal attention to my club all the season."

The meeting began the afternoon of March 2 at the Fifth Avenue Hotel in New York, with the status of the St. Louis club still in doubt, making the actual creation of a schedule all but impossible. As a result, three possible schedules were presented. Rumors were also swirling that Freedman was attempting to sell the Giants for a reported $65,000. He denied it. Expulsion of the St. Louis team was recommended by the magnates. Nothing was done to address the Louisville situation.

By this time, all Louisville players had signed and returned their contracts, with two notable exceptions: Wagner and Phillippe. According to Dreyfuss, Wagner had been busy "employed as star German comedian in the principal theatre of Carnegie, Pennsylvania, where he lives." He also had a billiard hall in Carnegie to look after. Phillippi was still holding out, but signed shortly thereafter.

A team meeting was held the evening of March 17 "in one of the parlors of the Galt House," and all players attended except Wagner and pitcher Pete Dowling. Plans for the trip to Thomasville were discussed, and several made speeches, including Harry, manager Clarke and Waddell. Dreyfuss asked the players to be on their best behavior while in Thomasville, noting that the Piney Woods Hotel was popular with millionaires and people of high status. Dreyfuss bought each player a pair of slippers to wear in the hotel, so as not to demolish the floors with their spikes. After the meeting, Wagner appeared and signed his contract.

On March 18, the assembly arrived in Thomasville, checked in to the Piney Woods, and promptly were informed that full evening suits were expected to be worn by all guests dining at the hotel. Clearly, the Colonels had moved up in the world, but this presented a problem; only Dexter had brought a suit.

"Dexter declared yesterday that he was going to don his dress suit as soon as he arrived at the hotel. The next day, according to programme, Clarke will eat his dinner dressed in the swallow-tail. The next day Woods can have it, and so on down the line. Dexter insists that Wagner wear the suit last, because Hans is so big that once he gets into the clothes they will be useless thereafter." - Louisville Courier-Journal.

Back in Louisville, Dreyfuss had met with the owner of League Park, and arranged for seating to be increased by 3,000, bringing it more in line with League standards at ten thousand. In the past, overflow crowds were occasionally forced to stand in the outfield, sometime as many as 2,000 to 3,000 fans at a time.

Tommy Leach

When Clarke arrived at the park in Thomasville to inspect the diamond before the first day of spring practice, he found the infield to be in unacceptable condition. He immediately "ordered a gang of men out to scrape the diamond. When the players reached the park, in the afternoon, they found a chain gang of negroes hard at work putting the diamond in shape, and a great many funny remarks were made in comparing the striped uniforms of the convicts and those of the ball-players."

On March 24, at 1:30 in the morning, there was an explosion in a paint shop across the street from the Piney Woods Hotel. To ensure everyone's safety, the night watchman blew the engine whistle, and the hotel quickly emptied. A great fire ensued, lighting up the night sky, and it soon caught the hotel in a blaze. The Colonels jumped to action, making sure everyone had escaped, and carrying several invalids down from the third floor. Then the players worked to extinguish the inferno.

"The scenes in the hotel were picturesque. Half-dressed men and women knelt here and there praying. Many were screaming for their money and jewels which they had left behind. Sparks dropped all about, and set fire to the church near the hotel. The Colonels quickly organized a bucket brigade, and extinguished the church fire. Manager Clarke stood at the top of a tall ladder and threw water until the fire in the church was entirely out. The players were drenched to the skin." – Louisville Courier-Journal.

Then, the players thought of Hoy, who would not have heard the cries of "fire!" They sprinted back to the hotel. As Clarke was preparing to kick in the door to Hoy's room, the door opened, and there stood Hoy and his wife, fully dressed, preparing to leave. The glare of the fire had awakened them, but they had not realized how serious the situation was.

Next, the Colonels began carrying furniture out of the hotel, and several people as well. At the request of a frantic woman, Wagner pulled a 200-pound chest from the third floor to the street. When he finished, the woman thanked the wrong player and gave him a kiss. Hans was not amused. Another woman, in her rush to safety, had lost a diamond alligator valued at $2,500. Waddell found it on the lawn and returned it to her, whereupon she offered him a fifty-dollar reward. He declined the offer.

The players did not get back to bed until 5 o'clock in the morning.

The weather in Thomasville proved most agreeable, and there was little interruption to the manager's schedule of activities. The biggest problem was mosquitoes. On Saturday, March 26, the Regulars played the Yannigans in a private workout, no spectators allowed. Clarke was unable to participate, confined to his bed by a leg injury that resulted from a collision with a tree. After the game, some of the players journeyed to Florida to go coon hunting. It was to be Billy Hoy's first coon hunt, and the boys were eager to show him a good time.

March 26 also brought the first shock of the new season. The 1899 League schedule had been adopted and published, and the Colonels had been robbed of eleven Sunday games, five at home and six on the road, depriving them of many of the largest gate receipts the season would have to offer. It would be a huge financial hit for the team, estimated by Dreyfuss in excess of $16,000. Brush and his cohorts, James Hart of Chicago and Frank de Haas Robison of the Browns and Indians, were trying to bankrupt Dreyfuss' team. Predictably, Dreyfuss was livid, and he threatened legal action to remedy the situation. If anything, it made him even more determined to stay in the National League.

On the evening of March 29, Dreyfuss boarded the six o'clock Chesapeake and Ohio train to Washington, determined to have the troubling schedule changed. His plan was to get the League to hold a meeting to reconsider the schedule, but this required a majority vote, seven or more of twelve, and Dreyfuss by then had secured only five –Boston, New York, Philadelphia, Pittsburgh, and, of course, Louisville. Harry was dispatched to New York to meet with President Ferdinand Abell of Brooklyn and secure his vote, but by the time he arrived, Dreyfuss had already received a telegram of support from Abell. One more vote was needed, with Baltimore the most likely ally, but Dreyfuss thus far had been unable to contact Manager Hanlon.

When asked about the grievance of the Louisville club, Brush responded, "I have no wish to discuss that matter at all. The schedule has been made out and adopted, and the League circuit fixed at twelve clubs. If there are any who do not like it they have a right to protest. Personally, I have nothing to complain of. "

Two days later, it was clear the Dreyfuss did not have enough votes. Baltimore and Brooklyn had not voted with Louisville, and Dreyfuss' plan was all but dead. But he wasn't giving up. "Our attorney, Mr. Zach Phelps, is working hard to determine on a plan of action, in the event that a reconsideration of the schedule cannot be effected, and you can depend on it that Messrs. Hart, Brush et al, will get what is coming to them."

Dreyfuss then announced that the Louisville team would not move or disband for the 1899 season. The club would prepare as usual for the opener and all games to follow. It had also been decided that no players were to be sold. Brush and Hart had failed, at least for the time being, in their efforts to kill the franchise. The schedule that had been adopted decidedly did not favor the Colonels, but they were prepared to fight it out in court.

"Louisville appears to be the only stumbling block to the path of the magnates' eight-club scheme," reported the Courier-Journal. "Washington, Baltimore and Cleveland are ready to quit, and the life of the present circuit seems to depend upon the length of time the Louisville club will stand the freeze-out gaff."

Two days before the season was to start, Dreyfuss met with Brush and Hart in Chicago and worked out a revised schedule, returning all the Sunday dates that had been taken away. The threat of litigation had worked. The new season could now begin without the worry of intervention by the courts.

Ten thousand enthusiastic fans turned out on opening day, cheering and singing long before the game began, and well after it started. "They had packed into slow trolley cars like sardines in a box; they had fought their way to the ticket office; they had lost collars and ties in the rush for the turnstiles; they had come with the enthusiasm oozing." Two hours and five minutes later, ten thousand left the ball park silently, their heads hanging, and made their way home. Final score: Colts 15, Colonels 1.

Poor attendance throughout the circuit in April brought new predictions of the League's pending demise. The Washington team was drawing fewer than 300 fans at its home games and had begun selling off its better players to make ends meet. Louisville players were convinced that the Senators, and also the Indians, would cease operations within days. When they hit the road for a four-game series in Cleveland on April 30, the Colonels were far from certain that the games would actually take place.

Dreyfuss was more optimistic; he thought that both teams would survive until the Fourth of July.

The games in Cleveland were, in fact, played, the first two a doubleheader on May 2. But there wasn't much cause for hope for the home team; when the first game started, there were fewer than 100 patrons in the stands. Although eventually 500 entered the park, it was still too small a number for anyone to feel good about. Those who stayed home, in droves, missed two exciting one run games, each team getting one victory. When the Colonels lost to Boston on May 19, they had lost ten of their last thirteen, and were clearly stuck in the second division. It was Ladies' Day, yet barely 1,000 showed up.

Two days later they lost to Cleveland in a wet and muddy game and fell to ninth place. Ushers were sent out between innings to sweep water from the field. Phillippe took the loss. Despite the weather, the Colonels had insisted the game be played, having spent $300 to make the trip and not wanting to lose their share of the gate.

"The salvation of the game, from a financial standpoint, lies in the dissolution of the Cleveland and Louisville teams, and the strengthening of other clubs besides Brooklyn and Boston with what good material there is in the disbanded teams," wrote a St. Louis reporter. "The expense of maintaining the Clevelands is a heavy tax on the ball-playing club of the Robison brothers, as it is all outgo. Louisville is losing money almost as fast as games, but the suggestion to drop the club is received with disfavor in Kentucky. However, they will both be dropped."

In Chicago, despite the Brush rules, McGraw was kicking again.

"The battle was sanguinary. In every minute the players fought and jawed, and McGraw, chaffing under defeat, almost incited the crowd to riot. He defied (Ed) Swartwood and heaped abuse on him until the last man was out. Swartwood gave an exhibition of bad umpiring and cowardice. He permitted McGraw to do as he pleased. Once, after he put McGraw out of the game, he ordered the belligerent midget off the field, whereupon McGraw sat on the grass near the plate and heaped abuse on the umpire to the end, defying him to carry out his order."

A story from a Chicago paper revealed yet another attempt to reduce the League, this one with Louisville still included. Asked to comment, Harry said, "Yes, I heard about that story, and I can say positively that Louisville is yet in the big League. As far as Louisville is concerned, there is nothing in the story, though I won't say that the League will not be reduced. I mean that Louisville will not be thrown out – whatever else may happen, I am unable to predict. The Louisville club is not on the market."

Despite Harry's optimism, the team was still losing money. To cut costs, pitchers Malachi Kittridge and William Magee were sold to Washington and Philadelphia. Kittridge took a parting shot at Dreyfuss, accusing him of making the team stay in shabby hotels. Harry came to the owner's defense. "President Dreyfuss has run the club with a liberal hand. He sent the players to the finest training quarters in the South; they stopped at a $5 a day hotel, and no team was ever treated better. Around the circuit the team was sent to the best hotels, and no player has any kick coming."

As the Colonels struggled for survival, Dreyfuss was approached by manager Hanlon, formerly of Baltimore and now leading the Bridegrooms, or Trolley-dodgers, as they were sometimes referred to, or Superbas, about a possible trade, proposing that he give Hugh Jennings in exchange for Wagner. The offer was declined. "Most positively Hans Wagner will not be sold," insisted Clarke, "nor will he be swapped for Jennings or any other player in the League. When Mr. Dreyfuss mentioned Hanlon's Jennings proposition for Wagner I yelled 'Murder!' Dreyfuss said: 'Don't be alarmed, I am just telling you what Hanlon said, and in reply I gave him the merry ha-ha; also, the glacial glare and face.'"

And then the Colonels got hot. The last game of July's Eastern road trip was played in Philadelphia. The Colonels bested the Phillies, 6-3, with former Colonel Billy Magee in the box for the home team. The Eastern journey was their most successful in years, with only two losses in eight games preventing a perfect record, and they were quickly making up ground on New York, Pittsburgh and Cincinnati. A finish in the first division seemed to be within reach.

Back home again in League Park, The Colonels whipped first place Brooklyn 5-3 with 11,500 in the stands on a Sunday afternoon. The added seats in the grand stand did not solve the problem it was intended to, as many in attendance had no seats and had to stand on the outfield grass. One week later, 10,000 cheered as the team took two from the Indians. Hoy and Wagner each hit two home runs. On August 1, in the fourth inning of a victory over the Giants, Hans Wagner became the first player in major league history to steal second base, third base and home in one trip around the bases. The Colonels swept the three-game series.

When the homestand ended, the team traveled by boat on the steamer "City of Louisville" for a pair of games in Cincinnati. Meanwhile, Dreyfuss was believed to be headed for Grand Rapids to make a deal for Waddell, who had not pitched for the Colonels all season, having been farmed out after spring practice. Rube had been pitching every other day for two months, winning 28 of 31 games. Dreyfuss thought Waddell would provide the final push for a finish in the first division. But the Grand Rapids manager refused to let him go, as was his right. He had been "loaned" the pitcher for the entire 1899 season.

While the team was out of town, disaster struck, one they would not be able to overcome. A large section of the grandstand was destroyed by a fire, thought to have resulted from an electrical storm. Dreyfuss was not deterred. "We are protected in our lease. We will not transfer any games unless we are compelled. The Bleachers are still intact, as I understand it, and if necessary we can hire circus seats. A new stand can easily be erected in two weeks, and as we do not return home until next Saturday the work may be started as once. It is in the hands of the owners."

Dreher was quizzed by the newspapers about plans to rebuild. "I will never consent to put up the same sort of grand stand which burned down this morning. It took up a great space, and its seating capacity, considering its space, was small. The next grand-stand that is built at the park, unless it is a temporary affair, will be much larger than the old one and will seat many more people." A reporter asked Dreher if he intended a brick and cantilever grandstand, similar to the one recently built in Philadelphia. "Well, hardly that," responded Dreher. Once, again, Louisville was not quite big league.

Harry left New York, where he had been traveling with the team, to return to Louisville and supervise the construction of temporary seating, to be completed by the time the team returned home four days hence. Additionally, 2,500 circus seats had been rented. The debris from the fire had already been removed by the time Harry arrived.

The players returned home to find the damage from the fire had been much worse than they had been told. All their uniforms, bats and other equipment had been destroyed. At Harry's request, League President Nick Young had given permission for the team to wear their traveling gray uniforms for the rest of the home games. The men went to the bat factory to have new bats made. Despite Harry's best efforts, seating was restored to a capacity of only 5,000. Offers to transfer games to other cities in the League were many, but Dreyfuss was determined to complete the home schedule as planned, and all offers were cordially refused. However, there was some good news; Waddell would soon be rejoining the team.

On August 22, the first home game after the fire, the Colonels blasted Cleveland 15-6. Centerfielder Hoy went 4 for 6. Prior to the game, Manager Clarke was presented with a baby carriage for his newborn daughter. Attached was a personal note to Clarke, signed by 25 admirers, including Harry and Dreyfuss: "The rooters whose names are added hereto desire to present to your infant daughter this carriage and robe. It is a token of our wishes for her constant good fortune, of respect and admiration for her mother, and out of good feelings toward you. We renew our wishes for a happy life for Miss Clarke, congratulate the fortunate mother and father, and looking to a succession of Clarkes to use it, now present you this carriage in the name of the following of your friends and admirers."

Following the ceremony, Clarke proceeded to bat and made a base hit. The hapless Cleveland team, with the loss, fell to a record of 13-92, by far the worst in the League.

Ten days later, Dreyfuss had reversed course, and it was announced that following the home game of September 2, all remaining games would be played in other cities. It was a stunning revelation to the people of Louisville. It was now fair and reasonable to ask if major league baseball would ever be played again in their town. Although the team was making money, the prospect of losing more than $200 a game for the rest of the season threatened to wipe out all that had been accomplished financially. There was talk Wagner and Clarke would be moved to Cincinnati for the 1900 season, and Leach to Boston.

In the last major league game ever played at League Park in Louisville, the hometown Colonels beat the Washington Senators 25-4. Fred Clarke had five hits and Billy Hoy scored five runs.

"The baseball season of 1899 in this city closed yesterday afternoon, and at eight o'clock this morning the Colonels will shake the dust of Louisville from their feet, board a B. and O. S.W. train for St. Louis, possibly never to return to the city whose name they wear across their shirt fronts. And there are no tears, no moanings, no crepe, no regrets." – Louisville Courier-Journal.

Many fans, though, those who were purchasers of season tickets, were angry.

Before leaving town with the team, Harry spoke to reporters. "The Louisville Club is not for sale, none of its players are for sale. This winter a new grand stand will be built, and the team, the best one that ever represented Louisville, will be in the field next year. I might add that all unused season book coupons will be redeemed at their purchase price."

The people of the town had always trusted and respected Harry as a man of his word. But this time, no one believed him. Now, the newspaper writers in Louisville began referring to their own team as the "Wanderers."

In Louisville, Dreyfuss told a business acquaintance that the Colonels would play three games at home before the end of the season, the three being October 5, 6 and 7, against

Cincinnati. The next day the news hit the Courier-Journal. But it never happened. On October 15, 1899, the Louisville Colonels of the National League played their last game ever. Clarke's men defeated the Pittsburgh Pirates, 4-1. The Colonels finished their last season with a record of 74 wins and 77 losses, their best showing ever in the National League. Following their final home game, when all seemed lost, they had won 23 of the last 36 games, a testament to the will and determination of the players.

When the war ended, attendance had picked up considerably in most cities. The final ledgers of the 1899 season showed that eleven teams had turned a profit totaling more than $350,000. Cleveland broke even.

Still, by the first week of November, Dreyfuss had decided to sell the club, most likely to the National League, from whom he believed he could get $10,000 to $12,000, simply to fold the club and reduce the League. Only one year earlier, the club was believed to be worth as much as $60,000. But there was still no new grandstand, and the profits from the 1899 season turned out to be a paltry $300.

The week of Thanksgiving, newspapers in Chicago were reporting that a deal had been reached for the Louisville star players to be sold to the Chicago team. Harry handled the negotiations, as Dreyfuss and Hart, the owner of the Chicago club, did not get along well, and Harry and Hart had become friends. Clarke would be the new team captain, and Harry would serve as traveling agent for the team. Though still a young man of thirty, Harry's business sense was well known, and he was highly respected among the owners.

"Chicago will probably not pre-empt very many players from the Colonels' bunch in any event. Fred Clarke, of course, is the one most sought, and Clarke is anxious to join the Orphans. The acquisition of Clarke would also tend to solve the difficulty of getting a field captain. Wagner would also be a welcome acquisition, and "Rube" Waddell probably could do a turn in the box should occasion require

it. And there is 'Foxy' Cunningham, somewhat ancient but still in the ring. Ritchie, Hoy and Phillippi might also do."
-Chicago Inter Ocean.

Sixteen days later it appeared that Pittsburgh, not Chicago, would be the destination for the intransient Louisville players. The headline of the Courier-Journal read, "Best of the Louisville Players Said to Be Slated for the Smoky City." Although at this point he denied it, Dreyfuss had secured a controlling interest in the Colonels for an undisclosed sum. He intended to attempt to sell the Louisville franchise during the League meeting beginning December 10 in New York. When asked directly about the future of the Louisville team, Dreyfuss responded, "The League meeting will decide it all, and I feel that the Colonels will not be here next season." Since the ten-year agreement still had three years left, it was felt that the franchise still had value, especially during the ten days leading up to the League meeting. The plan was to get the League to buy the Louisville franchise, and then fold it to contract to eight teams.

Before securing the agreement with Pittsburgh, Dreyfuss and Pulliam traveled to Chicago to make one last effort to sell the team to Hart. Dreyfuss refused Hart's offer, which he considered insultingly low, and the pair traveled on to Pittsburgh to finalize the purchase of the Pirates. Dreyfuss commented, "We are investigating to see what is the best thing that can be done. If we get a figure for our players that we regard as satisfactory we will sell and retire from the League. If we do not we will continue in the field."

Barney Dreyfuss became principal owner of the Pittsburgh Pirates on December 8, 1899. Then, for the sum of $25,000, he bought Hans Wagner, Fred Clarke, Rube Waddell, Tommy Leach, Deacon Phillippe, Foxy Cunningham, Patsy Flaherty, Jack Doyle, Walter Woods, Chief Zimmer, Tacks Latimer, Mike Kelley and Claude

Ritchey from the Louisville team. Louisville retained players Tom O'Brien, Art Madison, Deal, Fox, and Gould.

Still secretary of the Louisville team, Harry released a statement. "As a representative of a committee, consisting of Messrs. Dreher, Hammer and myself, appointed by the stockholders to make this deal, I today received the sum of $25,000 for the pick of the Louisville team. Leave tomorrow at noon with the money. This deal does not mean that Louisville is off the baseball map, but was made simply to lighten the burden of four men who have provided high-class League ball for Louisville at great expense to themselves." - Harry C. Pulliam.

On December 9, Harry arrived in Louisville to give a check for $25,000 to the local magnates. No matter the fate of the League, twelve team, ten teams, or eight, the thirteen players selected by the Pirates would not return to the Colonels. If the Louisville franchise did somehow survive, it would be a ghost of a team. The talented team that Harry had worked so hard to build in Louisville was no more. Before leaving, Harry admitted that he and Dreyfuss were going to try to sell the team to the League, which in turn would almost certainly fold it and reduce the League.

Not bothering with diplomacy, Dreyfuss announced plans to immediately relocate to Pittsburgh. "Just as soon as this meeting is over I will hasten to Louisville, pack my trunk, take my wife and babies and hustle back to Pittsburg. I like the town and expect to remain there."

Officials of the Pirates met on December 15 and elected Dreyfuss president of the franchise. Harry was elected secretary and treasurer, but did not immediately accept the offer out of his loyalty to the Louisville team and the uncertain future it faced. However, it was understood that he would accept the offer if the League were to buy out the Colonels.

"These baseball magnates are well supplied with dark lanterns and lead pipe. They are moving about ready to take a crack at each other's heads. The entire League is now fighting Baltimore and Brooklyn, trying to force one of them out in order to effect a reduction." –Louisville Courier-Journal.

The grand plan was to buy out Washington and Louisville and use the old tactic of schedule harassment to seal the fates of Baltimore and Brooklyn. In the end, though, only Brooklyn survived. Baltimore, Cleveland, Washington and Louisville did not.

"The melancholy days are come.

The saddest of the year.

Of absent cranks and empty seats,

And bleachers warped and sere.

The rusted turnstiles halting speak

Of pennant hopes long dead;

And echo faint alone now greets

The peanut man's dull tread."

Chapter Six

The Smoky City

In 1900, during the first week of January, Harry spent several days at the Louisville Hotel with malarial fever. His condition was deemed quite serious, but he recovered rather quickly, and went right back to work.

On January 9, the Pittsburgh Post-Gazette reported that Barney Dreyfuss intended to open a new office for the Pittsburgh club somewhere in the downtown area. Harry was expected to be in the city within the next ten days, and would probably look for a suitable location when he arrived. However, he had not yet resigned as secretary of the Colonels. Clarke was also expected to arrive in the same time frame.

According to the Chicago papers, Harry was going to become the new manager of the Cubs. Harry's response? "Report is all smoke."

After spending two days in late January visiting Dreyfuss in Pittsburgh, Harry headed back for Louisville, still uncertain of what the future held for him. Nothing had been made public by the circuit committee, the group responsible for deciding the number of clubs that would compete in 1900, and more importantly, which clubs were included. But Harry's actions were speaking louder than his words; he had been busy in the Smoky City, meeting with various employees and learning how things operated in Exposition Park, the home of the Pirates. His efforts were cut short, though, by a heavy rain and a snowstorm.

At the same time, his responsibilities to the Kentucky assembly were weighing heavy on his mind, in particular, the assassination of William Goebel, who had lost, then been declared the winner on appeal, the gubernatorial election. Goebel had been shot by political enemies while the appeal was pending, had survived long enough to be declared the winner, then died in his hospital bed. Harry resigned his position in the assembly before the matter had been settled.

"When Harry was in the legislature, Goebel was one of his warmest friends," said Dreyfuss, "and Harry has stood loyally by him ever since. He worked hard for Goebel in the last race, and lost considerable money on the result. He sent word to me yesterday that he was one of the warmest Goebel men in Frankfort, and that he was going to remain there until the matter was settled one way or the other. He said that if he did not report in Pittsburgh on time his friends would know that some Taylor man had used him for a target."

On February 17, Harry announced that he had accepted the position of secretary with the Pirates. Continuing to wear two hats, though, he worked to help Louisville land a franchise in the newly formed American League, which was to begin play in 1901. "If the Louisville people want a franchise in the American League the coming season I am satisfied they can get it, but they will have to be in a hurry. In case the town is not given baseball representation this year, it is my intention to obtain a franchise from the American League next year and run a club here myself. I believe it would pay."

When he returned to Pittsburgh, Harry declared that the team would hold spring practice in Thomasville, and would depart for that site on March 14. Clarke arrived in town two weeks early, delayed a day or two while his train was caught in a snow drift, and promptly made public a list of the 24 players who would make the trip. Combining the former Colonels and current Pirates gave him 36 players from which to choose. The twelve players who did not make the list of 24 were made available to the Louisville club. Billy Hoy had been released.

As they had every year in Louisville, Harry and Dreyfuss headed east to attend the League scheduling meeting in New York. It was expected that the final decision on reducing the League would be reached once and for all. At that point, most expected a reduction to ten teams, with Dreyfuss and his prediction of eight a notable exception. The big advantage to eight would be that it would force Freedman to strengthen his team. Since the Ducky Holmes affair, Freedman, out of spite, had been purposefully dismantling his Giants.

On March 9 the news broke; the National League was being reduced to an eight-team League, just as Dreyfuss had predicted. John T. Brush had gotten his way. As expected, the League purchased the Louisville franchise for $10,000, and then folded it. Freedman immediately announced plans to upgrade his team.

Harry returned triumphantly to Pittsburgh, jokingly referring to himself as a former magnate, an "also-ran", who was once again only a secretary. Two days later, he was scheduled to travel to Thomasville with the team to look after the financial details of the trip.

On the way to Thomasville, stopping in Columbus, big Rube Waddell joined the entourage, escorted by a large group of friends. It seemed everyone was Rube's friend. He proceeded to shake the hand of every individual there to see the team off, and then jumped into the car. Rube had a gun with him and made a point of sharing a look at the fine weapon with manager Clarke, who was disinterested.

"When the team passed through Louisville it was met at the Tenth Street station by nearly one hundred enthusiastic fans, who gave the former Colonels an enthusiastic welcome. A brass band played 'My Old Kentucky Home.'"
-Pittsburgh Press.

Upon arrival in at their destination, it was discovered that the Piney Woods hotel was full, and no rooms had been reserved for the players. In a pinch, an old and abandoned church building was procured, carpenters were hired to build rooms in the church for the men, and by the time the men arrived, twelve new rooms had been built, six on each floor. A baptismal pool was used for them to bathe. A hot water system was added.

The weather didn't cooperate either. On a day of heavy rain, Clarke decided to meet inside for a "suggestion" meeting. "I don't claim to know it all boys and if you have any ideas about the game, don't be afraid to spring them," he offered. Later he led them on a long walk on the muddy country roads. It is doubtful that this was one of the suggestions. When the rain did not end for several days, and the training grounds flooded, Harry made the decision to leave Thomasville early and head north. It was a disappointing spring practice. On the way, the new schedule arrived. The first home game was set for April 26.

Harry had made arrangements for the club to spend a week in Louisville on the way, for training and some exhibition games, and surely to visit some friends as well. Four exhibition games were scheduled; the first against A.C. Buckenberger's Rochester team, the second, in what must have been a somewhat awkward affair, against a ragtag team of extras left over from the merger of the Louisville and Pittsburgh teams. The Pirates won them all. Two more games were scheduled, but rain, a strong wind, and finally snow, intervened. Few of the jilted Colonel fans bothered to notice. The total gate was less than $200.

The Pirates started the season on the road at St. Louis. Clarke named Waddell as the starting pitcher for the three openers on the schedule – at St. Louis, at Cincinnati, and then the home opener at Pittsburgh, scheduled for April 26 against the Reds. In St. Louis, Waddell was to be opposed by Cy Young, said to be fit and ready for action to begin. The weather in St. Louis was expected to be gloomy.

Harry left the team before the championship season started to prepare for opening day festivities at home. By now he knew the routine well, even if it was a different city. Sell tickets, promote the team, make sure the field is fit for play, hire vendors, have scorecards printed, and one hundred other things, including putting out any fires that might start, at least figuratively.

The 'New Pirates," as they were now being commonly referred to by reporters, arrived in St. Louis on April 18, the day before the opener against the Browns. With 15,000 in the stands, Cy Young defeated Sam Leever and his mates, 3-0. Leever was hurt in the second inning and replaced by Waddell, who surrendered all three runs in the fourth inning. That was two more than Young needed. The New Pirates returned home on April 25 with three wins and three losses on their ledger.

Harry ordered a dress rehearsal, with all employees participating, the day before the home opener. He was determined that everything go as planned, without a hitch. A large contingency of fans from Carnegie, Pennsylvania, the hometown of Hans Wagner, were making the trip. Opening day in St. Louis had turned out 18,300 fans, and Harry wanted to top it. Reds president John T. Brush also planned to attend.

The opening game was a thriller. Down by eight, The Pirates scored seven runs in a raucous ninth inning, but fell one run short, losing 12-11 to the Reds. Harry was praised in the papers for the pre-game festivities. Fans were pleased to see several new entrances to the park had been added, and six different locations were now available for the purchase of tickets. A large crowd attended and heartily supported the team. The only blemish on an otherwise wonderful day was the final score.

"The attendance was a record breaker. Of that there is no mistake. Such a crush on the streets for hours before the game began was never seen on a like occasion. The turnstiles, new as they were and well-greased, fairly creaked on their axes, and the merry clink of the half-dollar must have been delightful to the treasurers of the Cincinnati and Pittsburgh ball clubs." - Pittsburgh Post-Gazette.

The Pirates won only four of their first ten, good for fifth place. But attendance at Exposition Park was among the highest in the League, and the fans cheered the team, even when things weren't going so well. Harry took notice. "Pittsburgh is a great town," he proclaimed. "We have been playing poor ball, but not a kick has yet been registered by the Smoky City fans. During our first three games at home the people came out and gave us the merry ha-ha for allowing the Reds to skin us. The boys like that kind of treatment and will hustle to give Smoky City enthusiasts a good run for their money."

Rube Waddell

Harry traveled with the team on their first road trip, making sure the hotel rooms were secured and adequate, taking care of expenses, and looking out for the players to keep them out of trouble. One particular player required more looking out for than any of the others.

"Since leaving home Rube Waddell has cut out all foolishness. He has a guardian in the person of Harry Pulliam, the genial secretary. Every evening promptly at seven o'clock Waddell makes a call on Pulliam, and when he leaves he is richer by one dollar, this being the amount agreed upon between the two to be paid Waddell for spending money when the team is on the road. This arrangement has been in force since the team went south. It saves money for Waddell and affords Pulliam a great deal of amusement." Harry and Rube were becoming fast friends.

On June 2, in a game played in a driving rain and thus shortened to four and a half innings, the Pirates lost to the League leading Phillies in Philadelphia, even with the home team missing sluggers Napoleon Lajoie and Elmer Flick. 10,000 loyal, perhaps deranged, cranks braved the storm. They hooted derisively in the fourth inning when Clarke called timeout and slowly walked in from the outfield to conference with Leever, his pitcher, and thus delay the game, hoping for a rainout. Then, he walked slowly back to the outfield, having told Leever to take his time and not be in a hurry. But the ploy didn't work, as Umpire O'Day apparently had a penchant for standing in the cold rain. He was a patient man.

Meanwhile, during the downpour, Harry had an issue of his own to deal with. "Secretary Pulliam assigned Rube Waddell to the carriage gate to-day, and when the man from Butler County failed to report after the storm broke, Harry started to look for him. He found the Philadelphia gate tenders well sheltered under the grandstand. Rube, instead of being with them, was at his post of duty, guarding the entrance. Lightning and rain could not drive him away."

On June 3, Harry took advantage of a rare Sunday off in the schedule to attend church. When he returned to the hotel, he advanced four dollars to Waddell, who used the cash to buy a railroad ticket to Atlantic City, and some cigars. Most of the other players spent the day resting. They were worn out from a heavy schedule, but still had the energy to lodge a complaint against their state rivals, the Phillies, whom they accused of the age-old baseball crime of stealing signs. Reserve catcher Morgan Murphy, a noted expert of the craft, had been spied at one of the clubhouse windows in deep center field, using field glasses to read the signs of the opposing catcher, and a large white blotter to flash it back to the batter. Wise to the ruse, the Pirate battery changed the signs, but they were quickly decoded again.

"George Edward Waddell was never east of Philadelphia until this trip, but he has a circle of acquaintances second in size only to that claimed by Secretary Pulliam. When the Pirates arrived from Philadelphia at eleven o'clock Wednesday night I won a dollar's worth of cigars by betting that Rube would meet a friend before he reached the hotel. He never has to carry his uniform bag and grip as some admirer is always on hand to relieve him of the burden. The only explanation his press agent can give is that Rube must be a member of some secret society." -Pittsburgh Press.

In Brooklyn, Clarke left the team to recuperate from an illness that was described as "kidney and liver trouble." It was not believed to be serious, but he was expected to miss as much as three weeks. Dick Cooley took over as temporary manager. Clarke tried to return on June 17 in a game at Chicago, but became ill in the seventh inning and had to leave the game. He returned to Cambridge Springs for more treatment and was now believed to be seriously ill. The next day they lost their seventh straight game, and found themselves in fifth place, having been passed by Chicago.

While on the road, the players were constantly looking for ways to amuse themselves. One popular distraction was the horse races. During a rainout in St. Louis on June 23, Harry Pulliam, the secretary, spent the day at the race track watching Harry Pulliam, the horse, owned by Senator O'Brien of Kentucky. Harry bragged that his namesake, the horse, would whip all rivals in the second race of the day, and backed his boasting by placing a four-dollar bet on the animal. Harry the horse finished last.

Heading back home to Exposition Park, the Pirates were scheduled to play Chicago on a Wednesday afternoon. Harry had hired a brass band of ladies to play from the bleachers before the game. It was Waddell's day to pitch, so he was ordered to report early, as Harry never really knew for sure that he would arrive in time to start the game. But, as usual, Rube arrived late, and was much put out to learn he had missed the performance of the brass band. Shortly thereafter, he was reported missing. When the game started, Jesse Tannehill was sent in by Clarke to pitch.

Harry was told of Rube's disappearance, and immediately called for a search party to track him down. Pawnee Bill's Wild West show was parked on the lot next to the park, and the search quickly led there. Pawnee Bill himself, told of the missing Mr. Waddell, suggested he might be in the big tent where the show was taking place. Several men were sent in to see. When one of them returned, he said he had seen "a man who looked very much like Rube dressed as a cowboy astride a mustang and carrying a repeating rifle. There was no way to prove the truth of this find. But it was noticed that Rube did not appear at the grounds until after the Wild West performance was over, and that Jack O'Connor discovered a trace of war paint on his face. As soon as Rube got on the grounds he started to coach with Indian yells, and in this performance, he was joined by a band of braves who were taking in the game from the top of some wagons just outside the grounds."

When multiple warnings brought no change of behavior, Clarke decided he had had enough, walked into Dreyfuss' office, and announced the suspension of Waddell. No reason was given, but it was assumed Clarke had simply lost patience with him and his unpredictable antics. In response to his suspension, Waddell emptied the clubhouse of all his personal items, and vowed never to pitch for Pittsburgh again. The Pittsburgh Press pondered the absurdity of it all.

"Think of Rube Waddell. While a member of the Pittsburg club he received twice as much money as he could earn in any other way, and lived on the fat of the land while away from home. In addition to all this he was under the care of Secretary Harry Pulliam, who took the trouble to manage his finances for him, with the result that on June 15, for the first time since he began playing professional, Rube found himself clear of debt. Now the unfortunate twirler is playing every day for a semi-professional team. He will be a loser to the extent of hundreds of dollars."

Independence Day brought a doubleheader sweep of Boston, lifting the New Pirates into third place, just .002 percentage points behind the Phillies for second. Total attendance for the day was 21,500, including 11,000 at the morning game and 10,500 in the afternoon. Harry was praised for the excellent work of his well-trained employees, and the handling of the overflow crowd. The players were given praise as well, although backhanded, for their failure to "suffer their usual attack of stage-fright." Clearly, this was a different breed of Pirates. The fans loved them.

They seemed to love Wagner most of all.

"Hans Wagner believes in variety. Sometimes he handles his bat as Vardon would a golf club, and other times he takes a full swing, and he is not above bunting. He made a funny play in the fifth yesterday. The Boston players were looking for a long hit and Hans fooled them and bunted with the handle of the bat. Dineen got the ball and in throwing to first he caught Wagner on the top of the head, and the ball bounded to the grandstand. Hans kept going, and when he reached third he sat down on the bag and rubbed his head, while the spectators enjoyed a hearty laugh." – Pittsburgh Press.

When Clarke returned to the field, the team got hot. His home run was a game winner on July 12, 7-6 over the Superbas, and moved the Pirates into second place, though still well behind Brooklyn. Clarke's blast hit the centerfield fence, and he was across the plate before the ball was returned to the infield. It was his second home run of the year.

The very next day the New Pirates were demolished by the Phillies, 23-8. Happy Jack Chesbro, in relief of Leever, who had only recorded one out, surrendered fifteen runs in only four innings of work. The game being a total wash, Clarke sent Wagner to the box to finish the monstrosity, and he fared only slightly better than his predecessors. Flick and the Frenchman, Lajoie, each scored four runs for the victors. After eight innings Clarke forfeited the ninth, called it a night, and sent everyone home, including 3,400 spectators, most of whom, for some inexplicable reason, were still there.

"The horrible nightmare consumed about two and a half hours of a pleasant afternoon, and at its conclusion the occupants of the stands were pinching themselves to find out if they were really awake, and finding that they were not entirely bereft of their senses they made a hurried departure from Exposition Park and sneaked up the side streets as though ashamed to even be seen coming from there." - Pittsburgh Post-Gazette.

On July 25, riding a four-game losing streak in the East, the Pirates' bats heated up, knocking pretty boy Winnie Mercer of the Giants out of the game in the third frame. In the first inning, a sudden downpour flooded the field, then subsided just as quickly. Eager to play, the men of both teams grabbed brooms and scattered bags of sawdust on the infield, soaking up the drenching water. Play then resumed. Down 9-3 when Mercer retired, the New Yorkers sent in rookie pitcher Christopher Mathewson for mop up duty.

One month after Waddell left he was still at large, causing Harry innumerable headaches.

"It begins to look as though Secretary Harry Pulliam will never succeed in disentangling himself from the mess of trouble into which the guardianship of Rube Waddell thrust him. Rube has gone, but he has left behind him a trail of trouble for the genial secretary. The latest bunch of woe comes in the shape of a crate of dogs which somebody shipped Rube from Punxsutawney. The railroad officials have notified Harry that they will enter suit if he does not pay the $16.50 charged up and take the dogs off their hands, as they are a nuisance with their constant howling and yelping. Harry doesn't want the dogs and has ordered the company to ship them to Milwaukee or some other warmer spot" – Pittsburgh Post-Gazette.

The first place Brooklyn team arrived in Pittsburgh on August 16 for a highly anticipated three-game series in Exposition Park. Rain seemed inevitable on the day of the first game, on a Thursday, but Harry guaranteed all that the full three games would be played before the Superbas would be allowed to leave town. "If rain interferes with to-day's game look out for a double-header to-morrow. Rain to-morrow will mean two games Saturday."

The Pirates had climbed within six and a half games of first, and a sweep of the series would bring them within three and a half. But Joe Kelley, the old Oriole who was now captain of the Brooklyn team, was not worried. "I don't see any club that has a chance to pass us," he said, disregarding the Pirates. Even so, Brooklyn manager Ned Hanlon had taken the precaution of giving Iron Man McGinnity, their star pitcher, extra rest before arriving in Pittsburgh, even though the Iron Man had proven time and again that he never got tired. He had not pitched in four days.

Unfortunately for the home team, the first game did not get rained out, and McGinnity was indeed well rested, shutting out the Pirates 8-0. A reporter for the Post-Gazette observed that, "Those Pirates of ours were as helpless before the curves and that famous raise ball of Pitcher McGinnity as a child would be in a tug of war against an elephant." Captain Kelley scored three runs for the winners, one on a home run.

Clarke and his men fought back bravely to win the second game by a score of 5-3, setting up a showdown in game three. Five different players scored, and Leever did the pitching. In the finale, the Pittsburgh faithful feared that Hanlon might send the Iron Man to the box again. But once again, rain posed an even bigger threat. "He (the weather man) will have to blow or wash the grounds away to prevent this game," Harry insisted. Hanlon did indeed turn to McGinnity, and close to ten thousand turned out to see the rematch. Clarke countered with Happy Jack Chesbro. To irritate McGinnity, who liked to work quickly, the Pirates slowed the game down, making him wait and disrupting his rhythm. The ploy seemed to work, with Pittsburgh scoring twice in the first, then twice more in the second, on the way to an 8-4 victory. The Pirates had won the critical series, but were still five games back in the standings. When the series ended, Clarke called for a team meeting.

"In the morning the boys indulged in a practice bout in the batting line, and in the afternoon, there was one of those heart to heart talks in the way of a players' conference. The subject upmost in the minds of the players, as well as the followers of the team, is the question of second place. It is conceded that the Brooklyn team has first place pretty well cinched, so that the only real fight at present is for second honors. To finish in second place means money for the players, because there is almost a certainty of a post season series between the teams finishing first and second, and such games in this city would draw immense crowds." -Pittsburgh Post-Gazette.

With the team scheduled to embark on its last Eastern trip of the season, Clarke and Rube Waddell patched things up, and Waddell was recalled from Milwaukee, where he had been seemingly pitching and winning every day for manager Connie Mack. All four regulars – Chesbro, Tannehill, Phillippe and Leever – had been performing well, but Harry and Dreyfuss were going all in. The ever-confident pitcher sent a telegram to the team: "I am coming to join the boys and hold the team in second place." Catcher Chief Zimmer was sent to accompany Waddell on the trip and make sure he didn't get sidetracked on the way.

The first destination on the trip was Boston, where Pittsburgh won four games in two days, back-to-back doubleheader sweeps. Chesbro outdueled Kid Nichols 9-0 in the first of the four, and Wagner stole home in the last, igniting a great deal of kicking by the Beaneaters, but Umpire O'Day held his ground and the run counted. Wagner scored nine times in the four games. The Pirates had won six in a row, and were now within five games of first place.

Next, on to Brooklyn, where they were scheduled to play five games against the Superbas. Leever was masterful in winning the first, 9-2. The second ended in a 6-6 tie due to darkness. The third game was shortened as well, for the same reason, the Pirates winning this one, though, and stepping with three of first in the standings. Brooklyn took game four on a Saturday afternoon, with plenty of sunshine left to finish the 6-6 tied game, but Hanlon refused Clarke's request to do so. The reporters called them cowards in the Pittsburgh newspapers, claiming that Hanlon was afraid of the Pirates, and they were probably right. The Bridegrooms seemed to be losing their grip at the top of the League race.

Having won 13 of 16 in the East, the team returned home on Thursday, September 2, trailing Brooklyn by just four games in the standings. They arrived on the third section of train number 19 over the Pennsylvania Road just before 9:00 in the morning. The locals, ecstatic over the results of the trip, began to gather hours beforehand, an immense crowd growing, blocking the road and access to public buildings.

A contingent of policeman were dispatched and attempted to maintain order. When the train finally arrived, though, it was a useless attempt.

The fans "joined in a veritable maddened elbowing struggling mass in their anxiety to shake hands with the local players as they stepped from the sleeper," wrote a reporter. "The crowd numbered thousands and it was only with the greatest difficulty that the committee in charge was able to get the players through the crowd out to where the carriages were waiting. The people wanted not only to see their idols but wanted to grasp hands with them, but they were finally rescued by the committee." A parade down the streets of Pittsburgh was staged that afternoon, organized by the fans, with Harry and Dreyfuss leading the procession.

Five days later, Waddell and Cy Young engaged in a classic pitchers' duel in St. Louis. In the seventh inning, first baseman Dan McGann of the Browns, now sometimes referred to as the Cardinals by the newspaper men, drove home Roderick Wallace, who had reached on an error. It was the only run scored in the game, which lasted one hour and twenty-five minutes. Each team collected but four hits, all singles, save for a double by Waddell. But Brooklyn also lost that day, and the next day as well, while the Pirates rested. With a scant thirteen games left on their schedule, the Pirates had pulled even with the Superbas in wins, at 73. Pittsburgh, though, had two extra losses. They were seventeen percentage points behind. It was close enough to inspire a poem.

"Black hung the smoke over Pittsburgh town,
Where the fires gleam red when the sun goes down,
And where the pavements echoed the hurrying feet
Of the jubilant fans in the crowded street,
For the news went flying from door to door
That the Pirates had captured a game once more,
And the fans yelled "Thirteen games to play,"

And the Pirates but eighteen points away.
Louder they yelled on Sunday morn,
And louder yet in Pittsburgh rolled
That roar for the Pirates uncontrolled,
And the offer to wager untold gold
On the Pittsburgh team in the pennant fray,
For the Pirates were seventeen points away.
Still sprung that volley of well-bunched hits
That tore the atmosphere all to bits,
From the big round bats of the Pirate crowd,
While their partisans cheered them long and loud,
Carrying terror to Brooklyn town,
Where faces paled as the sun went down,
For the score showed only twelve games to play,
And the Pirates fourteen points away.
Then came these boys bedecked in red,
With big Jake Beckley at their head;
They came with a rush and a hullabaloo,
And brought back with them that old hoodoo.
When the game was over there was deep dismay
For the Pirates were seventeen points away."

Pirate fever had spread to Louisville as well, where the locals had been following closely the exploits of their former favorites. A call to arms was ordered:

"Louisville, Sept. 25, 1900. – It's next Sunday, and the trains leave from First and Tenth street stations, via L&N, at 7:50 a.m. It's the last Sunday ball game. It's the last Sunday excursion to Cincinnati. Go up, and by your presence encourage Pulliam, Dreyfuss, Clarke and all the other boys in our old ball team. They deserve it. Help us get the boys in line. All the old rooters are going. The game is close and the fight on to a finish. Give us your encouragement. Yours truly, Jas. B. Camp, I.F. Whiteside, Lamar Herndon, Will W. Douglass, Henry Davis, Ed Gans, committee representing rooters."

Then, in heartbreaking fashion, they lost three of four to the Reds. The momentum was gone. Upon returning to the Smoky City, Harry was incensed about the treatment Waddell had received from the Cincinnati players while he was pitching. "I never saw nor heard anything like it in my life. The way that Peitz, Steinfeldt and others abused Rube would not be tolerated in the Bowery or even in Whitechapel district. It was outrageous in the extreme, and yet Umpire Emslie stood and listened to it and never even offered an objection. I know Waddell is an eccentric fellow, but there is one thing about him and that is he conducts himself as a gentleman on the field and is a favorite wherever he plays. Nobody ever knew of him insulting a spectator or a fellow-player, and he is certainly entitled to fair treatment as a gentlemanly player of the game."

During the last week of the season, the pennant lost, an ugly scene was witnessed by the faithful in a game at St. Louis against John McGraw and his new team, the Cardinals. At the end of the seventh inning, with the Pirates leading 3-2, Umpire Emslie inexplicably called the game on account of darkness, even though, by all accounts, including the Pittsburgh press, there was still ample daylight to play two or three more innings. Having realized what had happened and not at all happy about it, many of the fans rushed the field and attacked Emslie, several of them throwing rocks and sticks, and even bases, but none hit him. The rest jeered and threatened him until police established peace and escorted him all the way to his hotel room with many patrons still in pursuit.

The Pirates finished the year in second place, trailing only Brooklyn, led by former Orioles Hugh Jennings, Joe Kelley and Willie Keeler. Thus, the two met in the championship series, Brooklyn taking the crown three games to one. Tim Hurst umpired. When it ended, the Pittsburgh players expressed their gratitude to Harry for a job well done by presenting him with a diamond ring.

At the League meeting in December, among the items discussed was a proposal to abolish spring training trips, and the possibility of shortening the season from six months to five. But these issues were dwarfed by the seemingly never-ending concerns about rowdyism. Perhaps a switch to a two-umpire system was the answer. The players of the National League asked the magnates to have the rules to limit kicking more strictly enforced, and though the magnates seemed inclined to agree, no action was taken. To many of the magnates, it was really a matter of weak umpiring. And, a war with the newly formed American League loomed ahead.

The old rumors of Harry leaving Pittsburgh in favor of Chicago to work with his friend Jim Hart, perhaps as manager, resurfaced in the off season. A year earlier he had been courted but chose to remain with the Pirates. The Pittsburgh Press lobbied to keep him in Pittsburgh.

"The owners of the Pittsburg club need Col. Pulliam as much now as they did a year ago. What he did for the club last season can be fully appreciated only by persons who were with the team at home and abroad. The last Eastern trip, when the Pirates made their famous spurt, was one thorough test of his ability."

But other men had other ideas. W.W. Kerr, team treasurer and also one of the owners of the Pirates, returned from the League meeting with Harry, Clarke and Dreyfuss. In responding to questions of reported "internal troubles" among the club officials, he inferred that Dreyfuss was upset about attempts by Kerr and P.L. Auten, another one of the stockholders, to replace Harry Pulliam with Frank Baillet as secretary. Dreyfuss fought gamely in Harry's behalf, but combined, Kerr and Auten owned enough stock to prevail.

"Harry Pulliam, the clever and efficient secretary of the Pittsburg Baseball Club, formerly tendered his resignation, and it was reluctantly accepted," reported the Pittsburgh Press two days later. "Harry did this in order that there may be no fight for his position, which will be given to Frank

Baillet, a nephew of Mr. P.L. Auten, one of the largest stockholders on the Smoky City team. Harry will go to Scottsburg, Allen County, Ky., for a good long rest, as he is not in the best of health."

His future suddenly very much in doubt yet again, Harry spoke with the press in New York on December 22. "No, I do not know what I will do as yet," he said. "I resigned from the Pittsburgh club because Mr. Auten wanted to put one of his relatives in my place. This is a fine capable fellow who held the same position before I took it and it was but natural that Mr. Auten should want him back. Mr. Dreyfuss made a strong fight for me to hold my place – a fight, I might say, that I did not want him to make. Barney stuck to me like a man and when I left he pressed his personal check for $500 in my hand as his appreciation for my efforts and his regard for me. No, I have nothing to say about the Louisville situation as regards baseball. I do not know what I will do as yet."

Then he went home to Kentucky.

Chapter Seven

The Baseball Wars

In New York, the new American Association, in partnership with the National League, was launched at the Hotel Marlborough, with Harry in attendance representing the city of Louisville. He was said to have the backing of several distillers in Kentucky. This was the National League's attempt to stop Ban Johnson and the American League from getting a foothold on the baseball landscape. Boston, Chicago and Philadelphia were being considered for American Association franchises, with the blessing of the National League. The baseball wars were in full swing, with the American League actively trying to lure players away with bigger contracts and more money, and the National League trying to stop them.

One of the biggest threats was American League agent Connie Mack, who traveled to Goshen, Ohio, to court Pirate pitcher Sam Leever. "I find it much easier to do business with the National League player than I expected," said Mack. "Most of them are disgusted with the methods employed by the National League, and will welcome a change." Leever, however, chose to remain a Pirate.

Barney Dreyfuss was not concerned about American League attempts to raid his team of its best players. He was convinced the reserve clause would protect his investment. To him, the possibility of a players' strike was a bigger threat. He admitted having several younger players under contract, just in case.

Four days later, at a meeting of club Directors, Harry withdrew his resignation as secretary of the Pirates and resumed his duties, with the approval of Dreyfuss, who had fought off the challenge from Kerr and Auten. Now back in control, his first move was to reinstate Harry.

In early February, Harry was shocked to learn of the death of utility player Tom O'Brien, who had played in 102 games for the Pirates in 1900. The Post-Gazette described his illness as Typhoid-Pneumonia, likely contracted when he joined a touring team and traveled to Cuba to play ball during the off season. He was only twenty-seven years old.

In order to speed up the games, which were often taking more than two hours to complete, a new rule was adopted. Foul balls would now be counted as strikes, with the exception of strike three. Prior to this change, a player could foul off any number of pitches, and still not have any strikes against him, causing some spectators to become bored. Some players, such as McGraw, had perfected the technique, fouling off endless pitches while looking for a good one to hit. Opponents of the rule argued that it would significantly reduce hits and runs, which would also cause boredom.

A greater concern to some players, though, especially those who did not play every day, was a new rule voted in by the magnates that limited each team to sixteen players on their roster. Each team had until May 15 to reduce its roster, but after September 15, they would be allowed to add as many players as they wanted. Clarke's plan was to carry only five pitchers and three catchers. Versatile players like Tommy Leach, who could play all infield positions, suddenly became more valuable. In recent seasons, the Pirates had carried as many as twenty players, and most other teams did as well. Jobs were being taken away, increasing the likelihood that the players would indeed strike.

On March 5, Hans Wagner met with Harry and signed a contract with the Pirates for the 1901 season. He had been offered a larger contract with many incentives by an American League team, but chose to remain loyal to the city of Pittsburgh. It was great news for Pirate fans. Hans had been given a considerable raise in salary. Dreyfuss confirmed that more than a half-dozen other players had also signed contracts.

After getting Wagner's signature, Harry leased a room for team headquarters and quickly headed west, out of town, in an attempt to sign Phillippe, Tannehill, Leach, O'Connor and Fred Ely before they were swept off their feet by American League representatives. In other cities, the American League was having considerably more luck.

Two days later, he had signatures from Jesse Tannehill, who had won twenty games in 1900, and catcher Ely, a fan favorite. Both Connie Mack and Hugh Duffy had tried to lure them away, but Harry's personal approach and the team's recent success made the difference. Leach, on the other hand, was rumored to be headed to Detroit of the American League, but Dreyfuss insisted the infielder would remain loyal to the Pirates in the end. Thanks to Harry's efforts, the team avoided being raided by the upstart American League.

While Harry was busy saving the team, Clarke, Dreyfuss and Wagner decided to have a friendly little competition.

"President Dreyfuss and Manager Clarke will make a trip down to Carnegie this afternoon and take part in a clay bird shoot, which Hans Wagner has arranged for their benefit. Hans is the champion clay bird shooter of Carnegie, and, as President Dreyfuss has been doing a lot of talking about his particular merits in that line when he was a member of the Kentucky National Guard, and Manager Clarke has been spouting about his gun work in the wild and wooly west, Wagner is going to try and take a large sized fall out of them. In view of this invasion of wing shots it might be well for the citizens of Carnegie to have their lives, as well as those of their family and cattle insured at once." – Pittsburgh Post-Gazette.

Before leaving for spring practice in Hot Springs, Harry arranged to have a large quantity of black soil shipped in from Kentucky to Exposition Park to replace the yellow clay that was used for the base paths. Clarke had complained that the yellow clay was hard on the eyes, and hard on the feet as well.

Undeterred by having failed to secure Tannehill and Ely, Mack made a strong appeal to land Rube Waddell. He visited Waddell's father, gained his favor, and the two of them went on a thirteen-mile journey in a buggy, finally tracking down the pitcher, who was on a fox hunt. Mack made his best pitch, but was not persuasive. Waddell signed with Pittsburgh. Mack went home emptyhanded again.

Meanwhile, the superstitious Clarke looked for any advantage he could gain while in Hot Springs. "Manager Fred Clarke is on the lookout for a mascot for the coming season and anyone having a good healthy mascot will find a ready purchaser," read an article in the Post-Gazette. "Manager Fred ran across a man with a vampire yesterday and wanted to purchase it right off the reel, but the owner would not sell, as he needed it in his business. Clarke says that the vampire would have been just the thing, because all he would have needed to do would be to turn it loose, 'sick' it on the opposing team, and that would have ended all controversy."

In New York, American League President Ban Johnson announced that the winner of his League would challenge the winner of the National League to a championship series at the end of the season. But, with the National League's insistence that the American League was an outlaw league, such a series was not expected to actually take place.

In Baltimore, with the prospect of a summer of no baseball staring them in the face, Baltimore fans lamented the demise of the Orioles. "It was Muggsy McGraw's methods that turned the trick in the Monumental city, just the same as it was Patsy Tebeau's methods that killed the game in Cleveland," wrote fan James Nellis. "Rowdyism of the most flagrant kind on the part of the players aided and abetted by part of the spectators is what drove the decent people from the game in both Baltimore and Cleveland. This same rowdyism was not permitted in the other cities, and National League methods did not kill the game in them."

As an uneventful spring practice drew to a close, Harry decided to have a little fun with the team, and the fans as well, during the Cowboys vs. Indians game. "Col. Pulliam threw the gates open today and gave the fans a treat. This allowed the secretary his liberty. He utilized it by umpiring the game, swinging a swagger cane dangerously when any kicks occurred. Col. Harry stood all the sallies thrown at him without a flinch until Zimmer said he looked like Nick Young. The umpire convulsed with laughter at this one and asked for time to recover." The Cowboys defeated the Indians, 18-13. Only 150 fans attended the game, making a gate of approximately $42.

Heading north, Harry scheduled an exhibition game in Little Rock, only to find upon arrival the grounds were not in playable condition. They had not been tended to the entire spring. This angered the manager. Rain had washed away several work days in Hot Springs, and he was desperate to get the men ready for opening day, just five days away. With a free day on their hands, most of the player chose to spend it in a pool hall. Harry had more ambitious pursuits in mind. On the recommendation of a state official he met at the team hotel, he decided to pay a visit to the Arkansas state legislature. His reaction was noted in the Post-Gazette:

"Fully half of the legislators sat with their feet on their desks. Some read newspapers while others munched popcorn. While a watchdog of the treasury, 'the gent from Washington County,' was orating against the measure the sergeant-at-arms, a one-armed war veteran, fell asleep. His badge of office, a long spear, dropped from his hands to the floor with a bang, breaking off fully two inches of the steel point. A roar of laughter followed."

Early in the season, the Pirates had decided to part ways with the irresponsible Waddell, and he was sold to the Chicago Cubs. In his first start against his former team, he was defeated by the Pirates, 4-2, in Chicago. 12,500 attended, mostly to see the enigmatic Waddell, filling the grandstand and the bleachers. New Pirate pitcher Hooks Wiltse was the winner in his first game. The two runs he allowed were both driven in by Waddell. After a slow start, the team moved into first place with another victory over the Cubs. They had eight wins and five losses. More than five years had passed since the last time the Pittsburgh Pirates had held the top position.

On May 10, Dreyfuss returned from Louisville and was greeted with bad news from Harry. Clarke had been injured again. "I am afraid that Fred Clarke's injury is more serious than he thinks," he cautioned. "Something is wrong with his chest. I am not a surgeon, but I believe when Fred Clarke cannot straighten himself and has to bend over like an old man that his case is serious enough to deserve a careful investigation. Fred should not try to play until he finds out what is the matter with him." An incident with Tacks Latimer in a game against Chicago was believed to be the cause, but Clarke laughed it off and dismissed the injury as minor. Later, a doctor told him he should not play for at least two weeks. Others thought he might be done for the year.

So, the Pirates carried on without him. After a 2-1 loss to young Christy Mathewson of the Giants, they had little good to say about the pitching phenom. Said Tannehill, "Matthewson will not last long if he continues to pitch so many curves. I was four times at bat on Tuesday and he only gave me two straight balls. If he keeps this up something will give way." Said Dreyfuss, "I would not give Phillippe for three Mathewsons."

In a loss to the Beaneaters on May 23, Wagner once again wowed the crowd. According to newspaper reports, he hit a foul ball so far it landed in one of the cars of a passing train.

Unfortunately, it was a foul ball. Wagner then proceeded to strike out. The next day Clarke returned to the lineup and led the team to a 6-4 win. Captain Fred had two hits, scored two runs and had a stolen base to his credit. All was well again.

A torrential rain blanketed the city of Pittsburgh as the Pirates rode home on the rail to end the month. They arrived to find a flooded ball park in a flooded city. Two games were washed away, and more would have been if the schedule had not sent them right back on the road. "At the present time the park is in a deplorable condition. That position of the ground known as right and middle fields is covered with a foot of water, which will remain there unless the river lowers sufficiently to allow the sewers to carry it out. The water comes from the sewers which the high stage of the river causes to back up and overflow the grounds."

Throughout the League attendance was up, and baseball seemed to be more popular than ever. Reduction to eight teams had clearly been the right move. In an interview with the Pittsburgh Press, Harry spoke about the crowd in New York on Decoration Day.

"They say the scene at the Polo Grounds in the afternoon was worth going miles to see. Everywhere there was a sea of faces. The upper and lower tiers of the grand stand were packed, and spectators were lined many deep behind the chairs. All three open stands were overflowing. The lower bleacherites squeezed together until there was room for no more, and the gate to Burkeville was locked an hour before the game. A solid mass of humanity was banked from the field entrance to the ropes and stretched in a semi-circle from stand to stand. On the roof-tops and on the tops of the fences an eager multitude had gathered, while from the height of Coogan's bluff and the viaduct thousands more looked down upon the picture, throbbing with life and animation."

"The New York newspapers are printing more baseball news than ever before," he continued. "Papers that a year a year ago dismissed the sport with a few paragraphs each day cannot get enough of it now. Horse racing, the yachts and other sports get the minor positions and baseball is featured every time."

Back in Baltimore of the American League after one year in St. Louis, McGraw and his teammates were up to their old tricks. In a game against the Tigers on May 31, after a close call at the plate did not go their way, the entire team rushed Umpire Jack Sheridan, shouting in protest and making threats. Mike Donlin threw a bat at him. When Sheridan refused to change the call, the Orioles refused to continue the game, forcing him to call a forfeit, in favor of Detroit, by the customary final score of 9-0. Injuries had, by this time, pretty much robbed McGraw of his ability to play to his own standards, but as a manager he was proving just as combative.

But the actions of the Baltimore team paled in comparison to events in Pittsburgh in a contest against the Reds. Prior to the game, Umpire Bert Cunningham had announced he would not allow Pirates Claude Ritchey and Tommy Leach to play, allegedly due to comments they had made in a previous game. In response, Clarke altered his lineup, although the crowd was much displeased. On a sacrifice bunt attempt in the eighth inning, in a key moment of a tight game, Cunningham declared Kitty Bransfield out at first base, even though all in attendance thought otherwise. The Pirate rally died, the game was lost, and the crowd was incensed. As Cunningham was walking to his dressing room, the fans shouted at him when he passed the grandstand. Then he noticed a mass of people coming his way in a hurry. He stopped short and started to run to the Pittsburgh bench for cover. When the mob continued to follow him, several Pirates, in fear for his safety, rushed back onto the field and attempted to escort him out of the park. The angry fans, estimated by a newspaper reporter to number 2,000 or more, blocked his way, but the players did manage to get Cunningham onto the Cincinnati bus, where he eventually rode away to safety. Harry, opposed to rowdyism in all situations, was disturbed by the incident.

On Monday, June 10, the first place Giants came to town, featuring their trio of great pitchers, Christy Mathewson, Luther Taylor and Bill Phyle. In the first game, Phillippe bested Taylor 3-1, moving the Pirates within 2.5 games of the top and giving them momentum heading into the second game, where they would find the undefeated Mathewson waiting for them on Tuesday. The baseball community in Pittsburgh was salivating for the matchup, a midweek game that enticed a huge midweek crowd of 7,000 fanatics, all hoping to see their team be the first to top Matty in 1901.

Unfortunately, Mother Nature had never seemed to care much for baseball, and this game was no different. When the battle began, a major storm was heading toward the Steel City. Needing to complete the game, it was played at a frantic pace. In the fourth inning drizzle began to fall. Several minutes later the storm hit. Up 4-0 and hoping to avoid a rainout, the Pirates sprinted out to the field, but Manager George Davis of New York demanded a halt to the proceedings. Umpire O'Day, pointing to the legions of fans in the stands, would not do so, and the match continued.

"Under baseball law the umpires are required to keep the players in their positions as long as the spectators remain in the uncovered stands during a rain storm. This rule is a reasonable one, for the players should be able to endure any weather that the spectators can stand. Football, horse racing and athletic games go on, rain or shine, and it is not much to ask the knights of the diamond to take a drenching occasionally."

After the Giants batted unsuccessfully in the top of the fifth inning it was an official game, no longer subject to a rainout, and Umpire O'Day ordered a halt to the proceedings. With a huge assist from their fans, the Pirates had defeated Mathewson. Tommy Leach batted in all four runs scored. The next day Pittsburgh won again and moved into first place.

When the Giants returned to Pittsburgh again in July, with another large crowd expected, Harry had to deal with reports of ticket speculation. To make matters easier for fans, and to avoid long lines at the ticket office before games, he had arranged for tickets to be sold at various locations around town. For the Giants series the game tickets were in high demand, and enterprising individuals were buying large quantities of them at the different locations, and selling them at inflated prices outside the ballpark. Grandstand tickets, which normally sold for 75 cents were being resold for one dollar and bleacher tickets, which normally sold for 50 cents were being sold for 75 cents. Many of the fans who paid higher prices complained to Harry, but there was nothing that could be done to placate them. Demand for tickets was strong in the other cities as well. A four-game series between the Pirates and Cardinals in late July drew more than 60,000 to the ballpark.

"The national game usually takes a slump after July 4 until September, but this year seems to be an exception to the rule. Nearly 50,000 persons saw the National League games yesterday and about half that number witnessed the contests in the American League." – Pittsburgh Press.

After the series with St. Louis the Pirates had a scheduled one-week vacation. Many returned to their homes to spend time with family. With little more than two months to go, they were in a tight race with Philadelphia, St. Louis and Brooklyn. A little rest before the stretch run was welcomed by the players.

During the week off, while some of the players were doing light workouts on the field at Exposition Park, a stranger appeared who, having borrowed a uniform that belonged to Clarence Beaumont, began working out in the pitching line. He was a big and strong young man, and as Fred Clarke watched with great curiosity, he put on an impressive performance of control while throwing with impressive speed, and equally impressive curves and drop balls. The manager assumed he was there at the invitation of one of the Pirates, but when Clarke sought more information, no one knew who he was, and the young man mysteriously disappeared before Clarke could track him down. He was never seen nor heard from again.

Before resuming play at the end of the week, pitcher Sam Leever, having been injured much of the season with a sore arm, offered to let Harry send him on vacation with no pay until his arm was better. He had injured himself while shooting clay pigeons. Harry appreciated the offer, but declined. "Come to Pittsburg with me," he said to Leever. "I have a copy of "The Crisis", and if you have nothing else to do you can read it." Leever accepted the offer. "We do not treat our team as the American League does," Harry stated later, "so Leever will continue to draw salary whether he pitches or not."

In early August, Harry left for his annual journey to Saratoga for the races. One writer suggested he wasn't the only Pirate to have a horse named after him. "Harry Pulliam returned yesterday from Saratoga. He enjoyed his vacation immensely," reported the Pittsburgh Press. "While away he received a letter from Johnny Fay, the turfman and owner of Hans Wagner, the running horse. Fay is a great rooter for the Pirates in general and Wagner in particular. He wrote: 'If you win the pennant I will send my horse Hans Wagner to Pittsburg for my friend Honus to ride in the parade.'"

Whether this was truth or fiction is uncertain. Perhaps it was a case of friendly competition with the Pittsburgh Press' rival hometown paper, the Pittsburgh Post-Gazette. If so, the Post-Gazette was the clear winner:

"John Honus Wagner, the hero of Carnegie, was likewise the hero of Atlantic City this afternoon. John Honus was in for a dip this morning, and nearly frightened a party of women bathers to death, as they mistook his huge form for a sea monster of some kind. In the afternoon he nearly frightened Cy Voorhees to death by driving one of his shoots so far over the middle field fence that it rolled into the ocean, and by this time is en route for Germany with John Honus' name tagged to it."

To end August, last place Chicago, now referred to sarcastically as the Remnants by the Pittsburgh reporters, arrived in town for a Thursday doubleheader. Rube Waddell was not scheduled to pitch for the Cubs that day, but many fans showed up just for a glimpse of the pitcher, and to see what antics he might be up to. They were disappointed to find that he was not even in the ball park. When Harry was asked where he might be, he guessed that Waddell was probably in Butler County visiting friends and family. He also guessed that Rube would likely bring a hoard of friends back to the park to watch him pitch. Rube was anxious to shut down his former teammates. When the doubleheader was completed, a split, Brooklyn, Philadelphia and the Pirates each had 61 wins.

Two days later the Remnants left town with Rube never having put in an appearance. It was rumored his absence was related to an incident involving a woman, a jealous husband and a revolver, but this was denied by team president Hart, who dismissed it as "the imagination of one of his newspaper friends in Chicago."

On September 14, the Pirates returned home from a 15 game Eastern swing, having won twelve of the fifteen. In the process they stretched their lead to five games over the Phillies. The gap continued to grow as the Pirates continued to win. The run Hans Wagner scored in the bottom of the eighth inning in a 5-4 win over Brooklyn on September 27 clinched the first ever pennant for the Pittsburgh Pirates. At a meeting of representatives later that evening, Harry was among several who gave speeches. Although no text of his speech was taken, Clarke noted in approval that Harry's speech "was as eloquent as anything the Colonel ever said while serving his country as a framer of Kentucky laws."

The Pirate fans were crazed with pennant fever beyond reason. "Because his wife would not give him fifty cents for the purpose of seeing the Pirates wrest the pennant from the present champions, Harry Newman will have to answer at the September term of courts for assault and battery. He is 29 years of age and is a teamster, residing at Rock Alley, Allegheny." -Pittsburgh Press.

Once the championship had been clinched, plans for an elaborate season finale that would surpass opening day were made, including a parade, badges for the occasion, and private boxes for important dignitaries. Dreyfuss planned to give all of the team's share of the gate that day to the players, in appreciation of their great accomplishment. A trophy – either a loving cup or punch bowl – was commissioned to be presented to the team by the railroad men of the city.

The Pirates won the celebration game on October 2, an 8-4 dusting of the Beaneaters, in the frost, and then the rain and snow that followed. Nevertheless, despite the resulting small crowd, the pomp and circumstance played as scheduled at the insistence of the railroad men. Clarke, Dreyfuss and Harry were all asked to give speeches. Harry, the last of the three, simply said, "I can't talk but I'll buy." The next day the team held its annual field day, with the usual events scheduled.

The anticipated exhibition series between Pittsburgh and second place Philadelphia never came to fruition. Instead, a barnstorming tour was undertaken, with Harry creating the schedule. Before saying their goodbyes for the season, the team was honored at a banquet hosted by W.C. Temple, the man whom the Temple Cup was named for. As the evening wound down, Temple gave a speech about Harry, the man who was most responsible for putting the great team together, and keeping it together as well. As he finished speaking, he presented Harry a diamond stud on behalf of the players. Harry was humbled. "You shouldn't have done this, boys," he stated. "I thank you, on the square, I do."

The Pittsburgh Press had kind words for Harry as well.

"It takes a diplomat to keep eighteen ball players in fine humor at all times, particularly when, after a long trip, the club strikes a hotel that has failed to assign rooms, not bathrooms, to all the players; at another time trains are late and breakfast is no longer served when the hotel is reached; in such instances Pulliam never fails to rise to the occasion in dealing out the proper explanation and salve. The result is everybody is supremely satisfied, though nobody gets exactly what he wants.

"Putting sixteen ball players comfortably in twelve lower Pullman berths, each player in a berth, is another of the genial secretary's star feats.

"It's no wonder Pulliam is extremely popular with players, press and public alike. With him the other fellow wins at all times. All this diplomacy was acquired, we are told, while reading law in the office of the late Zach Phelps and subsequently while trying to put through the Kentucky legislature the now famous Redbird (Kentucky Cardinal) bill."

The League meeting was scheduled to begin on Tuesday, December 10, in New York, where the traditional first order of business was the awarding of the pennant to the League champion. Harry and Barney happily accepted. The two most important issues on the docket, however, were the creation of a new partnership agreement, and the election of the League president. Some felt a younger man might bring more energy to the job. Barney Dreyfuss offered Harry Pulliam as a candidate. "A year ago, Harry Pulliam was read out of the Pittsburg club by stockholders who had control at that time," he said. "Today he could be elected president of the National League by a unanimous vote."

The Sporting News seconded the unofficial nomination.

"H.C. Pulliam is not a candidate for the presidency of the national League, but he will, in all likelihood, be Mr. Young's successor when the factional fight is settled and the magnates get down to business. Mr. Pulliam has the good will and confidence of all the club owners, possesses executive ability, is versed in baseball law, is an enthusiast in the game, is progressive, is energetic and resourceful, and, what is of great importance at this critical time, can harmonize all the interests. His election to the office would be acceptable in all quarters."

Instead, the magnates elected Albert Goodwill Spalding, a life-long ambassador for the game. Brush and Freedman, who favored abolishing the position in favor of creating a three-man committee, were the only nay votes.

When the meeting ended, Harry traveled to Louisville, then on to Scottsville and Nashville to spend the holidays with his family. Despite the thrill of winning the pennant, he was weary from the grind and needed a rest to recoup his health. 1901 had been one of the best years of his life.

Chapter Eight

Anywhere but Louisville

1902 did not start out well for Harry Pulliam. After spending a couple of weeks in Winter Park, Florida, he passed through Louisville on his way back to Pittsburgh and spent a night at the Louisville Hotel. He was wearing the diamond stud the players had given him at the banquet to celebrate winning the pennant. While bathing, he removed the ring from his finger. It slipped from his hand, onto the floor, and cracked. Apparently, the contrast of the cold marble floor and the hot water in the tub caused the damage. It was a one in a million chance.

"Anywhere but Louisville," he sighed, "this wouldn't have happened."

Nobody, it seemed, was really happy about the selection of Spalding to be the new President of the National League. He had been, at best, a compromise candidate. Harry kept hearing his own name bandied about as a replacement, but he had moved on to other matters and was not interested. It was time to start preparing for the season of 1902. He publicly supported Spalding.

Spalding, on the other hand, was feeling less than secure in his new position. He asked Dreyfuss to call a meeting of the magnates to seek a vote of confidence. At the meeting, held in Pittsburgh, Harry and Dreyfuss were in attendance. Some magnates expressed support for Spalding, but others did not come forth.

On April 2, Spalding resigned, clearing the way for a candidate that both sides could support. That candidate turned out to be W.C. Temple, of the Temple Cup, who was then elected president of the League. James Hart had proposed Harry as a candidate, but Harry declined, and instead suggested Temple. Freedman and Brush had once again pushed an idea to vanquish the office and appoint a three-man committee to replace it. A long discussion ensued, but the plan was ultimately scrapped, at least for the time being. Temple's election was unanimous. However, there was one catch. Harry had visited Temple at his home in January, asked him if he was interested in the position, and was told that the position would not be accepted by Temple under any conditions.

It was hoped that he would change his mind, but he did not, and declined the offer. With no other option on the table, the three-man committee was adopted, to consist of John T. Brush, Arthur Soden and James Hart. Now, the magnates could finally turn their attention to the coming season, and the war with the American League. When the meeting ended, Harry immediately headed for Hot Springs to join the club.

When later asked about Hart's nomination, he was diplomatic. "Yes, I was gratified by the suggestion of myself for the presidency by some, but felt that Temple was the only man for the position. I was perfectly satisfied with my situation here with the Pittsburgh club and had no desire for the larger office even if I could have attained it."

On April 7 he arrived in Hot Springs, where the Pirates were once again holding spring practice. He shared insights about the League meeting and told stories about the people involved, which were received with great interest by the players. He was a gifted storyteller who knew how to command an audience, and people enjoyed listening to him.

In Pittsburgh, plans were in progress for opening day and the raising of the town's first National League pennant.

"The new flag pole from which the baseball championship pennant, won by the Pirates last year, will float over Exposition Park, will be erected next Tuesday or Wednesday. The unfurling of the pennant at the ball park on

Tuesday, April 22, will be one of the leading events in baseballdom in Pittsburgh this season." -Weekly Gazette.

"Instead of having speech making, which only few of the persons present could hear, it has been decided to allow the players to be the whole show," reported the Pittsburgh Press. "The members of both teams will meet at the home plate a few minutes before 3:30 and, headed by the Grand Army band, will march across the field to center, where promptly at 3:30 they will 'break' the pennant. As soon as the beautiful flag flies in the breeze the Pirates will scamper to their positions in the field and the Cincinnati Reds will hustle in to their bench. The game will start without delay."

The weather was perfect on opening day, and everything went without a hitch, just as Harry had planned. The fans turned out in waves, 15,000 strong. "Hundreds who had arrived at the park early were turned away at 2:40 because they found they could not get seats. So great was the jam at 3:15 that the club management decided to allow a thousand or more spectators to stand in front of the grand stand and the right field bleachers, although no ropes had been stretched." The icing on the cake was a 4-3 win over the Reds.

Dreyfuss, having tasted a championship and wanting another, schemed to find a way to motivate his players to repeat. In a joking manner, Harry suggested sending them on a trip around the world. Dreyfuss liked the idea.

On May 18, the Pirates played before a gathering of 15,000 fans in Chicago. Now referred to as the "Cubs", they were the Remnants no more, the team in closest pursuit of first place Pittsburgh. Led by stars Frank Chance, Bobby Lowe and Joe Tinker, the young Cubs were building a team that would eventually achieve greatness, but on this day, they were throttled by the Pirates, 11-3. Meanwhile, on the south side of town, the American League's White Stockings drew fewer than 2,000 fans while hosting first place Detroit.

John T. Brush

The Pirates started the season hot, and then got hotter still. By the first of June they were threatening to run away with the championship, winning thirty of their first thirty-six games. Being proactive and signing their players early was paying off for Barney and Harry. While most clubs had lost players in the war with the American League, the champion

Pirates remained intact. The war was still going full scale, and in turn, the National League had begun to raid American League teams.

The big news tip of the day on June 11 was that the St. Louis club of the American League was claiming to have stolen Hans Wagner and Jack O'Connor, and other players as well, from the Pirates by signing them to contracts for the 1903 season. "The telephone bells in all the newspaper offices jingled all evening at the demand of the fans, who wanted to know whether the rumor had been confirmed or not, and while waiting for word from Brooklyn and St. Louis there were many guesses as to the players captured." Barney and Harry both denounced the story, which soon proved false.

A month later the Pirates visited Chicago again. In the fourth inning of the game played on Monday, June 23, a fight broke out between the two shortstops, Wid Conroy of the Pirates and Joe Tinker of the Cubs. "The cause was an alleged clinch on Sunday, Tinker claiming that Conroy held him at second base. When the pair met at that station in the fourth a controversy was launched. Before the spectators realized what was on, the boys were at each other hammer and tongs. Tinker, the aggressor, let drive his right, which landed on Conroy's neck. It was an ugly swing and almost caused the Pirate to lose his feet. But he recovered in an instant and delivered a straight arm jolt under Tinker's left eye. Then both forgot everything else but punching, and swung wildly at each other until they were separated by O'Day and the other players, who crowded around and endeavored to restore them to good humor." Both players were suspended.

Otherwise, though, kicking and rowdyism seemed to be fading away. A new rule stipulated that any player who left his position to argue with an umpire was required to be immediately removed from the game, with the exception of the team captain. It was making a difference.

Harry, meanwhile, for the first time in a long time, was free to enjoy the fruits of his labor. His team was sailing along in first place by a comfortable margin, and there didn't seem to be any way he could possibly improve the roster. The Pirates had everything: hitting, pitching, fielding, speed and, best of all, persistence. They were out to prove that 1901 had been no fluke. As secretary, he continued to balance the books, pay the bills and speak to the press on behalf of the club. The writers admired his baseball acumen, and they admired the way he dressed as well.

"Harry Pulliam, the Pittsburg magnate, is baseball's Berry Wall. His wardrobe is a most extensive one. While there are many well-dressed players in the League, none compare with the Pirates' business man." -New York Evening Telegram.

In July, Harry put to rest rumors that the Pittsburgh club was being courted by Ban Johnson, who wanted to move it to the American League. "Under no circumstances will we form an alliance with the American League interests," he flatly stated. "The Pittsburgh club has been and will be loyal to the national organization. We cannot subscribe to a cut-throat policy, and for that reason, if no other, we would necessarily reject any overture from the American League." A few days later an even wilder rumor was spreading; Ban Johnson wanted Dreyfuss to sell his team to the American League. This one was also quickly put down by Harry.

Then, rowdyism returned in a big way. Following a loss to the Cardinals in St. Louis, a mob of fans followed the Pirate players as they left the park, hurling insults and threats. One threw a rock that hit Clarke in the face. Clarke pointed out the culprit, who was immediately arrested.

In its weekly edition, The Sporting News gave more details of the assault. "The Pirates were followed to their bus by a howling mob on Sunday, and had they not submitted in silence to taunts and insults they would have been mobbed. While going to the bus Clarke was struck in the face twice and other attempts were made to land on him. The riot call brought a platoon of police in time to prevent the Pittsburg players from being torn to pieces."

But perhaps the most disturbing part of the whole affair was yet to come. "The daily papers state that President Robison sent word to the police judge that he would pay the fines of all parties convicted of participation in the attack on the Pittsburg players."

Ban Johnson

Harry's nerves were strained by the incident. He took his yearly vacation to Saratoga for the races during the second week of August. Before departing he was asked to comment on the status of the war. "Pittsburgh would be glad to see peace," he said. When he returned he commented on the recent sale of the Cincinnati team by Brush to Garry Herrmann. It was to the benefit of every team in the League, he suggested, without mentioning Brush by name. He also predicted a "great and lasting revival of interest in baseball at Cincinnati."

In Pittsburgh, there were more important issues to deal with. On August 16, a group of miners formed a square facing all directions and began to sing to the crowd between games of a doubleheader with the Phillies at Exposition Park. When they finished, one of them addressed the crowd of 7,200, informing them they were there to represent striking miners in the anthracite coal region. An appeal for help to feed and clothe the families of the strikers was met with "a shower of money." Fifty people, including players from both teams, spent ten minutes gathering the coins, a total of more than $250 raised, from Pirates fans and Phillies fans as well. After the money was collected, the police force arrested six young boys who had pocketed the money they had picked up.

Throughout the summer, representatives of the American League continued their attempt to raid the National League of its best players, with mixed results. On the evening of August 20, American League President Ban Johnson and vice-president Charles Somers arrived in the city of Pittsburgh incognito. The pair, inconspicuously as possible, made their way to the Lincoln Hotel, where, as Johnson hid behind a lamp, Somers registered under an assumed name, and Johnson did not register at all. Pirates' catcher Jack O'Connor was evidently part of the scheme, as one by one he began escorting unsigned (for the 1903 season) Pirates to a hotel room to meet with Johnson and Somers.

But Harry and Dreyfuss had been tipped in advance, and for days had had men posted at every hotel in town to watch for the plotters. At some point one of them alerted Harry to the scheme, and he hurried to the hotel. Seeing Harry arrive, aware that their cover had been blown, Somers tried to protect Johnson, securing an enclosed carriage for him to escape. Then, changing his mind, he left alone, leaving Johnson to fend for himself. Johnson bribed the hotel porters to take him downstairs on the freight elevator, where he hid behind some garbage cans, then exited via the back alley and walked, or perhaps ran, to the depot to catch a train. Harry, though, arrived at the depot before Johnson did, and he watched the two conspirators board a coach bound for Cleveland.

The five Pirates who had met with Johnson and Somers were Tannehill, Happy Jack Chesbro, Jimmy Burke, Leach and Lefty Davis. When asked, all admitted to the meetings, but none had signed contracts or agreed to change allegiances. For his part in the shenanigans, Dreyfuss suspended O'Connor, gave him the rest of his year's salary, and kicked him off the team. "No player can be a stool pigeon for the American League and draw salary from the Pittsburgh club at the same time," he said.

Later Harry fended off another attempted raid. "Ban Johnson made a strenuous effort to secure Bransfield when the first baseman was ill at his home in Worcester, but I telegraphed Kitty," he boasted, "and the American League president got a very cold reception in Massachusetts. If our players live up to the contracts that we have with them we will not lose a man now with the team." He had just signed Leach and Conroy, and the core was under contract for 1903. The one exception was Chesbro. "We will pay liberally to retain him, but if he wants $7,500, he'll have to guess again."

In New York, having sold the Giants to John T. Brush a month previous, Andrew Freedman retired from baseball. This was both good news and bad news for the National

League, which would have benefitted greatly by having a competitive team in New York. Brush, however, had already proved himself difficult to work with, and was not liked by most of the magnates. There was no reason to expect this to change.

Five days after the Lincoln Hotel fiasco, the Pirates stretched their lead over Brooklyn to a whopping 21 games after defeating the Superbas, 8-6. On the last day of the season they won their 103rd game, setting a new National League record for wins in a season, and completed one of the most lopsided pennant races, if there even really was a race, in baseball history. Once again, there was no postseason exhibition between the top two teams.

On November 16, Harry met with Ban Johnson at the Waldorf-Astoria Hotel in New York City. Also attending were several other American League men: S.F. Angus, owner of the Detroit team, Ben Shibe of the Philadelphia team, and John Kilfoyl of Cleveland. Some reporters were speculating that the Detroit team was being dropped by the American League, and the Pirates would switch alliances to take their place. Others insisted that Harry and Dreyfuss would never be involved in syndicate baseball, which they felt stifled true competition. It was also known that Harry had earlier in the day spent several hours with John T. Brush.

"We may take Pittsburg in the League instead of Detroit," said Shibe. "And we may let Pittsburgh have the Baltimore franchise and give Detroit's franchise to New York. We may keep Detroit, and not have a team in New York. It is hard to say just now. We've got quite a few little details to fix up. We're getting along finely, but we're not here for our health."

The magnates returned home having not settled anything.

Harry sought a solution to the contract jumping, which was a boon for the players, but was hitting the owners where it hurt most – in the pocketbook. He suggested a committee be formed, with equal representation from both Leagues, to examine and rule on the validity of the contracts in question. It would not be easy. Many players had two contracts, both of which seemed to be valid. Some even had three. But the two Leagues weren't ready to trust each other, and the suggestion was tabled.

On December 8, Harry and Dreyfuss arrived at the Hotel Victoria in New York City for the annual winter meetings of the National League. The conversations around the hotel among the magnates centered on the decision of whether to re-elect the executive board that composed the three-man committee, or choose a president. President Hart of Chicago voiced his thoughts. "Unless W.C. Temple will accept the office as president I don't know who else will be talked of. I have heard nothing much regarding any other candidate."

Later that day, beginning near midnight, a dramatic meeting took place between Ban Johnson and Charles Somers of the American League and several representatives of the National League, including Brush, Garry Herrmann, Dreyfuss and Harry. The American League had made a proposition for peace, which was clearly rejected by the National League.

"So far as I am concerned the American League is dead," said Brush as he left the meeting. "We will have nothing to do with it. Yes, Johnson and his people are here with their ideas. We have refused to accept them. They declare they have New York and Pittsburgh. They have not. I admit they can get into Pittsburgh, but know that they dare not go. We know, however, that they cannot get into New York, or the island, at least. Their claims are nil and their journey of no effect."

Meanwhile, it was being reported in the papers that the men attempting to get an American League franchise in Pittsburgh were P.L. Auten of Chicago and W.W. Kerr of Allegheny, the two previous stockholders of the Pirates who had tried to wrest control of the team from Dreyfuss. The source of the information was Ban Johnson, who had not yet decided whether to award them a franchise in Pittsburgh or not.

At a meeting of team Directors in Jersey City, Barney Dreyfuss was re-elected president of the Pirates and Harry Pulliam was re-elected secretary. However, there seemed to be bigger things in store for Harry. Talk was that he was being considered again for the position of president of the National League.

Support for Harry to be the new leader of the League was strong among the magnates. They knew he was a good businessman, a hard worker, and a man who tried to do things the right way. Furthermore, he was a young man, presumably more energetic than the elderly Nick Young. "I am for Pulliam because he likes everybody, and everybody likes him," Garry Herrmann stated. To him, it was as simple as that.

On December 13, Harry Pulliam was unanimously voted President of the National League. He was thirty-three years old. He was also voted secretary and treasurer, with the right to hire his own assistant. Harry had let it be known beforehand that if the vote were not unanimous, he would not accept the position. John T. Brush, who had originally opposed Harry and would continue to do so for many years to come, changed his vote to make it so.

"We had to weaken Pittsburgh, so we took its most valuable man," joked James Hart.

"I am sorry to lose Harry, but the League needed him," said Dreyfuss.

Newspapers throughout the circuit, and across the country, enthusiastically endorsed the move, including the Pittsburgh Press:

"The only fault that the patrons of baseball in Pittsburg can find with the National League today is that the organization took from the local team the most popular secretary it ever possessed to make a leader.

"In the three seasons that he spent here Harry Pulliam made many friends, and while all will rejoice over his promotion there is sincere regret that it is not possible for him to establish his headquarters here. This, however, cannot be. The central office is now in New York, where it should have been established years ago, and the new president will have to be on duty there most of the time.

"There is no fear here as to his ability to make good. Trained in the game for years and broadened by studies of the law and his newspaper experience, he is better fitted for the place than any of the magnates of either League. He will succeed, but his success will not parallel Ban Johnson's. Pulliam would not steal a player one minute and turn around the next to denounce the practice. He believes that it saves time and money to tell the truth and that trickery does not pay in the long run. His policy is bound to be popular with the public"

"Colonel Pulliam, as he is commonly styled, is very popular is baseball circles. He is a great mixer, a raconteur who could have held his own with Tom Ochiltree, and an all-around good fellow. In addition to his social qualities, he is an admirable business man, keen, tactful and diplomatic and of sterling character. He is well fitted to harmonize and direct the councils of the League, which have been at cross-purposes so long." -Baltimore Herald.

Prior to the election, Nick Young, who had served the League faithfully as president for many years, was nominated for treasurer. He declined the nomination for reasons regarding his health. The magnates then voted him an honorary life member of the Board of Directors.

Ready to make another attempt at ending the war in favor of peace, the two Leagues decided to meet again to work out their differences, most likely sometime in January, at a location to be chosen by Ban Johnson. The key development was the decision by Johnson to include a provision in the agreement calling for the banishment of contract jumpers.

"There will be peace. That is certain," promised Johnson. "The American conferees are very likely to be the same gentlemen who took part in the meeting here yesterday. The Committee will be called together in the West – probably at Cleveland, although I may choose old Cincinnati. There was absolutely no discussion of terms. That will be for the committees. The unanimous expression in both Leagues is for peace, and there will be peace."

Over the holidays, Harry returned to Kentucky to spend a day in Louisville, and then several days in his hometown of Scottsville to rest and recover from a hectic December. Afterward, his plan was to return to Pittsburgh to handle business there, and to make arrangements for the transition, then on to Washington to meet with Nick Young. Before leaving, he spoke with the press one last time.

"The war in the Southern League has come to an amicable settlement, which I learned with a great deal of pleasure, as I never like to see a baseball fight. They result in no good to anyone. I believe the fight between the National and American Leagues will be settled in much the same way in Cincinnati next week."

Chapter Nine

The Quest for Peace

"Harry Pulliam says he would rather be secretary of the Pittsburg club than President of the League. He means it too." – Pittsburgh Press.

As the new year began, Harry expressed his belief that ending the war between the Leagues would increase the value of all clubs in both Leagues. Basically, this was based on the assumption that potential investors in the game would not want to get involved in any venture that was unstable, as both Leagues clearly were. In his estimation, the cut-throat methods of the war needed to end before they permanently harmed the sport.

He left for Washington to meet with Nick Young and collect the records, papers and books that belonged to the National League and were on file in his office. He had not yet named an assistant, and indicated that he probably would not do so for some time. Young had served the National League for 32 years.

Next, it was on to Cleveland to attend the conference with the representatives of the American League. Having met with new Giants owner Brush the day before, he was convinced the American League would not attempt to place a team in New York. "National League matters," Harry surmised "are in better shape than at any time during the past year."

On Sunday, January 4, Johnson postponed the much-anticipated meeting, citing the fact that the National League committee had not been granted full authority to act on any proposal that might be offered. It was a weak excuse, and no alternate date was being considered. The optimism that existed at the end of 1902 was beginning to fade.

"Ban Johnson and Harry Pulliam will bow gracefully to each other at the entrance to the peace factory meeting, and remark, 'After you, sir,' but it is our private conviction that Johnson has a brick and Pulliam a slingshot beneath the coattails," observed the Pittsburgh Post-Dispatch. "The desire to have the other go first, therefore, loses force from a peace standpoint."

On Monday, the original date of the meeting, Harry arrived back in Pittsburgh, seeing no need to go to Cincinnati for a meeting that might or might not take place. Hearing nothing from Johnson, he made plans to go to New York to start work on the business of the National League, which did not include the American League in any way. He did, however, remain in touch on a regular basis with the club owners, updating them on the situation. That evening he addressed the press:

"I cannot understand the reason for the position taken by Johnson. The National League made the first proposal for harmony, and it was in good faith. We realize that the baseball people demand peace between the two Leagues, so that the recreation will not suffer. I regret that Mr. Johnson is acting in the manner mentioned, for his conduct will apparently bring about a complete collapse of the move to have harmony. I shall go to New York tomorrow night, open up the National League office, and prepare to go along with the coming season on the old lines – that of antagonism to the American League."

The next day, after consultation with Garry Herrmann, Johnson agreed to hold the peace meeting on January 9. Harry was wired by Dreyfuss, urging him to leave for Cincinnati immediately. At 9:00 Harry boarded a train headed west. He arrived early, but many others were delayed, so the meeting at the St. Nicholas Hotel began late, but finally an attempt to achieve peace was at hand. The

American League was represented by Ban Johnson, Charles Somers, Charles Comiskey and Henry Kililea; the National League representatives were Harry Pulliam, Garry Herrmann, James Hart and Frank De Haas Robison. Taking a break after several hours, some expressed optimism to the many members of the press camped outside the conference room.

A proposal to create one twelve-team league was discussed, but in the end, Johnson, no doubt trying to preserve his base of power, insisted on two eight team leagues. His only other real interest, it seemed, was to cooperate on a plan to protect clubs from being raided by the rival League, the crime he himself was most guilty of. But the National League representatives favored two separate leagues themselves, so the only real issue, besides the pilfering of players, was territorial rights. Johnson was intent on having a team in New York, his insistence matched in intensity only by the National League's desire to deny him one. This issue, it seemed, was beyond compromise. There could be no gray area. Either the American League had a team in New York, or it did not.

Yet despite this seemingly impassable block in the road, negotiations continued the next day, with no break for lunch, then into the evening. The owners of the National League teams, whose approval would be required for any agreement, kept near their phones in their respective cities in anticipation of a long-distance call at any moment. Shortly after 7:00 p.m. an agreement was announced. Both Leagues were to have franchises in Boston, Chicago, Philadelphia, St. Louis and New York. Additionally, the American League had teams in Cleveland, Detroit and Washington. The National League would keep Brooklyn, Cincinnati and Pittsburgh. Thus, two separate eight team leagues. Despite the opposition of Brush, the National League had succumbed to the American regarding territorial rights in New York.

Also, both Leagues agreed to honor the contracts of the other League, and a uniform contract would be used by both Leagues for the sake of simplicity. This would, of course, keep player salaries down, enhancing the profits of the owners, but more vexing to the players was the agreement

Garry Herrmann

on a reserve clause that would bind each player to the team that owned his rights for the length of his career.

Finally, a list of disputed players and their fates was released. Mathewson, who had jumped to the St. Louis American League team, was returned to the Giants. Tommy Leach, who had recently signed with New York of the American League, was returned to the Pirates.

Having played a significant role in negotiating the terms of the agreement, Harry released a statement that night.

"The result of this conference will be prosperity in baseball such as the game has never known. The feeling between the two Leagues is entirely harmonious. We date a new era in baseball from today, forget the past, and look to the future for a strengthening of the ties that have been formed at this meeting."

Immediately after the conference ended, he called for a special League meeting to be held on January 19 to officially ratify the agreement, and also to create the new schedule for 1903.

Despite Harry's optimism, there was displeasure in New York, where the Giants were less than thrilled about having to share their territory with an American League intruder. Giants' secretary Fred Knowles offered his opinion.

"The committee in Cincinnati simply exceeded its authority. It was appointed to refer back to the League, and the New York club never was consulted on the terms drawn up in Cincinnati. To encroach on our territorial rights in that manner is so far as I can see decidedly unconstitutional. What will be done in Cincinnati next Monday remains to be seen. We will stand for anything fair and reasonable, but when a man goes into your pockets and takes something out you don't feel like coming around the next day and giving him what he left."

Remorse and second thoughts were also being expressed in Brooklyn, Boston and Philadelphia. When the vote was taken, only five "yea" votes would be needed, but if all four

Eastern teams voted no, the agreement would not be ratified. Herrmann, disgusted by the growing doubt, threatened to leave the League if the vote was carried by the "no" faction.

Harry remained confident, both publicly and privately, and moved on to other issues, including the assembling of a staff of umpires. Two days later he was in Philadelphia with Herrmann, helping to negotiate the sale of the Phillies, the result of which would probably secure another "yea" vote for the agreement.

When the sale of the Phillies was completed, John T. Brush saw the writing on the wall, and decided to make one last stand to protect his territory. He took the matter to court and obtained an order restraining Harry from taking an official vote on the peace agreement until Brush had a chance to present his stand to the committee.

"I do not propose to have Herrmann and the others walk roughshod over me and my interests without having a say, and naturally I was forced to invoke the aid of the courts," he said. "The committee which signed the peace pact never conferred with me while it was in session, and I most strenuously object to an arrangement which is opposed to my interests."

To protect the interests of the League, Harry met with attorneys himself, in Cincinnati. Herrmann joined him. Afterward, Harry insisted the meeting of January 19 would indeed take place, though he still did not know if a vote would be taken at that time. Most of the magnates had confirmed that they planned to attend, including Brush, indirectly, by way of the Boston club. He refused to address Harry directly.

On the morning of the 19th, Harry and Dreyfuss were ordered to appear in court regarding Brush's restraining order. Harry was able to keep a sense of humor. "I now have seven lawyers in my employ, and I am looking for a couple of more to play the outfield." No vote was taken that night, but on the afternoon of January 21, Brush withdrew his suit, opening the door for the vote to finally take place. At 2:00 a.m. the next day, the agreement was ratified by the National League by a vote of 8-0.

Brush had been given the opportunity to express his concerns to all the magnates, and having failed to convince them to oppose the agreement, found it useless to continue his opposition, and in the best interests of the League ultimately voted in favor of it. He also blamed newspaper reports for spreading inaccurate information that turned him against the agreement.

The Philadelphia Inquirer saw the vote as the end of Brush's reign of power.

"At every turn John T. Brush, the former dictator of the National League, and who for many years was referred to as the Napoleon of baseball, met his master in Herrmann and the other men in the National League who are for peace. He was beaten at his own game and in the future will only be known as the president of the New York club."

From there Harry traveled to New York, arriving at the headquarters of the National League in the St. James Building on the afternoon of January 26, and sorted through a mass of accumulated mail. He sidestepped a few probing questions from the New York writers about the territorial issue, expressed optimism for the future, then excused himself and went back to work.

The first order of business was to hire a staff of umpires. The first hire – O'Day was already under contract – was Gus Moran, who had worked the previous season in the Western League. Of the twenty-two umpires who had started the 1902 season in that League, he was the only one standing when the season ended. So, Harry reasoned, he must at least have some chutzpah.

When Harry took over as president, several rule changes were being considered. Some "purists" thought the pitcher's box was being raised too high in some parks. At the time, there were no guidelines for how high it could be, but over time home groundskeepers, attempting to help the home team's pitchers, had begun to raise the box. A limit to the height was being proposed.

Progressives, on the other hand, were suggesting it might be a welcome change to not have pitchers bat, but rather, have a tenth player added to the lineup who would not play the field, but would simply bat for the pitcher. Purists were horrified by the idea. Another option bantered about was to only have eight batters in the batting lineup, excluding the pitcher's spot altogether. This would allow the better hitters to get more at bats, making the game more attractive for spectators.

And, in the opinion of some, fielders' gloves were becoming entirely too large. "The rules committee should take up the mitt question once more, as some players are using mitts with pockets and can catch the ball as one would scoop a butterfly," noted the Cincinnati Enquirer. "Outfielders should not be allowed mitts under any circumstances, as it takes away from the beauty of the game."

Interleague play between the two Leagues was also a topic of conversation, some greatly in favor, others strongly opposed. And the foul strike rule remained controversial. Harry was content to let the rules committee make those decisions. He had plenty on his plate already.

In mid-February, the location where the American League New York team would play remained a mystery. When asked about it, Harry responded, "I am not worrying myself about American League matters. I have enough to do to keep track of the affairs in the National League, and I guess Ban Johnson is able to take care of the affairs of the American League. It may have grounds here, but I haven't the slightest idea as to their location."

The next day, New York reporters posed the same question to Johnson, who claimed he would announce the location sometime in the next ten days. It had become a source of intense curiosity around the city, and the League as well.

On February 23, the rules committee met and voted to keep the foul strike rule, despite opposition from the American League, which had not used the rule in 1902. They also voted to limit the height of the pitcher's slab to not more than fifteen inches higher than home plate and the bases, and put in place a rule that the baselines must be level, and home plate as well. The pitchers would continue to hit for themselves.

At the League meeting in March, "President Pulliam expressed a desire to improve matters on the ball field regarding players. He does not want to be a figurehead in this respect, and suggested that, instead of having to report all questions of rowdyism and finding fault with the umpire to the Board of Directors, he be vested with power to take immediate steps himself toward squelching outbreaks on the field and the causes thereof." – Chicago Tribune.

The next day, the magnates did indeed vest this authority in Harry, giving him, "absolute power to maintain order and discipline on the ball field." This included the power to discipline players and managers by way of fines or suspension for rowdyism and kicking, and other behavior issues that might happen during a game. Going one step further, teams were forbidden to pay fines for players, and also forbidden to pay salaries of suspended players. With this victory, Harry had already significantly increased the powers of his office.

As part of his attempt to cut down on kicking, Harry instituted a policy stating that umpires would not stay in one city more than one week, and would not travel with teams on their way out of town. Just as folks tire of relatives who stay too long, he said, so it was with umpires as well.

The location of the new American League park to be built in New York was finally announced by Johnson on March 12. The magnates had selected a site in northern Manhattan, near the Hudson River, in the Washington Heights neighborhood. It was only a few blocks from the Polo Grounds, which infuriated Brush. He and Andrew Freedman had, through corrupt political maneuvers, blocked several previous options, but this time they were unsuccessful. When construction began, Freedman organized a neighborhood protest, urging residents to claim the new park would lower property values. They signed and circulated petitions, to no avail. The matter was settled. The New York Times was not impressed:

"From Broadway looking west, the ground starts in a low swamp. It rises into a ridge of rocks perhaps twelve to fifteen feet above the level of Broadway. From the top of the ridge the land slopes off gradually to Fort Washington Road. As the property is today it will be necessary to blast all along the ridge, cutting off a slice eight-feet or more ... There are about 100 trees to be pulled up by the roots."

The tentative peace between the Leagues was threatened in 1903 by complicated cases involving players George Davis and Ed Delahanty. Davis, one of the best hitters of the previous decade, had jumped from the Giants to the Chicago White Stockings team in the American League in 1902. In negotiating the peace agreement, it was determined that he remain with Chicago for the 1903 season. However, by the time spring training arrived, he had been convinced to report to the Giants instead. Harry ruled that he could not play for the Giants, citing the peace agreement. In a related decision, infielder Kid Elberfeld, who had signed with both the Giants and Detroit of the American League, was granted permission by Giants' owner Brush to stay with Detroit. Then, in a move orchestrated by Ban Johnson, he was moved to the Highlander's team, much to Brush's displeasure. To placate Brush, Harry changed his mind and allowed him to keep Davis. It was a mistake. Chicago then sued for breach of contract, and Harry had a huge mess on his hands.

Delahanty, an even better hitter who played for the Phillies, worked as a recruiter for the American League, successfully wooing players such as Elmer Flick, Harry Wolverton and Al Orth, and himself as well. The Senators of the American League gave him a $4,000 contract, and a $1,000 signing bonus to boot. Unfortunately, he wasted most of it drinking and gambling. To pay his mounting debts, he signed another contract, this one with the Giants. It was a three-year deal, with a $4,000 salary advance to pay back the bonus he had been ordered to return to the Senators. At one point, Ed Delahanty had three active signed contracts at the same time, with three different teams.

After a tense meeting in New York that lasted several hours, Harry and Ban Johnson issued statements indicating final decisions in the cases of Ed Delahanty and George Davis. Delahanty was to honor his commitment to the Washington team, and Davis his commitment to the Chicago team of the American League. Elberfeld stayed with the Highlanders. Harry had reversed himself again, embarrassing himself, and angering Brush in the process. Brush opted to fight it out in court.

Manager McGraw of the Giants was not at all willing to give up on the two stars either. From spring training in Savannah, Georgia, he said, "I hardly think either of the League presidents care to be in contempt of court by refusing to obey the judgment of the courts, as both Davis and Delahanty have contracts in New York. I look to the courts to decide that the two players must fulfill their engagements with New York, regardless of the officers of the two big Leagues."

On April 4, George Davis announced that he would report to the Giants for the start of the season, in defiance of the agreement reached by Harry and Ban Johnson. His attorney, John Montgomery Ward, had advised him that he was well within his rights to do so. In the interest of peace, Brush agreed not to play Davis, at the suggestion of Garry Herrmann. He appeared in only four games.

Early in his tenure as president, Harry came up with the idea of a Hall of Fame, to be located in his office in New York. When he learned of this, 1902 batting champion Clarence Beaumont posed for a photograph to give to Harry for his office museum. Harry and Clarence had become friends from their days together in Pittsburgh. It was a source of great pride for Beaumont to have his picture hanging in Harry's office.

"I want a good picture, Clarence," Harry wrote to him. "I am proud of the record which you made last season, and I want that smiling face of yours to look upon me every time I wheel around in my office chair. So go at once and get the photo. I will attend to all the other details."

"I'll tell you, that's the kind of man to have at the head of the League," Beaumont beamed. "Who wouldn't try to do good stick work when he knows that Harry C. Pulliam is watching his batting average and helping him along. I'll bat better than ever this year, just to please the dear old president."

Harry's Hall of Fame soon became well known around the League, and its contents a source of discussion among the players. It included, among other things, a large photo of his friend, Rube Waddell.

Prior to the start of the season, Harry sent a letter to every player clearly outlining what was expected regarding behavior on the field in the National League. "If there is rowdyism it will not be the fault of the umpires or players, but my fault. I intend to have clean ball, and to carry out that intention and to enforce my authority will be a test of my executive ability." Harry apparently also meant to have clean ball in the literal sense. His edict further stated that players were not to wear dirty uniforms during games.

"Pulliam may be a great man and all that," said noted tough guy Jesse Burkett in response. "But he has seen few games where the uniforms of the home club were soiled except during the game. A visiting club does not wash uniforms on a trip, but the color of the cloth hides any part of the uniform that may be soiled. Next thing they will be wanting us to wear ribbons on our bats and fancy hosiery."

He also sent a written interpretation of the new rules to all National League umpires. Part of his plan to end kicking and rowdyism for good was to back up the umpires in all matters, thereby empowering them in the eyes of the players. "You're the whole thing," he told them. "All you've got to do is remember that."

The Chicago Tribune heartily endorsed and supported Harry.

"President Pulliam has chosen a wise policy so far in the matter of doing away with rowdyism on National League diamonds. There have been several outbreaks among players long accustomed to doing as they pleased on the diamond. The first outbreaks were in Cincinnati and New York, where two of the worst disturbers on the diamond are in control – Kelley and McGraw. Instead of swinging the ax immediately, Pulliam considered the bringing up of the lawbreakers and simply sent a firm warning to them to the effect that the day of such things was past and that another break would be severely punished. It is not likely the warnings will have any lasting effect when a team strikes a losing rut. It will then be up to Pulliam to act. No one who has watched his methods so far doubts he will act and in a way that will convince all rowdies he means what he says. It is going to be no easy task, nor does anyone envy him."

Several days before opening day in Pittsburgh, Harry received an invitation to attend the first home game and participate in the raising of the pennant at Exposition Park. He accepted the invitation. The celebration called for the players of the two teams, the Cardinals and the Giants, to line up at home plate and salute President Pulliam, who would lead the way to the flag pole in center field. The old pennant was then to be lowered and the new one raised. The players were to escort Harry to his box for the game to begin.

Once the season started, so did the kicking. The players were testing Harry's resolve, including his good friend Hans Wagner, whom, after reading a game report from Umpire James Holliday, he suspended for an altercation with Reds' second baseman Jack Morrison. Later, Holliday contradicted himself on the details, leading Harry to reprimand him and cut back his work schedule, pending a decision on his continued employment by the League. Backing his umpires "in all matter" apparently had its limits. Yet, for the most part, he did. In some cases, he probably went too far.

"Previous to the game yesterday President Pulliam, of the National League, sprang a surprise on the locals. Tuesday, he suspended Doheny, not for tossing his bat in the air, but because he gossiped after the game," reported the Pittsburgh Press. "Yesterday Mr. Pulliam walked up to (George) Van Haltren and said: 'You are out of the game for five days. Your sensational methods of holding up (Billy) Lauder's injured finger during yesterday's game so that the spectators could see the bloody bandage is a thing we don't want in baseball, and I intend to make an example,' and President Pulliam lit a cigar and turned his back."

"I suppose the next thing in order," mocked Van Haltren of the Giants, "will be a sentence to attend a pink tea."

Despite the complaints, Harry's heavy-handed approach to kicking and rowdyism was making a difference. In its edition of August 2, the St. Louis Post-Dispatch declared that, "the day of the umpire is here. No longer can the pugnacious player bullyrag the arbitrator and make him the target for sarcastic abuse."

By late July, a total of forty-six players in the two Leagues had been suspended for bad behavior during a game. Twenty-five of them were National Leaguers, the worst offenders being Napoleon Lajoie, Joe Kelley, Heinie Peitz and, predictably, John McGraw.

Kicking and rowdyism aside, baseball continued to thrive. A Saturday afternoon game in May between the first place Giants and defending champion Pirates at the Polo Grounds in New York was attended by 31,500 patrons, establishing a new record for the largest crowd in baseball history. The game attracted more fans than attended all American League games played that day combined, a clear public relations victory for the National League. Harry was quick to gloat. "I am free to confess that the attendance at today's game gave me the utmost surprise. I knew that people loved baseball, but that a single game would draw 31,500 people exceeded my greatest anticipations. It is a demonstration that the people love clean sport, and that is what I intend they shall have."

While most of the National League teams remained profitable, the American League was on very shaky ground, leading many, including Harry, to believe that Ban Johnson was behind talk of amalgamation. Reporters had linked him to a plan floating around that would combine the two Leagues, then drop the weakest four, and return to the days of a one major league system. Harry, no doubt, had no interest in the plan. His teams were, on a daily basis, outperforming and out drawing Johnson's teams.

Magnates representing all eight National League teams met at the Victoria Hotel on July 20 to discuss and act on the George Davis matter. At 3:00 p.m. they went into executive session and stayed there, pausing only to take a short break for dinner, until midnight. It was reported to be a contentious meeting, with tempers flaring and emotions boiling over. At 11:00 the next morning, a weary group of men reconvened to make known their agreed upon course of action. Harry addressed the awaiting reporters:

"The matter having been thoroughly and carefully considered, it is the opinion of the League that the assignment of Norman Elberfeld to New York by Detroit was not a violation or breach of the Cincinnati peace pact, and George S. Davis still remains ineligible to play in the National League, except the courts decide otherwise. The National League is desirous of maintaining peace among organized professional baseball leagues and favors the adoption of a national agreement to that end."

He continued:

"The Davis case is in the United States courts, and their decision is far above any action which the National League might or could take. Our members are satisfied to await and abide the decision of the courts, and in the meantime Davis cannot play in our League. This is how the matter stands, and every phase of it has been gone over very carefully."

Harry had been shown up by the magnates. Some newspapers opined that such a blow to his position as president might cause him to resign, as he often threatened or offered to do when he was criticized, or did not get his way in a matter of importance to him. He did not handle criticism well, and often overreacted when it came his way. In this case, he did not, and when asked, simply stated that he had no intention of resigning.

The very next day, Brush decided to end court proceedings and, in the process, dropped his team's pursuit of Davis. The only option left for Davis was to play for the Chicago White Stockings of the American League. The matter having been settled, Ban Johnson announced he was ready to try to work out a new national agreement.

In response, a meeting was scheduled to take place in New York City for that purpose, with Johnson, Pulliam and minor league president Patrick Powers expected to attend on July 28. But Johnson inexplicably failed to show, much to the irritation of Powers. "Johnson may be sick, and then again he may not. We have heard other stories coming from the American League which turned out afterwards to be pipe dreams. We will not put off our business to wait on him. He has been delaying this agreement ever since the peace meeting last winter by his tactics, and we have decided to act without him since he has failed to come at our call. I am tired of Johnson's high-handed methods, and will no longer place any confidence in his promises." Harry agreed to proceed without Johnson. The two exchanged ideas without taking any action.

Johnson seemed to have changed his mind about the whole thing. "What is the use of going to the trouble of forming a new national agreement? We will respect all contract rights. Why Pulliam should be in a hurry I cannot imagine. Perhaps the National League wants to cut salaries. The American surely does not. We will sign an agreement when the time comes, but at present I see no reason for forming any."

One month later, Johnson had changed his mind again. The three presidents met in Buffalo, and a new national agreement that was much more far reaching than anything considered before was negotiated. There were nine main tenets:

1. The major leagues will make all rules for professional baseball.
2. The eight-member circuits currently in each major league will remain as is.
3. Neither League may change circuits without a majority consent in both Leagues.
4. All contracts with players must be respected subject to agreed-upon penalties.
5. A reserve clause for players protected teams' rights to each player until released or traded.
6. Farming of players was prohibited. Rights of a major league team cease when a player joins a minor league team.
7. A draft of minor league players was instituted, with minor league teams being compensated.
8. Playing games for a stake (money for winning) was prohibited.

9. A national commission composed of three members to settle disputes was created.

The three-man committee for settling disputes was to consist of Pulliam, Johnson, and Garry Herrmann. The minor leagues, much to the dismay of Patrick Powers, received no representation on the committee. Herrmann, a National League owner, was a good choice for the pivotal third slot, as he was a childhood friend of Johnson, who trusted him.
The good news had been preceded by tragedy. On Saturday, August 8, in the city of Philadelphia, six people died and fifty were injured when the left field balconies at the Philadelphia Base Ball Park collapsed during a game. Five of the injured were not expected to survive. An inspection of the debris revealed joists that were inadequate to support the weight of the crowd, and rotted out as well. A check of city records indicated the balconies and bleachers had not been inspected since 1895. Hearing of the disaster, Harry rushed to Philadelphia to offer assistance, arriving late Sunday night.
An inquiry determined that several hundred fans had rushed to the balcony to witness an incident taking place outside the ball park on Fifteenth Street. Once the balconies began to collapse they panicked, worsening the situation in the hurry to save themselves. Spectators reported that more than half the injuries occurred after the balconies had already fallen.
"After the crash," said Lieutenant Magee, "the police had all they could do to keep hundreds of others from rushing up and falling into the street. At least a dozen times crowds climbed out on the broken ends of the balcony to try and see what happened. We had to drive them back again and again. Our men must have saved hundreds from adding their names to the roll of injured. The crowd was absolutely panic-

stricken. The people seemed to have lost control of themselves entirely."

On the last day of September, Harry arrived in Boston to watch the first World Series game ever played. The betting line favored the Pirates, much of the core consisting of players he had scouted and secured as far back as his early days in Louisville. They had been Colonels.

In game one, Pittsburgh sent Deacon Philippe to the box to face Boston ace Cy Young. Just before the first pitch, Phillippe said to Fred Clarke, "I think I have my curve working in pretty good shape. You don't need to worry about this game." He was right. The Pirates attacked for four runs in the first inning and never looked back. The final score was 7-3.

"The actual attendance yesterday was 16,242, and the park could not accommodate another person," wrote the Pittsburgh Press. "As it was, hundreds who paid to see the game did not get a glimpse of the field and left early. Not a single free ticket was given out. Theatrical people, politicians, and even newspaper men went through the gate on paid tickets."

"I never saw better ball in my life than the game put up yesterday by the Pittsburghs," remarked Harry the next day. "They are certainly the greatest aggregation of tossers in the world and will win the present series in a walk. The performance of Clarke and Beaumont in the field was a revelation of speed and cleverness, while Phillippe's pitching was simply wonderful. The pleasure I feel over Pittsburg's victory cannot be described." But Harry's prediction did not come to pass. In the end, the series went to Boston, five games to three.

By almost all accounts, Harry Pulliam's first year as President of the National League had been a successful one. Kicking had been reduced, and rowdyism as well. Peace between the two major Leagues had been achieved. A new national agreement was in place, designed to maintain cooperation between all leagues at all levels on a permanent basis. And the first World Series had been a rousing success. When the matter of his re-election came up in December, he had a great deal of support.

"Harry Clay Pulliam will be his own successor as President of the National League. His election is assured. The memory of the misunderstanding of the early summer days has faded away, and all the antagonisms then born have died of inanition." - Cincinnati Enquirer.

Others had a different view:

"'We do not intend that Pulliam,' said a western magnate who had recently visited New York, 'shall have power to place the League in the embarrassing position he did when he told John T. Brush to sign George Davis, a player under ironclad contract to the Chicago American club. Pulliam may be an enterprising young man, but the League cannot afford to place him again in a position where he could, by his rash acts, precipitate a baseball war. As secretary, Pulliam would be bereft of all dangerous power, and might thus be useful to the League.'" -Louisville Courier-Journal.

But the opposition was not nearly strong enough to endanger his position. On December 9, Harry Pulliam was re-elected for a second one-year term. He would continue in office in 1904.

Chapter Ten

Nothing Comes Easy in New York City

I'll never forget one experience I had in a theater fire at Chicago," remarked Harry Pulliam yesterday. "It was during the year of the World's Fair, and I attended a performance of 'The Girl I Left Behind Me' at the Schiller, afterward the Dearborn and now the Garrick. When the alarm was first given the General in the cast stepped to the footlights and announced that there was no danger. The people began to move out in order. There was no panic. When we got to the door we were offered 'rain checks,' or fire checks, if you will, good for a subsequent performance. 'You don't owe me anything,' said I to the doorkeeper. I got my money's worth and was glad to escape." - Cincinnati Enquirer.

Harry Pulliam enjoyed the finer things in life. He attended the theater, ate at the best restaurants, and was often seen about the town, albeit, usually by himself or with friends who were male. A single man with no family of his own, he was never linked romantically with any woman at any time. He guarded his privacy, and there is little, if any, public record detailing his private life. Some historians have concluded that he was probably homosexual, and there is circumstantial evidence to support this contention, but he never stated it or in any way confirmed it publicly. In the early 1900's, virtually no man would have. In most states, including New York, it carried the implication of criminal activity.

As 1904 began, there was reason to be optimistic about the future of organized baseball, and there was reason to be pessimistic as well. The Louisville Courier-Journal covered both ends of the spectrum in the same issue:

"The inducements of baseball now are as good as they ever were and the player who is earnest in his endeavor and a hard worker with the same skill that he has shown in war times can do practically as well as in any time of his career. Many of the baseball men draw salaries which exceed those of most of the presidents of ordinary business firms and scarcely any fall below the income of bank clerks and ordinary salaried men."

"Stormy days in baseball are in sight. Salary cuts are coming, says a Pittsburg writer. Less than ten weeks remain before the League teams start for the South, yet few of the teams have started in to sign their players, which is taken to confirm the opinion shared by the fans that a general wave of economy will sweep over the pay-rolls. The magnates dodge the question, but thinking fans are positive that salaries will be cut and that a salary limit will be established. That will not apply to all players. One or two teams will not slice salaries."

In New York, the Highlanders were once again involved in conflict over territorial rights, this time with the team from Brooklyn. They were considering a plan to move some games, including Sunday games, from Washington Heights to Ridgewood Park in Long Island. When asked his thoughts, Harry declined to comment, although he did note that their territorial rights were confined to Manhattan. But the Superbas reacted differently. They filed a formal protest against the plan, claiming it was an intrusion on their territorial rights. Brooklyn requested immediate action by the National League to deal with the situation.

By mid-January the Ridgewood Park issue had become more than just a nuisance, and was an indication that perhaps real peace wasn't as certain as thought. Harry had filed a formal protest, with the matter to be considered by the National Commission in special session. He pointed out that permission to play games at Ridgewood Park had not been asked of the National League, and certainly had not been granted. He then wired Johnson to arrange a date for the Commission to meet.

In support of the Brooklyn team, Cincinnati Reds President Herrmann suggested that "if the New York Americans can go to Ridgewood, then there is nothing to prevent them from opening up next door to Brooklyn, if they so elect." Ridgewood was, after all, immediately adjacent to the borough of Brooklyn. But Ban Johnson argued the peace agreement had not limited the New York Americans to Manhattan in any way, and any part of the city of New York was within their territory. The peace had become tenuous at best.

Meanwhile, according to the Louisville Courier-Journal, Harry had been summoned to Boston by the owners of the Beaneaters. Having lost $100,000 over the previous two seasons, two of the three primary owners had come to the conclusion they wanted to sell the team. The popularity of the American League team in Boston, having just won the world's championship series, had served as the final straw. The Beaneaters couldn't compete with them. Harry arrived on January 31 to discuss options with the owners, including the option of purchasing the team himself.

But Harry denied the entire story. The Boston team was not for sale after all. "The story was a barefaced fake. I have not been near Boston since last October," he said. "The whole thing is the work of an American League press agent in New York City, and the purpose was to jolly along Frank Farrell." The Boston team denied the story as well.

By this time, notes were beginning to appear in newspapers throughout the circuit about players taking salary cut, including stars like Sam Crawford of Detroit and Elmer Flick of Cleveland. With the war over, at least as far as contracts were concerned, there was no longer competition and bidding to drive salaries up, and it seemed that owners, at least some of them, were trying to work their way back to pre-war salaries that were more profitable for their franchises. Said New York Giants' team secretary Knowles, "We pay a man every dollar he's worth - and no more."

On February 12 the Baseball Commission, now more officially being referred to as the National Baseball Commission, met in Chicago, their main purpose being to resolve the Ridgewood Park conflict. In executive session both sides made their arguments, which still balanced on the wording in the peace agreement of 1903. The meeting adjourned after a long afternoon of debate with no decision announced. Of the three votes to decide the matter, it was assumed that Johnson would vote in favor of the Highlanders, and Pulliam in favor of the Superbas. Therefore, the third vote, belonging to Herrmann, would be the deciding one.

Two days later there was still no decision. "No other meeting is necessary, and I will not call one," replied Herrmann when pushed. "In a few days I will hand down my decision in the matter. I do not want to prejudge the case. All the evidence is in and I want a little time to prepare my finding."

According to the New York Times, the Highlanders had grown weary of waiting on Herrmann, and had turned their attention elsewhere:

"It was said in Long Island City yesterday that the project of the New York American League baseball team playing Sunday ball at Ridgewood Park had been abandoned and that representatives of the American League had practically closed negotiations for a lease of a plot 460 feet by 800 feet on Borden Avenue, near the old Puritan Athletic Club House, and that the grounds would be converted into a ball park and athletic field and would be used by the New York Americans for Sunday games.

"The property in question belongs to the Roswell P. Flower estate. It is made land, the bottom filling being ashes. It is perfectly level, and beyond building the fence and stands and the work of laying out the diamond will require no alteration. It is within three minutes' walk of the Thirty-Fourth Street Ferry. It is also within a minute's walk of the bridge from Greenpoint to Long Island City."

On March 3 in New York, the National Baseball Commission finally ruled on case. Charles Ebbets of the Brooklyn team had threatened to take the dispute to court were it not resolved in his favor, but such action was not necessary, as Herrmann cast his lot with the Brooklyn team, resulting in a 2-1 vote against the Americans. They lost the foul-strike decision as well, but at least schedules amenable to both sides had been created, with the season ready to start in little more than a month.

Johnson, though, soon flared up again, accusing Dreyfuss, head of the National League scheduling committee, and Harry, of changing several dates after they had been agreed upon by both Leagues. Harry could no longer hold in his frustration. He had had enough.

"We have met with Mr. Johnson, in the spirit of fairness, and we are sick and tired of his unprovoked outbursts," he said. "He talks like a boy, rather than a grown-up. We have come to feel that we have been dealing with an irresponsible party, for no sooner are agreements made than he begins to cry aloud. He does more than any man in either League to cry down the game and hurt it."

Then Harry chose to go one step further.

"Now, finally, let me say, and say positively, that if Ban Johnson in his utterances represents the sentiment of the American League, the sooner we know it the better. War costs money, but war is infinitely preferable to this sort of peace. The sooner he breaks away the better."

But the Philadelphia Inquirer, in a city with a team in both Leagues, put the blame squarely on Harry. "Old Tecumseh once said that 'war is hell.' But of what of that to Harry, who would seek glory at the cannon's mouth? His voice is for war; he is hunting after gore, and, like the Jibbenainosay, he wants bucketsful of it, and the 'sooner the better.' But, distressing thought, can this be the rashness inseparable from youth?"

Harry doubled down. "I stand exactly by the proposition of yesterday. The sooner Ban Johnson begins his much-heralded war and stops talking the better for everyone concerned."

In Louisville, the Courier-Journal was incredulous over the whole affair. "Whenever the National League and the American League sit down another year to make out a schedule it wouldn't be a bad idea, after the dates have been properly put together, to have two copies signed, place them in a strong box and then hire a guard, never to leave the treasure until the announcement of the games has been made in safety to the public."

Harry took a break from it all in Pittsburgh, where he had been invited to attend a dinner, and was asked to speak. Bypassing the subject of baseball altogether, he chose to have a little fun with the locals. "Since arriving at Pittsburg I have discovered that you can teach us of the Blue Grass how to drink whisky. There we take it straight. Here you make high-balls by pouring water into the liquor. This is sacrilege in the eyes of all true sons of the South." He was a hit.

From there he went to New Bedford, Massachusetts, to watch the opening game of the New England League with his friend Fred Doe, who was associated with the New Bedford team. Rain was in the forecast, and Harry knew it before he went, but he didn't want to let his friend down. When the game was canceled, New Bedford Mayor Charley Ashley, perhaps star struck with a celebrity in town, intercepted Harry and took him on a day long tour of the town.

"Before he left the city, Harry Pulliam got an idea of the pride the mayor took in his charge. The latter escorted the baseball magnate all over the city, and if there was a nook or cranny connected with the city that was not investigated, Harry does not know where it is. It was walk and walk and walk, upstairs and down, downstairs and up, for almost an entire day, and if there was a man who left a town almost tired to death, it was Pulliam." - Pittsburgh Press.

Next, he began a tour of the National League circuit, showing up in the Queen City, home of the Reds. He watched a game with Herrmann in his private box and attended a luncheon for local reporters the following afternoon. One of them mentioned in the Enquirer that Harry appeared to be in good health and good spirits. From Cincinnati, he was planning to go to St. Louis, then Chicago, and on to the Eastern cities.

Before leaving town, he handed down a three-game suspension to Reds Manager Joe Kelley, guilty of kicking in protest of a call at first base in a game his team was leading 11-1. Kelley had been escorted out of games by umpires more often than anyone else in the League, and Harry was growing tired of it. He was still having to frequently hand out fines and suspensions, but less often than in 1903. All in all, things were going well in the National League, and for Harry Pulliam as well. The biggest problem so far? Too much rain on the weekends.

In St. Louis, Harry was asked to name his National League all-star team. He chose Johnny Kling as his catcher, Fred Tenney at first base, Lajoie at second, Wagner at short and Jimmy Collins at third for his infield. The outfielders selected were Clarke, Willie Keeler and Clarence Beaumont. Rounding out the team were two pitchers, Cy Young, and Iron Man Joe McGinnity of the League leading New York Giants.

After explaining his other choices, he spoke of Young. "Cy Young ought not be insulted with any comment on his ability. He is beyond all question the greatest that ever wore a toe plate."

In June, Harry introduced to baseball the whisk broom, which is still used by umpires today. "President Harry Pulliam, of the National League, is a man of ideas. He is as careful of the little things in baseball as the big, and his interest in the welfare of the players as great as that in the magnates. This explains why the umpires of late have been armed with whisk brooms to dust off the home plate when occasion requires.

"Time was when the old-fashioned house broom was generally in use for that purpose, but a couple of weeks ago (Jack) McCarthy, of the Chicagos, stepped on the time-honored article in use at St. Louis in running to the plate, and has been on the hospital list since, with a badly turned ankle. In order to obviate the recurrence of such accidents, Mr. Pulliam has banished the broom from the ball field and supplied each of his umpires with the smaller but equally useful article, which is carried in the pistol pocket." - Pittsburgh Press.

By July, John McGraw and John T. Brush had both publicly stated that the League-leading Giants would not participate in the World Series if they finished in first place. A deep animosity between McGraw and Ban Johnson still existed from the year and a half McGraw played for Baltimore in the American League. Their personalities clashed, and they truly hated each other. "I know the American League and its methods," spouted the confrontational manager. "I ought to, for I paid for my knowledge ... they still have my money."

Brush simultaneously insulted the American League, saying his team would not play any "minor league team" for the championship. Johnson responded, "I have suggested to Mr. Pulliam that the arrangements for a world's series be made at once, and that conditions and games be under the control of the National Commission. A motion to play the games at the end of the season was formally made and passed at a joint meeting of the two Leagues last spring, and I do not see how the National can go back on the proposition. As to what Brush says, I have nothing to say at present. I will let the baseball fans throughout the country be the jury. I think they will agree with me that Brush hasn't got the nerve to send his team against the American League pennant winners, whichever club gets the flag." Harry was powerless to do anything about it, though, as the new national agreement contained no mention of any championship series. It was left to the discretion of the owners.

"The series for the world's championship last fall awakened interest from the Atlantic to the Pacific, and was productive of more good in its advancement of the national game than anything that has happened in years," surmised the Philadelphia Inquirer. "In their blundering work they weigh lightly the fairness and intelligence of the patrons of our great national sort."

In August, Harry again suspended Reds Manager Joe Kelley, this time indefinitely. He had been tossed from a game for the fifth time, most in the League. "Not until I have been given guarantee by some responsible person that he will obey the rules of the National League will Joe Kelley be permitted to play another game of ball," he said. Then, after pausing a second, he added, "And if Cincinnati doesn't like my indefinite suspension of Joe Kelley she can lump it. It goes." Shortly after, Harry left for his annual week-long vacation in Saratoga. Accused of leaving town to avoid a meeting with the temperamental manager, Harry defended himself, stating, "I came to New York on Monday, and after an investigation settled the matter, I passed Mr. Kelley within three feet at the Polo Grounds, and he made no overtures; neither did he call at my office Tuesday. Having by this time my matters in hand, I came here to finish my vacation."

He also fined catcher Goldfish Dooin of the Reds, who remarked, "I've just contributed my salary for three days to buy fancy vests and a peacock blue band for Harry Pulliam's hat."

But Kelley and Dooin weren't the only protesters. Grumbling was being heard from other players as well. Many were complaining that the umpires had become power hungry, booting players from games for minor infractions, and sometimes even baiting players to kick. Sometimes the complaints were valid, yet Harry stood firm in supporting his umpires in all matters. And above all, he remained publicly optimistic.

"President Harry C. Pulliam, of the National League, is a man who always tries to look on the bright side of things. On the wall just above his desk in his New York offices he has hung three mottoes, all of which are worthy of note. One says: 'Good manners wear better than good clothes.' The second one bears this legend: 'A smile beats a sneer every day in the week.' The third is also good: 'There is some good in everyone, even a Malay pirate.'" -Pittsburgh Press.

Harry's personal life, on the other hand, was not going well at all, and he was struggling to keep it together. In the spring, he and his good friend James Hart, the president of the Chicago club, had made plans to travel together to Europe in the fall. But the two had a falling out of some sort, and Hart decided not to go. He claimed the disagreement was anger over Harry's assignment of umpires for Cubs' games, but that seemed a trivial matter for such a drastic step. Harry was heartbroken.

The Pittsburgh Press decried that, "It has now come to pass that he has been deserted by a man who for years was Pulliam's best and most influential friend – Jim Hart of Chicago."

Three days later the report in the Press was much more ominous:

"The news dispatches of the past week continued the intelligence that Harry C. Pulliam, president of the National League, is on the verge of a nervous break-down. The reasons assigned was the strenuous work that has attended his occupancy of the presidency. I incline to believe that this is not the real reason."

Chapter Eleven

A Little Closet Under the Grandstand

By any standard, 1904 had been a banner year for baseball. Attendance for the season in the two major leagues had reached nearly four million, with the National League outdrawing the American only slightly. There was peace, or something very close to it, when the season ended, the friction between Ban Johnson and the Giants notwithstanding. Kicking and rowdyism had continued to decline. Harry Pulliam hoped to build on that success in 1905.

At the League meeting in December, the National Commission had taken over the World Series, mandating that both League winners participate. Harry wasn't yet ready to give up on the 1904 World Series. "I am heartily in favor of spring championship games between New York and Boston," he exclaimed. "Now that the National Commission is to have absolute charge of the games there is no reason why they should not be played. If they wait until fall, Cincinnati, Pittsburg or some other National League club may be champions, and Boston also might be out of it."

As 1905 began, it was Harry's physical health, more than his mental health, that needed tending. "The illness of President Harry Pulliam, which reached the state to-day that medical attention was necessary, may develop into baseball history," reported the Philadelphia Inquirer. "Pulliam is to-night quite sick and confined to his room and bed and the physician attending him, while expressing no decided opinion, intimates that his patient is by no means in condition to meet the strenuous work of the active discharge of his duties, and probably will not to-morrow. Pulliam's symptoms are those of grip (influenza) and also not different in important details from typhoid fever." Various other newspapers described his illness as nervous prostration, pneumonia and a severe cold.

He was staying at the St. Nicholas hotel in Cincinnati when he fell ill, in town for a meeting of the magnates. His good friend, Barney Dreyfuss, cared for him the entire week, not leaving Harry's room for any length of time.

The meeting went on without him, with Garry Herrmann holding Pulliam's proxy vote. It was arranged that if an executive session should become necessary, it would be held in Harry's room, with all members present. The event was, in comparison with the year before, quite tame and peaceful. It was a calm start to the year. The biggest news was that a 154-game schedule would be played in both Leagues in 1905, an increase of fourteen games. Johnson and Pulliam were named as independent commissions to create their own League schedules. The season was to begin on April 14 and end on October 5. Harry's wish to have a spring championship series was not acted on, possible owing to his illness. Thus, it did not happen.

Several days later Harry had recovered and returned to work. Having greatly reduced the occurrences of kicking and rowdyism in baseball, he now set his sights on a new goal; the elimination of betting at the ball parks during games. This was another step in his efforts to "elevate the sport," by wiping out every element that tended to make ladies hesitant to attend. In Pittsburgh, Barney Dreyfuss issued an order that all betting cease at Pirate games, even though betting was already outlawed throughout the National League. But the fans in Pittsburgh didn't take the ban very seriously, or in any of the other cities as well.

"In the private boxes the millionaires wrote checks for hundreds which they risked on a single swat; in the grandstand, though, Bill Schneier and Shad Gwilliam and that bunch used to clean up enough in one inning – maybe – to buy drinks for everybody in town. Out in the bleachers they bet everything from a dollar to a bottle of pop, and if the loser of the bet was dissatisfied, the man on the field who executed the play got the pop bottle. It is even said that the players made quiet little bets among themselves, but this is denied by Jack Taylor, as well as other."

Harry had just started focusing on the elimination of gambling when the kicking returned in a big way, and rowdyism as well. "I am trying to enforce the laws of the League and to have clean baseball. But we are having a lot of trouble in the League at present. The laws are there for me to enforce, however, and I am going to do it."

On April 22, first baseman Dan McGann of the Giants physically attacked catcher Fred Abbott of the Phillies. McGann was one of the worst offenders of Harry's conduct policy in the League. Harry suspended him for ten days and fined him one hundred dollars for his role in the confrontation with Abbott. Abbott, who was apparently something less than an innocent bystander, was suspended seven days and fined fifty dollars.

"The Giants as a team need disciplining," read an editorial in the Pittsburgh Press. "They are starting off to make trouble wherever they strike a team that is capable of putting up a close contest against them, and unless President Pulliam makes it plain to them from the very start that the rules which govern other teams apply to them as well, he will have a lot of worry from them."

How right they were! On the very same day that Harry announced the suspension of the two players, the Giants and Phillies played again in Philadelphia. 17,000 were in attendance. In the ninth inning the Giants came from behind to win. This didn't go over well with the Philadelphia crowd, which was already mad about the suspension of Abbott. Having seen the attack for themselves, they firmly believed McGann to be fully responsible, and their man innocent.

Sensing trouble, scores of police officers, many in plain clothes, had been sent by the city to maintain order, far beyond normal security for a ball game.

After the game, as the Giants were exiting Huntington Park, a large mob attacked them. "The mob went to the grounds all primed for trouble, carrying eggs, vegetables, and bricks. The New Yorkers had to fight their way into their coach with the assistance of police. Thousands followed, pelting the players with eggs and stones."

On Broad Street, Roger Bresnahan was hit in the face with a dirt clod thrown by a boy. Exiting his carriage, he chased the boy down and hit him. A furious crowd quickly surrounded Bresnahan. He was rescued by police before any serious harm was done. But the crowd grew larger, and soon passage at Dauphine and Fifteenth Street became blocked. Some tried to pry the player away from the officers, who were forced to draw their guns. Bresnahan was taken into a grocery store for protection while he awaited a patrol car to take him to the police station. In response, vegetables on display in the front of the store were thrown, and the store looted. When the patrol arrived, and took Bresnahan into custody, hundreds followed, bombarding it with potatoes, eggs, and anything else the crazed mob could find.

In May, Fred Clarke, a pretty good kicker himself, joined many others in making a public plea for Harry to do something about McGraw and his Giants. "I cannot understand why McGraw is allowed to act as he does," he ragged. "He has no right to be exempt from punishment when he violates a rule. If ever McGraw repeats the words he said to me on Saturday, he and I will fight, as sure as I am living, and I will land hard on him if I start. Had he not been removed from the grounds just when he was Saturday, I am sure he and I would have come to blows. The way he talked to quiet Mike Lynch was simply scandalous. He called him all the vile names in the category, and a few that I had never heard before."

The next day, Clarke contacted Harry to file a formal protest against McGraw. When Pulliam responded that he would refer the matter to the Board of Directors, many accused him of not doing his job, and giving preferred treatment to McGraw. Dreyfuss also filed a protest against McGraw, for using offensive language against him as he sat in the grandstand during two games in the Polo Grounds. "He accused me of being crooked, of controlling the umpires, and made other false and malicious statements."

McGraw shot back, accusing Harry of showing favoritism toward his old club, the Pirates. "The fact that Dreyfuss used his influence to have Pulliam made the president of the League should not blind the young man to his duties to the other seven clubs that pay his salary." Harry did as he had promised, referring charges against McGraw to the Board, and calling for the members to meet in Boston on June 1 to consider the matter.

Dreyfuss spoke further on May 24.

"The time has come when the leader of the Giants must be put on the rack for his conduct. He has been defiant of the rules entirely too long. It's amazing the way McGraw runs matters at the Polo Grounds. Umpires seem to be afraid of him. He browbeats them as in the old Baltimore days and gets away with the tactics."

Then, he brought up a new charge.

"There must be a ruling on the habit of McGraw when ordered off the field of going into a little closet under the grandstand. It leads to a passageway to the clubhouse. McGraw has holes cut in the partition and can coach his team from that conning tower. Why, he might as well go up into the stand and coach his men. He is clearly violating the rules and knows it. He is not off the field."

McGraw was suspended fifteen days and fined $150 for his tirade against Dreyfuss. The accusation that Dreyfuss was crooked, a much more serious charge, would be handled on June 1 in Boston.

Brush defended his manager. "I am completely nonplussed by the severe sentence imposed on our manager. I do not know just now what we will do in the matter. So far as I have been able to learn McGraw's offense consisted of saying, after a bad decision by Umpire Johnstone, that he would as soon have Barney Dreyfuss umpire the game as Johnstone. This was not addressed particularly to Dreyfuss, who occupied a seat in the upper tier. It seems to me my club has been dealt with harshly, and I will hold that opinion until Pulliam shows me evidence that McGraw has committed a serious offense."

McGraw simply said, "At present I only want to say I think I got a raw deal."

Soon, the dispute became a national sensation. Even the newspapers were taking aim at each other. A reporter for the Philadelphia Inquirer wrote, "The disciplining of Manager McGraw, of the New York Nationals, was discounted by the New York papers, nearly all of whom are 'right' so far as the Giants are concerned. They pretend to see in it a conspiracy to kill baseball in New York, and threaten all sorts of reprisals."

Upon arriving in Boston for the meeting, Pulliam made a forceful statement.

"I have been the butt of joke and ridicule because I considered the charges filed by President Dreyfuss of Pittsburg, against Manager McGraw of New York, of sufficient importance to refer to the Board of Directors. If the manager of a team that has won the pennant one year can publicly proclaim on a National League ground that the president of another club that has won a pennant three-years is crooked and controls the League umpires, I want the Board of Directors to stand up like men and say so. If, after they meet here in Boston, they say my action was a joke, I am willing to admit that my sense of humor is dull, and that the laugh is on me.

"I believe the profession of baseball an honorable one, and that a man can be a success and still be a gentleman. If any club president thinks that it is necessary to the success of the game to allow a player to brazenly insult another player, he is entitled to his opinion; but I, for one, will not agree with him for a minute. If I cannot stop such brutal indecency on the ball field I will retire from the presidency of the National League at the conclusion of my elected term. It will not be necessary for anyone to start a propaganda aimed at my defeat for re-election."

Once again, Harry had threatened to resign if he did not get his way.

McGraw was exonerated of the charges made by Dreyfuss by the Board of Directors, based on a lack of evidence, but not content with that, he filed suit in court to have the fine and suspension lifted, which Harry had emphatically declined to do. A hearing on the injunction was scheduled for Monday, June 5, in Boston.

Now on a roll, through the newspapers of New York City, McGraw accused Dreyfuss and Pulliam of conspiring to rob the New York Giants of the pennant by depriving them of the services of their manager. This charge infuriated Harry. "Anybody that says there is collusion between Dreyfuss and me is a rank liar. Everything that I have done in baseball, beginning as president of the Louisville club, then with Pittsburgh, has been on the level. My letters and books are open to the public."

The day before the hearing, Harry maintained that he wasn't losing sleep over the matter, but still hired two attorneys to represent himself and the League. He knew that his power to maintain peace on the playing field was at stake, and he wasn't willing to let it go without a fight. "If he is bigger than I," he said, "then I want to know it quickly, so that I can act accordingly."

At the hearing on June 5, Justice Sheldon of the Supreme Court issued a temporary injunction against Harry, restraining him from imposing both the fine and the suspension, pending a hearing to take place at a later date. According to the judge, McGraw had been denied the opportunity to appear before Pulliam in his own defense prior to the imposition of the penalty. He had not been given the chance to refute evidence and defend himself.

McGraw boasted about his victory in court. "President Pulliam cannot compel me to stay away from the Pittsburg baseball grounds this afternoon. I will do as I see fit. He is not governing my actions." It was reported in the Pittsburgh Press that a dozen or so private detectives had been hired to escort the New York players to and from the ball park in Pittsburgh, to ensure their safety.

On June 13, Judge Sheldon in Boston ruled that under the terms of the peace agreement between the American and National Leagues, the Brush resolution was still in effect, and the only punishment allowed was a maximum of ten dollars per offense. Any larger fine would require a hearing and proof of guilt. McGraw had won again.

Harry issued a statement in response. "I regret very much the outcome of the so-called McGraw litigation, not so much that it affects me personally, but on account of the encouragement it will give to so-called rowdy ball in professional baseball." Always intent on following the letter of the law, he resolved to return fines in excess of ten dollars that were previously imposed on several players. This included, but was not limited to, ninety dollars for Dan McGann, twenty dollars to Hans Wagner and twenty dollars to Joe Kelley.

After the verdict was announced, Harry was castigated in the papers.

"It might be just as well for Harry Pulliam to cast about for another job. They are after his official toupee, and incidentally they are animated by a Christian-like desire to throw the harpoon into Barney Dreyfuss. The keynote has been sounded by the New York papers – 'the one-man power has been tried and found wanting.'" -Philadelphia Inquirer.

Later, Harry admitted that he did not vote in favor of Dreyfuss in the McGraw hearing, causing a major rift between the two men, and ending their ten-year friendship. "We were willing enough to punish McGraw," he said, "but the evidence submitted by Mr. Dreyfuss did not warrant it, and so there was nothing for us to do but to dismiss the charges."

Harry Pulliam, it seemed, had been too honest and too fair for his own good. Dreyfuss vowed never to speak to him again. In July, he threatened to leave the National League, implying he would receive better treatment in the American League. Harry told him to go ahead and leave. It was the wrong thing to say.

"It seems to be the general opinion among the magnates of the National League that President Harry Pulliam is losing his head. It is a strange proceeding for an employee to tell one of his employers to quit the business," responded the Chicago Journal. "Pulliam has become very unpopular since his administration began abusing the National League club owners, the men who pay his salary. They are beginning to grow tired of it."

In August, a sportswriter in Pittsburgh asked John McGraw if he believed Pulliam would return as League president in 1906. "Bet a nice suit of clothes that Pulliam will not be re-elected President of the National League. I know what I am talking about and I will willingly pay for the suit if I lose. The League has had enough of Mr. Pulliam."

Having learned a lesson from the McGraw fiasco, Harry ordered better record keeping, with a file for every reported incident and all related paperwork to be maintained and updated. This was to be handled by his secretary, John Heydler. Additionally, he ordered that players, just like umpires had always done, were required to submit their version of the proceedings when thrown out of a game.

Soon enough, another incident involving McGraw and his Giants took place in, of all places, Exposition Park in Pittsburgh. In the ninth inning with the game tied, a Pittsburgh baserunner was called safe at third base on a close call. Several Giants kicked, including McGraw, and he refused to have his team take the field to continue the game. Umpire George Bausewine, after waiting for several minutes, declared the game a forfeit, a 9-0 win for the Pirates. 18,383 witnessed the incomplete game.

According to the League constitution, when a team forfeited a game, it was to be assessed a fine of $1,000. Also, a manager who refused to continue play was to be fined $100. The penalties and fines were required to be paid within ten days. If not paid in a timely manner, the team would become ineligible to participate in a championship game.

"I am impatient to see what the League will do with the champions," quipped Fred Clarke. "If we had disgraced ourselves at the Polo Grounds before a record-breaking crowd as the Giants did here yesterday, we would have been mobbed."

Harry ruled that the forfeiture of the game on August 5 would stand, but McGraw would not be fined. Some observers felt the case should have gone before the Board of Directors, making it likely that Brush would appeal. Others criticized Harry for imposing no fine. Less than a week later, Brush did indeed appeal the decision.

As the World Series approached, likely to be a showdown between the Giants and Connie Mack's Philadelphia Athletics, players from both Leagues began expressing dissatisfaction with the plan for distributing the gate receipts from World Series games. The National Commission was to receive ten percent, the club owners would equally divide sixty percent, and the 38 players would share the remaining forty percent. However, the players were to only share in the first four games. They were to receive nothing if games five through seven proved necessary. It was estimated that each player would receive approximately $475.

The rules of play for the World Series stipulated that each League president select one umpire to work the entire Series. Pulliam selected veteran Hank O'Day, long considered to be perhaps the best umpire in all of baseball. Johnson chose Jack Sheridan. Harry was charged with handling the financial details of the Series.

Barney Dreyfuss chose to skip the World Series, choosing instead to visit his sister in Louisville. Meeting with the newspaper men, he said he was tired of baseball and glad to have a break from it. He predicted that Harry would be re-elected as president of the National League, and furthermore, that it would be unanimous. This surprised the reporters, having heard much of the fallout between Dreyfuss and Pulliam. "I have not seen Harry since June 14," he said, "but I have no hard feelings against him. I know that he is capable and I want him to be retained in office. The only trouble with him is that he takes everything so seriously."

In November, Harry sent a letter of welcome to the new owner of the Cubs, Charles W. Murphy, who had recently purchased the club from James Hart. He also wrote to Hart. "The position the Chicago club occupies today is certainly a monument to your ability and enterprise and full adherence to all that has been best in baseball."

The day before the League meeting was to begin, a story broke in the Cincinnati Enquirer, exposing a plan by Brush to replace Harry as president of the National League with former player turned attorney John Montgomery Ward. It was alleged that Brush had the support of Dreyfuss, and Soden of Boston as well. At Harry's request, arrangements were made for Jim Hart, who was still one of the Directors of the League, to attend. New owner Murphy had asked him to participate as well.

"Morning reports from New York differed greatly from each other," observed the Pittsburgh Press. "One paper had it that a conspiracy had been formed to oust President Pulliam, and said that he 'wore a drawn, worried look all day,' while another paper said, 'All is lovely, and there is no look of worry on President Pulliam's face.'"

When the League meeting officially began, the pennant was presented to the New York Giants, who had gone on to win the World Series over the Philadelphia Athletics of the American League. Christy Mathewson had pitched three shutouts. Following, Harry presented the end of year financial statement, confirming what all had expected: 1905 had been the most profitable year in League history.

Next, the magnates turned to the issue of electing a president. Barney Dreyfuss entered Harry's name in nomination. Then Brush intervened with the surprise nomination of James Hart, who in turn refused to be a candidate. Still, Hart received the votes of Brush and Herrmann, but the other six chose Pulliam, and since the votes for Hart were technically illegal, Harry was again chosen unanimously.

In a further show of support that much ingratiated Harry, he was given full power to determine the amount of fines and length of suspensions of players in all matters of discipline. The ten-dollar limit was no longer in effect.

Later, Hart said of declining the nomination, "There is almost no job I would less like to hold than that occupied by Pulliam. It certainly is thankless, and one's path constantly is beset with troubles."

Chapter Twelve

I Had an Audience with the Pope

Harry's flair for fashion always made an impression on the people he met.

"Among those present was the Hon, H. Pulliam, the human haberdashery. Without saying a word Harry can make himself heard above the hum and turmoil of traffic which grows pretty loud in the city. It's the clothes. On this occasion, however, Mr. Pulliam has calmed himself down to a subdued autumnal tone. His garments did not shriek as of yore. The polite and talented president wore tan shoes and black velvet spats, or overgaiters. If not walking on velvet Harry comes quite close to it. He had a plain gray suit and a pickled beet in his buttonhole, cheese colored vest, and a New York Central shirt, with four parallel tracks on the bosom. The little college yell hat of last summer has given way to the sedate derby, and Harry wore no cane of any kind." - Chicago Tribune.

The off season leading to the summer of 1906 was a relatively uneventful one, and had a calming effect on Harry's nerves. The baseball wars were over. Harry and Ban Johnson, albeit through great tribulation, had found a way to work together in the best interests of the game. Johnson had learned that he could trust Harry, that he was a man of his word, and a tireless worker. Harry had learned to accept Johnson for what he was: a demanding but dynamic leader who could be combative one minute, and respectful the next.

On January 1, Harry visited the home of Nick Young in Washington, where he found the former League president to be in excellent health, working in his garden. Then he returned to New York, back to work, where the offices of the National League and the offices of the New York Giants were now in the same building. The biggest issue on his plate was his continued defense of the foul strike rule, which pitchers continued to love, and hitters continued to hate. There was, however, agreement that it did speed up the game, so the rule remained in place. Even Ban Johnson had tempered his opposition to it.

Hank O'Day, the senior umpire in the National League, dutifully signed and returned his contract, expressing his eagerness to start another season. Harry's new power to levy fines and suspensions with no limits would, it was hoped, make the job of the umpires safer and easier.

"No president of the National League has ever received the power to discipline rowdies on the ball field that has been delegated to Harry Pulliam," suggested the New York Sun. "Next year (1906) he will be a czar, and it is generally hoped that there will not be a revolution among his subjects, the magnates and players."

Player salaries were rising and talk of a strike was rarely heard anymore. "Nowadays the ball player, if he is at the top of his class," wrote one reporter, "is paid better than college presidents, newspaper editors and other men of intellectual pursuits."

In Chicago, expectations for the young Cubs were running high. They already had an outstanding infield, consisting of Frank Chance, Johnny Evers, Joe Tinker and Harry Steinfeldt, and a bevy of talented but inexperienced pitchers looked promising. On the south side, White Sox outfielder Ducky Holmes asked for and was given his release. The formal Louisville Colonel had been hired to manage the Lincoln, Nebraska team in the Western League.

Harry was in Philadelphia for the first game of the National League season on April 12, where the Phillies hosted the champion New York Giants. Hank O'Day served as umpire. After Philadelphia Mayor Weaver threw out the ceremonial first pitch, he turned to the grand stand and announced the names of the starting pitchers; Ames for the Giants, Lush for the Phillies. Those who had expected to see Christy Mathewson pitch were disappointed. Matty was down with a nasal condition. On a warm spring day, in a well-played contest, the Giants prevailed, 3-2. The following week, Harry himself threw out the first pitch at the home opener in Pittsburgh.

On his first trip to Chicago, Harry too was impressed with the Cubs. "I saw the Chicagos early in the season, and I have no hesitancy in saying that there is not a more evenly balanced team in the National League. They seem to be proficient in all departments of play, their base running, team hitting and fielding being of the highest order. Their pitchers are as good as any in the League, and their catching department could hardly be improved upon."

In June, nineteen-year-old Grace Grant, a Chicago native, submitted an application for the position of umpire in the National League. She was five feet six inches tall, and according to the Pittsburgh Press, weighed 150 pounds when wearing umpire gear. Her experience as an umpire was limited to a handful of amateur games. Harry did not hire her.

June 12 was a day of celebration in New York City for the champion Giants, where in the morning a parade marched, beginning on Union Square East, down Broadway to City Hall and then to the Battery. A team of police led the way, followed by a succession of amateur teams, all in uniform, and a car carrying Harry Pulliam, Garry Herrmann and Secretary John Bruce of the National Committee. Last came the players, the Giants, who were cheered lustily at every opportunity, and then the Reds.

"Business was practically suspended on lower Broadway while the parade went by. Every huge office building had its windows crowded with clerks and stenographers, who abandoned their duties to get a glimpse of the champions." - Cincinnati Enquirer.

At the Battery the parade disbanded, and the players from both teams were escorted to the Polo Grounds, where fireworks were exploded, and a big mortar discharged, opening to reveal a very large paper balloon with an oversized American flag hanging from it. The assembled watched in amazement as the balloon carried the flag over the viaduct at One Hundred and Fifty-fifth street and drifted out of sight. Then followed a speech by Herrmann, and finally, the raising of the silk championship pennant.

The next day, after a game with the high-flying Cubs, John McGraw was busy denying accusations that he had ordered the groundskeeper to mix a "soapy substance" in with the dirt around the pitchers' slab and home plate to handicap the visiting team. But the Cubs were insistent that it was a fact, so owner Murphy alerted Harry Pulliam, and announced that next time his team played at the Polo Grounds he would bring a chemist along to examine the dirt. If any foreign substances were found, he said, the Cubs "will carry their own dirt with them in valises."

Harry had a different use for soap in mind. He issued an order to his umpires that any player who started a game with a dirty uniform was to be fined five dollars. Aside from dirty uniforms, though, for the most part, everything was going well for Harry Pulliam and the National League in July of 1906. Attendance was strong, thanks to Harry's expanded powers kicking was down, and best of all, at least to fans outside of New York, the Giants were not in first place. On July 21, Harry arrived in Chicago on his latest tour of the circuit looking happy and care free. Then everything seemed to fall apart.

Harry fined players Heinie Peitz of Pittsburgh and Joe McGinnity of New York for an altercation during a game on July 24 in Pittsburgh. More importantly, he also fined Hank O'Day fifty dollars for failing to prevent the altercation.

O'Day, though, refused to pay the fine, claiming there was no way the fight could have been prevented by him, or anyone else. On July 31, he refused to officiate his assigned game at the Polo Grounds, leaving Harry no choice but to suspend him. The rule in question, rule 58, stated that base coaches were only allowed to talk with base runners, not opposing players. Pulliam had fined O'Day because he had allowed Peitz, the third base coach, to speak to Giants pitcher McGinnity, which led to the fight. O'Day defended himself, saying he had done the best he could, but that the rule was virtually impossible to enforce.

When Harry suspended him, O'Day threatened to leave the National League in favor of the Tri-State League. Harry had gone too far, and now was in danger of losing his best umpire. O'Day paid a visit to Pulliam's office, where an angry confrontation ensued.

"I'll quit my job before I'll pay the fine," threatened the umpire.

"You'll quit your job if you don't pay it," Pulliam shot back.

Meanwhile, McGinnity planned to appeal his fine.

"I lose about $500," he quipped. "for being a man."

Suddenly, things weren't quite so rosy in the National League.

The newspaper men jumped to O'Day's defense.

"There seems to be a general opinion that Pulliam has made a vital blunder in antagonizing the best umpire he has on his staff, exaggerating it far too much by the punishment he has inflicted and the manner in which he has inflicted it." - New York Telegram.

"O'Day has been a good umpire, and regarding the Pittsburgh matter stated that everything happened so quickly that he did not have time to stop it. That very likely is true, for Hank is aggressive enough, and with half a chance would have stepped in between the players and cut off any rough house that had been started." - Boston Globe.

"Every player in the land will grieve over the loss of Hank O'Day. Well they might. Every club in the National League is glad to meet O'Day on the road. It means a square deal. Something should be done to stop the wild rampage of Pulliam." - New York World.

Then the attack turned personal, and from the Pittsburgh Press, a long-time supporter of Harry.

"Before leaving our city after hoodooing the Spuds so the terrible Phillies could beat them, President Pulliam completed arrangements for extensive Parisian importations. He does not care to purchase his gowns on this edge of the water. Mr. Potter, the owner of the Phillies, has sailed for the other side as the authorized agent of Mr. Pulliam, whose cable address is Glad Rags, Polo Grounds. While abroad Mr. Potter has carte blanc d' tear the lid off in his search for chic creations. His foreign cable address is Jimpot, Paris.

"Former President Potter's last evening in town was spent on the Bellvue Stratford roof garden listening to Mr. Pulliam's clothes, which spiked the big horn in the orchestra. Harry made up a partial list of what he wants from abroad and will cable for the things he forgot. Here is the list:

Two peter pan shirt waists – one of baby blue and the other green, with seashore sleeves.

One highball gown for roof gardening in New York, Philadelphia, and Louisville, Ky.

Three new form straight fronts, trimmed in real Irish fillet de sole.

Box of hat pins.

Twenty-five yards of chiffon.

One wrist band of owlskin, like Harry Lehr wears at Newport.

Two princess frocks of fancy voile, trimmed with poplinette and Swiss cheese insertion.

Two dozen white buckskin pumps and fawn colored gloves, elbow length.

One diamond studded breast medallion in which to wear Hank O'Day's picture.

"On the 15th of September, Mr. Potter will return from Paris bringing the foregoing creations and perhaps a few more. Meanwhile, Harry intends to struggle along in the cheap and inartistic togs the real garby chap must put up with in New York. He long ago exhausted the limit in that abode of wealth and fashion and was compelled to send an agent to Paris. When the new things come over we would like to see Bill Shettsline, Jim Hart, or any of those near-dudes wedge Harry out of his job as one best bet in the National League.

"If Mr. Potter's trip to Paris isn't a scheme to keep Mr. Pulliam in the chair then we don't know anything about the inside affairs of the League."

O'Day visited National League headquarters in New York on August 6. Harry was gone on his annual trip to Saratoga, so the umpire left a proposal with secretary Heydler. He was willing to return to work under protest, delaying a resolution of the matter until the next meeting of the Board of Directors.

Harry agreed to the plan, allowing the umpire to return to work. O'Day paid the fine, pending a hearing at some future date. His first game back was on August 10 in Brooklyn, where the crowd cheered and hollered his name. Out of character, he tipped his hat, bowed, and smiled back at them.

While Harry was still on vacation, things heated up again in New York. On August 7, the Cubs were in New York to play the Giants. On orders from McGraw, the gatekeeper refused to allow Umpire Johnstone into the ball park. The Cubs refused to play without an umpire, so Johnstone forfeited the game in favor of Chicago. Harry was forced to cut his vacation short and return to New York to handle the matter. He ruled that the Giants had violated the League constitution, upholding the forfeiture.

Brush bit back, insisting that a police officer, not the gatekeeper, had denied Johnstone entrance, due to safety concerns caused by his horrible calls from the game the day before. The crowd might have killed him, Brush suggested. When questioned, the police officer claimed to have done nothing of the kind.

McGraw, for his part, insisted that since Johnstone was never actually in the ball park, there was no way he could declare a forfeit. Brush called Harry incompetent and threatened to contest the matter in court.

Another game between the two teams was scheduled for the next day. Harry escorted Umpire Johnstone, and Umpire Emslie as well, into the park, nodding at the gatekeeper as they passed. He watched them walk onto the grounds, then hopped into a car and was whisked away. The umpires were loudly cheered as they took their positions on the field. Once again, Harry suspended McGraw indefinitely.

"That deed has turned the whole baseball country more decidedly than ever against McGrawism, and has at last shown him to Gotham fans in his real light," a reporter wrote for the Chicago Tribune. "It was probably the most serious mistake of his career, and probably marks the beginning of the end."

McGraw was reinstated on August 24. He said, "I knew that the suspension would last until after the Chicago and Pittsburg series. I think these are the clubs that Pulliam favors." He hinted at legal action.

The Chicago Cubs won the National League pennant race of 1906, finishing a full twenty games ahead of the second place Giants. They won 116 games, setting a new major league record. In the World Series, though, they lost to their cross-town rival, the hitless wonders, the White Sox. Neither ballpark was large enough to hold the tremendous crowds, so the Chicago Tribune set up mechanical boards to recreate the games, play by play, in various locations throughout the city.

When the World Series ended, Harry left Chicago for New York, to prepare for a much anticipated six-week vacation in Europe. His health had improved, and he felt the ocean air would be good for his future prospects. The Pittsburgh Press followed his journey abroad, reporting that he had traveled the European continent, and the British Isles as well. On December 1, he set sail for home from Liverpool, England, a six-day voyage. His friends back in Pittsburgh, having received cards and letters from abroad, believed the trip had been good for him, and he would be well prepared to resume his duties in New York. The winter meeting was scheduled to begin on December 11.

He arrived in New York on December 9 and was immediately sought out by the press.

"I came the nearest I ever have in my life to forgetting baseball while I was away," he told them. "I had an audience with the Pope, visited the battlefield of Waterloo on a rainy day when I was the only person on the grounds, and saw the tomb of Juliette at Verona. On this occasion I had another wet adventure, for the River Adige was on the rampage and almost prevented me from getting back to town."

On December 12, Harry Pulliam was again re-elected President of the National League. Although some favored a three-year term, in the end it remained as always, one year. The vote was 6-1, with Brush opposed and Herrmann choosing not to vote, despite having endorsed Harry the day before. To lighten his increasing workload, amid concerns for his long-term health, he would no longer also serve as secretary and treasurer. John Heydler, formerly Harry's personal secretary, was elected to those positions. Some felt Harry had been overworking himself; he had developed a nervous disposition, with a touch of paranoia, and was more and more isolating himself at his apartment. He wasn't the same old Harry.

On December 22, he was back home in Kentucky, staying with friends Harry Russell, Johnny Fay, and Henry Wehmhoff, and wearing the latest fashions from London. Later, he was in Scottsville with his family. Another difficult year had passed.

Chapter Thirteen

I Think Mr. Pulliam has it Dead Right

"Take nothing for granted in baseball." The above is President Harry Pulliam's choice motto, hung in conspicuous places around League headquarters in the St. James building in New York. I think Mr. Pulliam has it dead right. – Cincinnati Enquirer.

Harry Pulliam lost his father in the spring of 1907. He was seventy-seven years old. There had been a long, lingering illness, and when the end seemed near, family was called to Nashville, where he had been staying with Harry's sister. Harry was at his father's bedside in the hospital during the final hours. The funeral was held on March 27 in Louisville, his home for many years, and he was buried in Cave Hill Cemetery. Harry's five living siblings – one had died as an infant – were in attendance. Like his personal life, not much is known of Harry's family. There is little recorded history, and he rarely spoke about them in public.

"The indications at this time," wrote Ralph S. Davis of the Pittsburgh Press, "are that the coming season in the two major Leagues, and in the numerous minor organizations(s) which flourish wherever the American flag waves defiantly, will be unqualifiedly the most successful in history."

After meeting for twenty-four hours over a two-day period, the presidents of the two major Leagues finalized their 1907 schedules, having eliminated most of the conflicts from the original draft. A new policy was also approved; each ticket sold was to have a raincheck attached. This was expected to save much time and money in the ticket office any time a game was rained out, or canceled for some other reason.

On April 17, Harry was in Pittsburgh for the opening game between the Pirates and the National League Champion Cubs at Exposition Park. It was a freezing cold day, but a large crowd attended nonetheless. Harry threw out the first ball to Umpire O'Day, who caught it, then turned to the crowd and promptly announced the starting pitchers. The champs bested the Pirates, 6-2.

By 1907, Hank O'Day's reputation as a top-flight umpire had begun to fade.

"Hank O'Day can create more disturbance in one game than all the rest of Harry Pulliam's staff in a season," wrote a Brooklyn Times reporter. "Hank is as popular here as a bull pup in a gathering of Thomas cats."

"That fellow Hank O'Day is a queer mortal," said a fan. "President Pulliam has given the umpires to understand that they must signal balls and strikes to the crowd by wave of his arms. This O'Day refuses to do despite the fact that it would relieve his voice of considerable strain. O'Day has for weeks been under the care of a throat specialist, yet he refuses to do what would not only be a great benefit to himself, but the spectators as well."

A new rule in place for the National League in 1907 required all ball parks to provide "special clubhouses" for the visiting team to use for changing into their uniforms before games. Most of the players opposed the rule, to the surprise of League officials. They preferred to dress in their hotel rooms. The majority of the 'special clubhouses', it seemed, weren't so special at all. They were cramped and built on tight budgets. Teams who did not provide visiting clubhouses at all were subject to a daily fine of twenty-five dollars.

In May, Fred Clarke filed a protest against catcher Roger Bresnahan of the Giants and his new invention, claiming the 'armor' he was wearing on his shins was an unfair advantage to the Giants' team. According to Clarke, when wearing the shin guards, Bresnahan had no fear of being spiked, and therefore was better able to block the plate when a baserunner tried to score. When Clarke learned that Harry had ruled in favor of Bresnahan, he went on a shopping trip and bought a suit of armor from ancient times. It was put on display in the Pirates' clubhouse, and Clarke let it be known he planned to use it, or rather have his catcher use it, when Bresnahan's Giants played in Pittsburgh on June 12.

"On this date Bresnahan and his shin guards will look like ten and a quarter cents in Hindoo money," predicted the Post-Dispatch. "Mr. Gibson, who does the lion's share of the catching for the Pirates will emerge, stroll or be carried from the Pirate dressing room enwrapped, tangled up in, or locked inside of this Louis XIIV battling suit. He will not be compelled to wear the regulation breast protector, guards nor a mask, or in fact, not even a catcher's glove."

Added Clarke, "I am also figuring on rigging my infielders in football armor."

Early on, Harry's enhanced power to fight kicking and rowdyism was clearly making a difference. On May 19, Ralph S. Davis reported that to date, not a single player had been suspended for complaining to an umpire, compared to eighteen on the same date in 1906. Even the Giants were behaving themselves, and playing excellent ball as well. They had won 23 of their first 26 games, a remarkable record, but still only led the Cubs by 1.5 games.

Harry, while pleased with the behavior of the players so far, expressed his belief that when the weather warmed, as it had yet to do, so would the rowdyism. Still, by mid-June, he had suspended only one player, and his name was not McGraw. The Giants manager had seemingly changed his ways, and Harry was quick to give him credit for it. The whole team, according to Harry, had been behaving like perfect gentlemen. And so was the rest of the League.

But Harry had no means of subduing the crowds. At the Polo Grounds on May 22, the Giants, with Mathewson pitching, were edged by Mordecai Brown and his Cub mates, 3-2. As the last out was made, the fans, infuriated by a questionable call, invaded the playing field and encircled umpires Emslie and O'Day. The two made a run for it toward their dressing room with dozens of angry men in pursuit. Some of the Giants aided them, led by Iron Man Joe McGinnity. The police were enlisted, saw bottles being thrown, and one of them fired a shot in the air. The fans quickly regained their composure and went home. If McGraw could no longer do the dirty work, his fans were apparently more than willing to do it for him.

Harry penned a letter to Joe McGinnity:

Dear Sir:

I was present at the Polo Grounds Tuesday and noted with pleasure your manly action in assisting to prevent an assault on Mr. Emslie. On behalf of the National League and myself I desire to return thanks to you for your courageous action.

Harry Pulliam

In July, Harry was forced to suspend the usually mild-mannered Frank Chance for throwing bottles during a game in Brooklyn. The suspension lasted one week. Harry noted that it was Chance's first offense in an otherwise spotless career.

The hometown paper defended Chance: "The Brooklyn club was more to blame than was Chance for the outbreak last Monday. There is absolutely no protection for players or public. The presence of one cop or special policeman would have prevented the trouble. Chance was goaded to frenzy by a bunch of filthy tongued galoots and he stood it until they pelted him with bottles. Then he lost control and retaliated, which would pass for human nature anywhere except baseball. Mr. Pulliam should give Chance two errors in the official averages for missing the rowdies he aimed at."

The throwing of pop bottles was becoming commonplace. Later in the season, in a game at St. Louis, a fan threw a bottle at Umpire Billy Evans, hitting him in the head. Evans crumpled to the ground, was helped off the field, and required several days to recover. Both Harry and Ban Johnson announced their intention to ban bottles at ball parks, but it would require the approval of the magnates, who would not meet again until December.

Late in the summer, during a three-game series at Exposition Park, eight New York Giants were thrown out of games by Bill Klem for misconduct, including Bresnahan, McGraw, Art Devlin, Bill Dahlen, Dan McGann and Frank Bowerman. Having watched the pennant slip from their grasp, the New York team was resorting back to their old habits.

"From what I can learn of what occurred here during the Pirates' series with the Giants, I guess that Billy Klem got a taste of what I have been up against from McGraw and his bunch ever since I broke into the National League as an arbitrator," commented fellow umpire Ed Johnstone.

When the season ended, the Cubs had prevailed again by a wide margin. The Pirates finished second, followed by the Giants. Harry named Hank O'Day as the National League umpire for the World Series, then set sail for England.

"Mr. Pulliam's real objective in visiting England was to supervise the building of a blue serge suit in which Mr. O'Day will umpire the world's series," wrote a reporter for the Chicago Tribune. "The worthy president has his own clothes built abroad, and knows what is what. He brought back with his own fair hands the suit, which was made by Poole, the man who chops out clothes for King Ed. The pants are creased down the sides of the legs instead of fore and aft. Do not fail to observe the king of the umpires when he splashes into the arena this afternoon."

Although he was certain to be re-elected at the League meeting in December, Harry's true desire was to buy a team and leave the presidency. As each year passed, the stress inherent in the job affected his health and his nerves more and more. He had fond memories of his days in Louisville and Pittsburgh, where he had excelled at building and running a baseball team. However, there were currently no teams available, so he marched on.

He announced that the winter League meeting, scheduled for December 10 in New York, would be held at the Waldorf Hotel. "I see no reason why a rich organization like the National League should not progress," he explained. "You know we started in meeting at the old Astor House many years ago, and by degrees have progressed up Broadway as far as the Victoria. We now feel that we are fully able to take care of ourselves in the Waldorf," he commented.

According to Harry, all of the magnates now were familiar with dress suits, and, having practiced a great deal, "can now walk on a rug without tripping."

"Mr. Pulliam's tailors refuse to give out any particulars as to the wardrobe being made for the National League president for this occasion, but the haberdasher let slip an information that lavender and purple will be the general color scheme in hosiery. Mr. Pulliam, being slim of ankle, will wear silk lavender hose with an embroidered cloister of wisteria winding its way over the pedal knuckle to partly allay the angular effect. In the mornings he will wear the famous Hearst collar all wound round with a purple tie, bearing in modest yellow the coat of arms of the National League. His waistcoat will be of watered gray silk and around his soft hat he is to wear a girdle of fluffy mousseline de sole to carry out the general effect." –Pittsburgh Post-Dispatch.

On November 12, Harry left New York for a visit to Indian Territory in Oklahoma. He stayed two weeks with his friend and former Pirate Bill Stuart, who had struck oil in the region. From there he went to Washington for the opening session of the Congress, and on to New York for the League meeting. He had lost fifteen pounds from worry before going on his trip, but had gained back twelve, and thought himself to be in excellent health.

In addressing the magnates, Harry reported that there were 112 cases of players being thrown out of games, and seventeen suspensions. This was the lowest total in five years. He recommended that pop bottles be prohibited in all League parks to ensure the safety of all in attendance at games. He called for an end to doubleheaders whenever possible, in order to increase profits, and also the practice of playing only seven innings in the second game of doubleheaders that are necessary. And, he asked for improvements to visiting clubhouses, and the requirement that postponed games be played, to insure the integrity of the pennant races.

Harry was re-elected President of the National League by a 7-1 vote. John T. Brush opposed. The magnates gave him a $2,000 raise, but they did not act on any of the reforms he had suggested. Before adjourning, Harry presented Hans Wagner with a silver loving cup, on behalf of the National League, for his services to the League.

Harry spent the holidays in Nashville with his sister. It was the first without his father.

In December, a newspaper article in the Post-Dispatch noted a battle brewing for the New York Giants' first base job, with veteran Fred Tenney being pushed for the position by youngster Fred Merkle. Tenney had held the job for fourteen years, but McGraw was very impressed by Merkle. "It is almost a pity to keep Merkle on the bench," said McGraw to the newspaper men, "for he has in him all the elements of a great ball player and he is so anxious to make good." Merkle was nineteen years old.

As 1907 came to an end, no one could possibly have predicted the unbelievable events that would take place in

1908. It was to be the most fantastic and controversial season in baseball history. Harry Pulliam and Fred Merkle would play the leading roles.

Chapter Fourteen

A Fateful Day in September

"President Pulliam says that a man is ridiculed, libeled, cussed at, laughed at, cajoled, thrown down, tramped on, disregarded and 'worked' oftener to the square inch in baseball than in any other profession, calling or trade in the world." -Pittsburgh Press.

In a letter to the Press Harry wrote:

"I am a hockey enthusiast now, and am here todaywith the Ottawa team as one of their rooters. They play the Victorias of Montreal tonight, and every seat (7,000) is sold. All Canada is excited about the game. One of these teams will be the champion of All-Canada, and this carries with it the championship of the world.

"If I do not turn up at the League meetings, you will know that some indignant Montreal rooter put me out of the running. If I live, I am going to Quebec – it is too warm here.

Harry Pulliam.

His jovial demeanor in Canada notwithstanding, Harry's friends were urging him to take a long break before the season started. He was reportedly not in good health. The Pittsburgh Press reported that "his nervous system is in bad order." The Cincinnati Enquirer defined Harry's condition as being worn out. He made plans to go to Muldoon's Institution north of New York for three weeks to rest and recuperate. Although the reporters were kind to Harry and did not use the word because they liked him, Muldoon's was something like a sanitarium.

Meanwhile, the New York Times made light of Harry's habit of threatening to quit if he didn't get his way.

"Col. Harry Clay Pulliam passed through a strenuous week with Johnson and Herrmann holding tight to the safety valve. Pulliam hasn't threatened to resign since Monday night."

The St. Louis Post-Dispatch did so as well.

"The latest reports are that President Pulliam is still busy on the $10,000 job. Somehow, the ink would not flow when he attempted to sign his name to the resignation."

When he arrived at Muldoon's "physical culture farm," as some called it, Harry soon realized that while recuperation was indeed part of the plan, rest definitely was not. He sent for his gym clothes in New York, stating that he was going to partake in strenuous physical activities. His training schedule was personally attended to by Professor Muldoon himself, and he kept Harry hustling. First thing every morning he took a brisk walk to breathe in the early morning air. The rest of the day was spent engaging in various strenuous exercises. It paid off. When he left, he declared himself practically fit to be a ballplayer himself. His mental stability was entirely a different matter.

While at Muldoon's, Harry learned of the retirement of his good friend Honus Wagner. "Say to Honus I regret his decision to quit the game just now," he said. "He is beyond a doubt the National League's greatest player, and his loss will be a severe one. However, I hope it is for the best. He will always have my friendship and esteem, for he is certainly one of the most manly men I ever knew, and I am proud to call him my friend." Wagner was actually simply holding out for a bigger contract. After meeting with Harry in Pittsburg, he was persuaded to return to the Pirates. Harry impressed upon him, during the three-hour visit, that not only did his team need him, the League did as well. He was probably the most popular player of all, with the possible exception of Mathewson, and the other teams needed the large gate he attracted. After signing his contract, Hans left that evening for Cincinnati to surprise his teammates.

When the season began Harry was asked to assess the race. "I do not desire to pose as a prophet," he responded, "but at the same time I think I can safely go on record and say to the patrons of the National League that in 1908, for the first time in a number of years, we will have a championship race of more than ordinary interest."

In a letter sent out to all managers, Harry asked them to do what they could to speed the game along so that spectators didn't lose interest. Outfielders were asked to hurry in and out from the field between innings, and Harry suggested having the groundskeeper in each park mark out a spot halfway between the dugout and home plate for the next batter to wait for his turn at the plate, instead of waiting in the dugout. This, he reasoned, would cut down the time lost between batters.

Around the circuit, Harry was taking heat for his directive that any player who left his position to argue a call was subject to immediate removal. One critic was Frank Chance, who remarked, "Whole infields will be tossed out at one time. I don't believe the rule can last long." In June, he suspended John McGraw for remarks made to Umpire Johnstone during a game played in the pouring rain. The next day, from the hidden booth behind the Giants' bench, McGraw continued his verbal assault.

"This cubby-hole is a unique feature on the Polo Grounds," read the Cincinnati Enquirer the next day. "Whenever Manager McGraw is put off the field or suspended he retires to it and is out of sight, but far from out of mind. Through a small hole cut in the boards he can survey the field and give directions to his men, to say nothing of attacking the umpire at critical times. The result is that the suspension of McGraw, while his team is playing at home, amounts to nothing except to keep him off the coaching lines."

Hearing of this, Harry said that he would likely extend McGraw's suspension, while expressing frustration over not being able to stop McGraw from continuing the practice. "I don't see my way out of it," he said. "The umpire orders McGraw off the field, but he cannot enforce his jurisdiction beyond the limits of the playing field. The umpire certainly cannot leave the game and go swooping around behind the players' bench to find out if McGraw is there."

Otherwise, though, suspensions continued to decline. "It's been a case of 'peace on earth, good will toward most men,' since the season opened," Harry remarked. "There have been so few banishments by the umpires that there are times when I can't realize that the baseball season is on until I look at the scores." He had been correct in his assessment that it was going to be a tight race for the pennant in the National League. On July 1, Pittsburgh stood in first place, but the Cubs were only three and a half games behind, and the Giants five and a half back.

"The present championship race in the National League is the best the old organization has ever been able to present for the delectation of the baseball public and it is little wonder that enthusiasm is running high in many of the cities." - Pittsburgh Press.

Harry spent the first week of August at the Laughery Club in Cincinnati as the guest of Garry Herrmann. The rest was good for his health, and the culinary variety at the club, where he insisted six meals a day were served, benefitted him as well. He returned to New York fit to endure the rest of the season.

On September 4, Cubs owner Charles Murphy filed a protest about a play that ended a game between the Cubs and Pirates that day. The bases were loaded with two men out in the bottom of the tenth inning, when Owen Wilson hit a single to center, scoring the winning run. Hank O'Day was the umpire. There was no second umpire. Murphy sent a telegram to Harry Pulliam:

"Chicago protests Friday's game here. With the bases full and two out, Wilson hit safely to center. Gill, of Pittsburg, failed to run to second base from first. He ran a few feet down the line, then turned out and went to the clubhouse. Evers, who covered second base, received the ball from Slagle and called the attention of the umpire to the force-out. The umpire simply said: 'Clarke has crossed the plate.' Chicago claims Gill should have touched second base before he ran to the club-house, and will prove by the affidavits of a number of persons that he failed to do so. This protest is filed by Chicago despite the fact that you have never yet allowed one, because Clarke's run should not count, as Gill was plainly forced at second base on the play."

Murphy also discussed the play with the newspaper men. "I do not expect the protest will be allowed, but it is certainly a just one, and should prove a strong argument in favor of the double-umpire system. Had there been another umpire on duty yesterday to look after the plays in the field Gill would have been declared out and Clarke's run would never have been allowed."

In Chicago, Hank O'Day was vilified, blamed for a loss to the hometown team in a tight pennant battle, including the local papers:

"Posted in the office of President Pulliam of the National League are several signs which read: 'Take nothing for granted in baseball.' None but an experienced baseball man like Mr. Pulliam knows how essential it is to remember that injunction at all times," lectured the Chicago Tribune. "If Umpire O'Day, dean of Pulliam's staff, had permitted the motto, which he has seen so often in the League's New York headquarters, to become photographed on his memory, he would not have taken for granted certain things in Friday's game of baseball between the Chicago Cubs and Pittsburg. The chances were 1,000,000 to 1 that hit would win the game, so O'Day took it for granted it did win the game, and started off the field with the crowd. And because O'Day neglected his duty, Chicago lost even that one-millionth chance. Not only is the double umpire system needed, but there is the equally great need of umpires who will remember not to 'take anything for granted in baseball.'"

Hank O'Day

In denying the protest, Harry, as usual, backed his umpire one hundred percent.

"The umpire in charge of the game, Mr. O'Day, reports that in the last half of the tenth inning, with the bases full and two outs, Wilson hit safely to center field and that on the hit Clarke scored the winning run; that after this run was scored the crowd ran on the field and that he(the umpire) went to the Chicago bench, considering the game ended; that at the bench Evers, of the Chicago club, told him that Gill, the runner at first, failed to touch second base.

"This is simply a case of fact and judgment and the ruling of the umpire is final. The question of whether there was a force play or not cannot be established by the evidence of players or spectators. It rests solely with the umpire. The umpire in this case, by allowing the winning run, ruled that there was no force at second, because if there had been the run would not have scored."

Nineteen days later, on a fateful day in late September, history repeated itself.

On September 23, the Cubs were in New York to play the Giants at the Polo Grounds. The Giants had moved into first place, but the race was tighter than ever, with Chicago, New York and Pittsburgh all within a game and a half of each other. Interest in the national game was at a new all-time high, spurred by the extensive coverage of the press, and attendance was skyrocketing. More than 20,000 turned out on a Wednesday afternoon to watch the game of September 23. They were about to witness the most controversial play in baseball history.

Shortly before game time, Giants' first baseman Fred Tenney, suffering an attack of lumbago, was replaced in the starting lineup by rookie Fred Merkle. Tenney had won the spring training battle for first base, but Merkle also made the team, as his backup. It was the first time all season that Merkle had started a game.

Two umpires had been assigned to call the game – O'Day and Emslie.

Christy Mathewson, in the midst of another great season, was the starter for New York. Manager Chance of the Cubs countered with Giant killer Jack Pfeister. It was a tight pitchers' duel into the ninth inning, with the score tied at one run apiece. Chicago shortstop Joe Tinker had hit a home run in the fifth, but the Giants had manufactured a run in the sixth to even it up.

In the last of the ninth, with two outs, McCormick had reached third base on a single by Merkle. Al Bridwell singled to center, scoring the winning run for New York. Then all hell broke loose.

Merkle, seeing McCormick cross the plate to end the game, trotted toward second base. Then, seeing a huge rush of fans coming from all directions, stopped short of second base, turned, and headed for the clubhouse. Evers, nicknamed the crab because he looked like one and had a crabby personality, saw Merkle's failure to touch second, ran there himself, calling for center fielder Hofman to throw him the ball. But Giants' third base coach Joe McGinnity ran over and intercepted the throw.

Fred Merkle

Next, according to some witnesses, McGinnity was tackled by Tinker, and perhaps Evers as well, in an attempt to recover the ball and touch second base. McGinnity broke free and threw the ball into the stands. Others claim he threw it high in the air and it landed near third base, where a spectator grabbed it. By now the affair had turned into a riot, with thousands of people on the field, some in celebration, others trying to figure out what exactly had happened.

"Some hot-heads in the crowd shouted that O'Day had given the game to Chicago and the umpire was instantly surrounded by angry fans," wrote one reporter. "For five minutes there was a free-for-all fight. Policemen and the New York club's specials wielded their clubs freely and fought their way back to the New York bench, forming a square, with O'Day in the center."

In the only action photo known to exist from the most controversial game in baseball history, Fred Merkle leads off first base in the bottom of the ninth inning, just prior to the single by Al Bridwell. The first baseman is Frank Chance of the Cubs.

With the field now unplayable, Frank Chance immediately protested the game. Murphy did also, hoping for a more favorable verdict this time. O'Day ruled that McCormick's run did not count, due to Merkle not touching second, and declared the game a tie. But Chance rallied for a forfeiture, claiming the game could not be continued due to New York fans having invaded the field, and the darkening sky as well. The final decision would be made by Harry Pulliam, who waited until he received a report from O'Da

Manager McGraw chimed in. "As a matter of fact, Merkle tells me, he did reach and touch second base. No Chicago player was on second base with the ball, anyway. It's a simple case of squeal. Chicago has been trying to get away with this all season.   We won fair and square. No impartial spectator who saw Bridwell's hit and McCormick score would want to take it away from us."

The New York papers defended Merkle. "It has always been a custom for the players to leave the field immediately after the winning run has been made, and as a matter of fact, many of the Chicago players left the field themselves."

Mathewson also defended him. "I had started from the field when I heard Evers yell to Hofman, 'Throw the ball to second.' I remembered the trick they had tried to play at Pittsburg, and I got Merkle by the arm and told him to go to second. In the meantime, the ball had been thrown in, high over Evers head, and fell near where the shortstop ordinarily stands. Merkle touched the bag, and I was near him when he did it."

Both teams protested, claiming victory in the disputed game. Harry's intention, as always, was to follow the rule of law, which in this case was unclear. He would have to set a precedent, one way or the other. And, one way of the other, he was going to make a lot of people very angry.

Another game between the two teams was scheduled for Thursday. One hundred extra policemen were recruited to handle security, because no one really knew what to expect. Once again, 20,000 fanatics turned out, this time seeking revenge. "When the Chicago team took up their positions for preliminary practice they were hissed and hooted, and cries of 'yellow' were hurled at Chance when he stepped up to the plate." The verbal assault continued throughout the entire game. The Giants won.

With yet another game set for Friday, Chicago demanded a doubleheader be played, the second game to be the replay of the protested game. Brush and McGraw refused. When the New York players did not show up for the second game, the Cubs claimed a forfeit. However, no umpires had been assigned, so no forfeit could even be considered.

The St. Louis Post-Dispatch saw one way out of the mess. "It seems now that the only way that a scandal can be avoided is for Pittsburgh to win all four of her remaining games and for the Giants to lose two of the five on their schedule. Then Pittsburgh could carry off the pennant and that tie game of Sept. 23 between the Giants and the Cubs could not alter the standing one bit."

But that didn't happen.

When he received O'Day's report, Harry considered the matter carefully. It was a no-win situation. By the strict interpretation of the rules of baseball, the run should not count, and the game ended in a tie. Yet by the standard of fairness, perhaps the game should be awarded to the Giants. For a man who all his life had honored both fairness and the rule of law, it was the ultimate quandary. Eventually, he did what he had promised he would always do. He supported the decision of his umpire. The game was declared a tie. New York's claim that Merkle had indeed touched second base was trumped by O'Day's insistence that he had not. Chicago's claim of forfeiture was denied on the grounds that it had become too dark to continue playing anyway. Should it be necessary to decide the pennant at season's end, the game would be replayed.

Harry explained to the public his decision. "Much as I deplore the unfortunate ending of a brilliantly played game, as well as the subsequent controversy, I have no alternative than to be guided by the law. I believe in sportsmanship, and will go as far as anyone to achieve its ends, but would it be good sportsmanship on my part, as president of the League, to repudiate my umpires simply to condone the undisputed blunder of a player?"

In New York, Harry was demonized in the press like never before. The fans called him crooked, and so did John McGraw. It was not safe for him to be in the city where he lived. The next day the Giants appealed his decision. A meeting of the Board of Directors was called for Monday, October 5, in Cincinnati. Chicago appealed, as well. With two days left in the season, the race was very much in doubt:

Chicago	98 wins	55 losses
Pittsburgh	98 wins	56 losses
New York	95 wins	55 losses

The Cubs had finished their season and clinched a tie of first. New York would have to win all three of its remaining games to catch them. Two days later, the regular season ended in a tie between the Cubs and the Giants.

At the hearing, several affidavits from Giant players were read, including Merkle, all swearing he had touched second base. "I would never have believed that men could swear to such statements as are made in some of these affidavits presented by the New York club," responded Emslie. "Several of these affidavits are absolutely false. It is a revelation to me that such documents could be obtained."

"The Giants protested so vigorously and long that the Board of Directors finally had to settle the matter," said Evers many years later. "I'm not so sure they would have decided in our favor at that, but Jack Ryder, the old Cincinnati writer, who is now dead, broke into the meeting and delivered a helluva speech in our favor, claiming there was no choice but to play the game over and vowing that the League would make itself a laughingstock if it let the Giants get away with the pennant on a bonehead play."

The Board of Directors ordered the game replayed.

On October 7, the Cubs made a fourteen-hour journey to New York aboard the Twentieth Century Limited supertrain. When they arrived, thousands taunted and insulted them as they climbed into a line of automobiles under police protection. When Giants' fans discovered where they were spending the night, they surrounded the hotel, "blaring horns and noise makers" to keep them from sleeping. The next day, the Cubs made their way to the ball park via the subway, dressed in street clothes, and keeping very low profiles. At the park they had to push their way through the frantic crowd outside the gate. Chance was hit on the neck by a beer bottle and bled.

The scene at the Polo Grounds on October 8, 1908, was unlike any that major league baseball had ever seen before, or has since. At dawn, lines had already begun to form at the ticket booths outside the ball park. Many had traveled from distant cities to see the epic match.

"Immediately (after) the gates swung over, hundreds upon hundreds fairly hurled themselves within the enclosure. The stands rapidly began to fill. By noon the sale of tickets ended, and soon there was not a seat – hardly standing room. And out beyond the enclosure every overtopping structure – chimneys, derricks, roofs – had their precariously hung swarm of rooters. Outside the grounds for an hour preceding the calling of the game at 2:45 o'clock there was an almost uncontrollable crush of many thousands, desperately anxious to get inside. Suddenly the corner gates to the diamond were flung wide, and hundreds rushed madly to the sides of the field, fighting for places, stopping the practice of the nines, and causing confusion which seemed likely to be unchecked. But the police fought the crowd back, and finally a sufficient margin of field was maintained around the diamond." - Philadelphia Inquirer.

Two men died in their eagerness to see the spectacle. One climbed and fell from a fence, breaking his neck. The other had ascended an elevated railroad platform and lost his balance. Police had to stop others from trying to ascend their vacated spots. In the distance, rooftops of houses were crowded with people who had no hope of getting into the ballpark. The cliffs beyond the grandstands had become a mass of spectators. Shortly before the game started, two men fell from the roof of the grandstand. They later died as well.

Several years later, Mordecai Brown recalled the scene. "The elevated lines couldn't run for people who had climbed up and were sitting on the tracks. The police couldn't move them, and so the fire department came and tried driving them off with the hose, but they'd come back. Then the fire department had other work to do, for the mob outside the park set fire to the left-field fence and was all set to come bursting through as soon as the flames weakened the boards enough. ... It was near a lunatic asylum as I ever saw."

Harry needed a police escort to get to his seat.

Earlier in the day, McGraw had said to his players, "I don't care whether you play this game or not. You can take a vote." As a team, they voted to play, although some had voted not to. With the park already well beyond full, the umpires decided to start the game early. Outside, speculators continued to sell tickets. Mathewson strode confidently to the box, took a few warmup pitches, and declared himself ready to proceed. There was a hushed silence of anticipation, then a large cheer when he struck out the first batter, Jimmy Sheckard.

The starting pitcher for the Cubs was Jack Pfeister, nicknamed "Jack the Giant Killer" for his history of mastery over the Giants. But he struggled, and when the Giants took an early lead, Chance yanked him in favor of Brown. Mathewson struggled as well, and when the Cubs plated four runs in the fourth inning, Brown had all he needed. The Cubs won the game and the pennant. The most sensational pennant race in baseball history had come to an end.

Harry did nothing to endear himself to the people of New York when he commented later. "It was the greatest race in the history of baseball. The best team undoubtedly won. But there was great glory for other teams besides the winners in the battles that were fought right down to the last day. All honor should go to the New York team for the gallant fight they made to bring the flag to Gotham."

"What a tremendous amount of argument, trouble and ill feeling might have been saved if Fred Merkle had been bright enough to run down to second base instead of making the champion bone-head play of the year," wrote a reporter for the Cincinnati Enquirer. "From all reports the League chief was forced to call the game a tie, owing to the wretched stupidity of Merkle." Since the infamous game of September 23, Merkle had been ridiculed by newspapers across the country. He had lost his appetite, lost fifteen pounds, and was having trouble sleeping at night. And he was still only a teenager.

Believing that Harry had stolen the pennant from his Giants, John T. Brush swore that he never would again attend another League meeting while he served as president. In his absence, the seven other clubs re-elected Harry unanimously. As the meeting neared its end, Harry revealed to the magnates that umpires Klem and Johnstone, who had been on duty in the makeup game of October 8 between the Cubs and Giants, had told him attempts to bribe them had been made prior to that game. Names of the persons involved had been passed on to Harry, but he declined to reveal them in lieu of an investigation. He did state, though, that none of them were involved in organized baseball. It was, to say the least, shocking news.

In December, Harry flew to the West Coast with Ban Johnson. They went to San Francisco to help the Pacific

Coast League deal with the California State League, an outlaw league. The plan was to get them into organized baseball. Securing star first baseman Hal Chase from the renegade league was the real motivation. They were unsuccessful. As usual, the newspaper men felt the need to comment on Harry's appearance. "Mr. Pulliam blew in from New York at four o'clock yesterday afternoon," wrote one. "He was attired in a checked gray traveling suit, a black sheath top overcoat, blue bow tie, a gray crush hat, tan shoes and white spats. He carried an orange wood cane and mauve gloves."

This was actually Harry's second trip to California. Before leaving San Francisco, he shared tales of his first visit with a reporter for the San Francisco Call.

"I will never forget my first visit to San Francisco. That was away back in 1891 and I was just turning my twentieth year then. Shortly before that time I had accumulated $1,100. Now, you know that such an amount looks fabulous in the hands of an inexperienced youth and I started out to see the world and do things to it. Well, the bank roll lasted until I hit the Coast, but then it gave out and I faced the ordeal of seeking my first job.

"I took stock of my accomplishments and found that they amounted to simply a good education, a willingness to work, a healthy appetite and a world of inexperience at doing anything useful except spending money. When I sized myself up and took stock I thought I was best fitted to turn San Francisco upside down as a journalist, and I accordingly applied to a local paper for a job as a reporter. The city editor was a nice, suave little man and after he allowed me sufficient time to cool my heels he invited me to become one of his staff. My assignment that night was to see the family of the captain of a little sloop. It seems that this captain had disappeared and caused consternation in the breasts of his relatives. I was on the job all right, but when I got out to the home of the missing captain there was no one to receive me and I perched on the stoop waiting for the return of the family.

"I had pictures of frantic women, wailing and gnashing of teeth and all the little scenic effects that usually make the settings at the home of a captain who is rash enough to want to play penuchle with the whales.

"I had guarded that stoop for about four hours when the family returned. Imagine my surprise when there was no gnashing of teeth nor wailing nor weeping. The family had just returned from the theater. That's how much the good people thought of the captain's disappearance. When I told the women folk I was a reporter they put up a show of excitement, and one of the ladies said she felt just 'turble' about papa, but the son-in-law of the captain took me aside and tipped me off that the captain was merely piloting a few large schooners of 'steams' into port and that he would be back again in the port of living men.

"I had my story all right and hustled back to the office. I thought the editorial staff from the managing editor down to the office boy would be on hand to greet me as the fair-haired child when I got there, but when I did arrive it was to meet an irate city editor, and he said things to me I did not think it possible for such a nice, suave man to get off his system. That was my one and only assignment in San Francisco. I guess the paper thought I was too good to keep. Anyhow, they let me out."After the tryout at journalism on the coast I beat it down to Fresno and went to work in a prune dryer. That was a soft berth for me. I got all of $9 a week, and as I only had to pay $6 a week for board, you can see that I had a great surplus to spend on wine, women and song.

"When I had finished my great labors of teaching a plum how to behave as a prune I went up to Calaveras County to see the home of Mark Twain's famous jumping frog. And say, believe me, I think every word of that story is true, for I had a little experience up in that county that had it even on the jumping frog episode.

"When I hit Calaveras I had a companion, a Pennsylvania graduate. Neither of us had any money, but we consented to join hands and fight a cruel world. We hit a lumber camp one dreary night, and say, we were the hungry kids. The fellow who ran the outfit was a Maine man, and he had a lot of fine, big Swedes working for him. I almost forgot my hunger in my open admiration for these great blonde Vikings, but the call of the appetite finally got the better of my artistic sense, and I asked the old boy if we could get something to eat. He curtly told us he was not running a boarding house, but I put up the long talk about being hungry, and he finally told us to go back in the kitchen and gorge ourselves. We did. That meal was no table d'hote affair, but I never relished a dinner more than I did that one, and I have dined in every first-class restaurant in America and Europe. Our fare was pork and beans, with molasses gravy and a huge, bumping cup of coffee. Say, I wish I could enjoy a meal now like I did that one. I've got half a notion to seek out that lumber camp and go against that chow again. One thing certain, I am going down and take a look at the prunes in Fresno before I return to New York."

Chapter Fifteen

That Man was Poor Harry Pulliam

"Baseball is in its infancy. It is just really started. Watch it grow in the next ten years. Don't laugh. I mean it. As it is handled now, baseball is a crude affair. In years to come the game will be played in magnificent amphitheaters. It is the only logical outcome of present conditions." - Harry Pulliam.

In January of 1909, while in Cincinnati for a meeting of the National Commission, Harry made a side visit to his old stomping grounds in Louisville. As usual, a reporter from the Courier-Journal was there to meet him. "No man ever left Louisville and made such a national success as Harry Pulliam and retained such universal popularity at home as he has," he wrote. "He counts his friends by the scores, and no matter how great are his surprises in store for them in dress and ultra fashion, he wears the same old smile and his glad hand is as it was in the days of old."

"'Hello, Harry; glad to see you back again,' said an old friend at he offered his hand.

"Never felt better in my life," was Harry's quick reply, followed by his usual merry laugh.'"

On his way back to New York, he visited the family of personal friend Edward McLaughlin, who had passed recently in Pittsburgh. He reflected on his chosen profession. "The job of president of a baseball league is no sinecure, and I have come in for more abuse than ordinarily falls to the lot of the common mortal. I don't mind attacks on myself as an official when there is truth behind these tirades, but I do object to stories that are falsifications aimed at myself or my organization. Since last spring I have settled up past scores with two men who questioned my honesty. When I am able to yell, 'Three!' a la Edmond Dantes, Count of Monte Cristo, then I will be satisfied and ready to go back to Kentucky."

Harry's health had not been good for some time. There had been plenty to tax his nerves. To the public, it seemed the Committee on Bribery was doing nothing. "Why," people asked, "was Brush named the chairman of the committee? Wasn't he one of the bribers?" Adding even more stress was the investigation of a ticket scalping scandal during the World Series that had brought into question the integrity of Charles Murphy, causing a great strain on their relationship. Now, of Hart, Dreyfuss and Murphy, none remained true friends.

Furthermore, a movement was afoot to assist the poverty-stricken Cap Anson by making him supervisor of officials in the National League, even though Harry had plainly stated that he intended to continue doing the job himself. But Anson was not ready to give up that easily.

"I think I'll get the job, all right," he said. "just as soon as I see Pulliam. I've had lots of experience with umpires and know how to handle them, so there's no doubt about my making good. Charley Murphy, owner of the Cubs, is for me and so are some other club owners. The National League ought to have a man to keep an eye on its umpires, and I think I can convince Mr. Pulliam that I am the right man."

Harry, however, could not be persuaded. Some accused him of being insensitive. At the same time, Charles Murphy accused Harry of holding a grudge against the Cubs because he had unsuccessfully tried to buy the team before Murphy did. Harry denied it. It became a very public feud. Harry became bitter. Arriving at a National Commission meeting in Chicago, he released a statement:

"I have given six years of my life to the upbuilding of the National League and helping to make men like Murphy rich, and all I have got from it is abuse and ridicule from the very men I have served faithfully. I have gained no riches and I am sick and tired of the whole affair. I am going out to California next week to take a much needed rest, and out there under the sunshine I am going to try to forget the genus 'magnate' ever lived. If anyone offers to sell me a newspaper while I am on this vacation I will not hesitate to fill the offender full of lead."

George Dovey of the Boston club asked Harry to dine with him that evening. "Nothing doing," he laughed. I refuse absolutely to be the guest of a magnate."

At the meeting, "Pulliam was in a genuine rage. His black eyes snapped with determination and his fingers twitched with eagerness for the battle. He decided he would upset the fuming pot of baseball scandal and expose its contents to the public gaze. He hinted that Charles Webb Murphy would be splattered with the debris."

"I'll find out if there was scalping of tickets during the last World's Series and I'll find out if Charles Murphy or any of his hired men had anything to do with it. I'm tired of Murphy's insulting remarks, and if baseball has to put up with such things, I'm through with it forever."

Murphy had not planned to attend the meeting, claiming to be in the hospital at his ill wife's bedside. However, when a blizzard postponed the opening session, he showed up.

On February 17, Harry hosted a dinner for the Baseball Writers of America. He joked about becoming one of them, as soon as the League was done with him, which could be any day. Then he totally lost control. "I am through with that body," he declared. "I will not attend the meeting of that body today, nor at all until I am convinced that they mean to do the square thing. Besides, I am not well." At that point he could not stop himself. "These baseball magnates are a lot of cheap people. They are built like Durham Bulls. They delight in nagging me to a point of desperation and then bawling me out. They win because I have neither the voice nor the humor to reply. Money madness is the trouble with some of them. They have flung discretion to the winds and are going after gold regardless of sport or the welfare of the game. They are killing the goose that lays the golden egg. I am going to let them go downhill their own way."

The headline in the St. Louis Post-Dispatch described Harry's rantings as hysterical. Later, he claimed there was a plot to remove him from his post, and it was led by none other than Barney Dreyfuss. "I expect that there are enough of the opposition to depose me as president, and as a matter of fact, I would not regret such action on their part. The job is a thankless one for the most part, and the friction that one has to contend with is not worth the trouble. As a matter of fact, I did order Dreyfuss and Ebbets out of my office in New York, and I would do the same thing again if the circumstances were similar."

Later that day Harry was granted a leave of absence by the magnates, though he had not requested one. Most assumed he would never return. John Heydler was named acting president.

"Pulliam, since the memorable Merkle incident in the League championship race of last year, at New York, called upon him to make an unpleasant decision, has felt the strain of his official duties. He himself says he has been overwrought and overworked to the point of a breakdown, and he shows the effects of the strain." - St. Louis Post-Dispatch.

"Pulliam's health has been impaired for some time, he being frail, nervous, and unable to withstand the heavy drain upon his constitution." - New York Times.

He was no longer thinking rationally. At 11:30 p.m., on February 18, he decided to leave for St. Louis, rebuffing the efforts of friends to detain him, worried about his well-being. Harry's brother, who had been summoned from Kentucky, was unable to convince him to stay as well. Hailing a cab, Harry climbed into the back seat. George Dovey, desperate to intervene, jumped into the front seat to convince the driver not to leave. Harry then jumped out and started running down Congress Street in a heavy rain, with several magnates in pursuit. They caught him at the corner of Wabash and Congress and tried to hold him from leaving by force. He began to scream, so they released him, but continued to follow closely. A block later he hailed another cab and headed for the train station. The magnates began to run after the cab, as fast as they could, the rain now "descending in torrents." They caught up to him just as he jumped onto the rear of the train, which was already pulling out of the station. He was gone.

In St. Louis the press was waiting for him. By most accounts, he told them he was in town to call on a certain young woman who he planned to marry, and that he was making plans for a wedding trip to Hawaii. Later he denied saying anything of the kind. Finding St. Louis less than hospitable, he departed for Cincinnati the next day.

In Cincinnati, Harry immediately checked into a hotel room, refusing to comment. Garry Herrmann visited, and insisted that he see a doctor. The doctor advised a long period of rest in a secluded area. His brother-in-law, George W. Cain, and a close friend, Mr. Russell of Louisville, had met Harry at the train station and escorted him to the hotel.

One day later he was on the move again. The newspapers charted his progress.

"President Harry C. Pulliam, of the National League, passed through the city (Atlanta) this evening, en route from Nashville to Florida, where he will spend five weeks in recuperating his health and strength. His rest at the home of his sister in Nashville has done him a world of good, and he is in better physical condition than he has been for the last two years. While in Nashville he walked from ten to twenty miles every day and went to bed at eight o'clock each evening. He discovered that a large part of his nervousness was due to trouble with his eyes, and he is now wearing glasses to correct his vision. He is on his way to Naples, a little village on the west coast of Florida, where Henry Watterson and other well-known Kentuckians have winter cottages. He will spend the next five weeks in fishing, bathing and playing golf. Early in April he will return to Nashville for an operation on his eyes, and he expects to resume his duties as head of the National League about April 20."

The operation on his left eye on April 10 was deemed a success. He had gained fourteen pounds. On April 16, he attended a game in Cincinnati between the Reds and his old friends, the Pirates, as the guest of Garry Herrmann. His prospects seemed to be improving. In Chicago, Murphy began openly campaigning for Anson to become president of the National League. Brush had promised a vote for Anson as well. But they didn't have Herrmann's vote. "I'm for Pulliam," he declared. "When he went away for a rest during the late winter we promised him that his place would be ready and waiting for him when he recovered. I mean to stick to that promise."

While Harry was staying at his brother John's home in Oshkosh, Wisconsin, in early June, a meeting of League magnates was held to discuss his return as League president. Attempts to remove him were not successful. They extended his leave of absence, and he returned to Cincinnati to visit Herrmann again. "I feel strong again, and entirely capable of again performing my official duties. I will remain in Cincinnati a day or so, and then go to St. Louis and visit all the club owners on my way east," he said.

On June 18, one of Harry's strongest supporters, Boston owner George Dovey, died of a hemorrhage of the lungs. He was onboard a train headed for Cincinnati when the death occurred. He was 48-year-old. Harry left immediately for Pennsylvania to console Dovey's family. There was immediate speculation that Harry would buy the Boston team. Instead, on Sunday, June 29, the New York Times reported that he would return to his position as president of the National League the following day. He had arrived in New York the day before. On the last day of June, back on the job, he attended the dedication ceremonies for the new ballpark in Pittsburgh. As envisioned by Barney Dreyfuss, it instantly became the most impressive ballpark in the National League. Supporters in Pittsburgh suggested they call it Pulliam Park, in honor of Harry, but Forbes Field was chosen as the official name.

The Cincinnati Enquirer noted Harry's much improved health on July 17. "Mr. Pulliam has lost considerable weight, but otherwise his health is good. He has good color in his face and is taking the best care of himself." It seemed he had completely recovered.

On the morning of July 29, Harry arrived at his office in the St. James Building and started looking through a stack of mail. After a period of time he stopped, according to his stenographer, Miss Caylor. He sat at his desk for a while, looking out the window. At approximately 1:00 that afternoon he informed her he did not feel well and was going home for the day.

At 9:30 in the evening, the telephone operator on duty saw a light flash on his board, indicating that Harry was trying to reach him. He tried several times to call, but got no response. A bellboy was sent to check on Harry in his apartment. When he entered he found Harry on the sofa, blood on his head, a revolver on the floor near his hand. He was dressed in underclothing, half hose and garters. He was alive, but unconscious.

The physician for the New York Athletic Club, Dr. J.J. Higgins, was called. He pronounced Harry mortally wounded and called the coroner, who called the police. According to some newspaper accounts, Harry was arrested for attempted suicide, but this was never confirmed.

Coroner Shrady released a statement.

"I was notified by the New York Athletic Club between 9 and 10 o'clock a man had shot himself. I got Detective Tobin of the East Fifty-first station. We went to the New York Athletic Club and were taken to the third floor to Mr. Pulliam's room, and found him lying on a sofa. He had on only an undershirt, a pair of socks and garters. His body was entirely covered with blood. He was in a very pitiable condition. He was semi-conscious, but irrational. He could talk just a little. I asked him, 'How were you shot?'

'What do you mean?' he answered. 'Don't understand what you mean.'

'He could hear me talk, but he could not comprehend what I said. He lapsed into unconsciousness. His right eye was out and he was blind in his left eye. His right eye we picked up off the floor. The ball went entirely through the skull and fell on the floor. It cut the optic nerve and blinded him. Had it been a little further back it would have instantly killed him. It would have passed through his brain. As it is, there is no chance at all of his recovery.'

Some accounts stated Harry's response to the detective as "I am not shot." He left no note. As of 2:15 the following morning he was still alive, but had lapsed into a coma.

The lead story in the Louisville Courier-Journal shocked and saddened untold thousands in his home state. "Harry C. Pulliam, president of the National League of Baseball Clubs, attempted suicide last night in his rooms on the third floor of the New York Athletic Club. Standing in the center of the room, Mr. Pulliam held a revolver to his right temple. He fired only one shot. It went in at the right temple and came out several inches away on the left side of his head. The bullet destroyed the right eye and passed through the upper part of the left. It is not believed that he can recover."

He died at 7:40 a.m. that day. He was forty years old. His body was taken to the undertaker Winterbottom at 620 Sixth Avenue. Dr. Walter Gilday, a friend and personal physician for Harry, saw to the removal of the body. Many of his friends stopped by to view that afternoon.

Harry's last act as president had been to send a letter to all teams telling them to raise the flags which had been lowered to half-mast since the death of Israel Durham, president of the Philadelphia club. The flags remained lowered to honor Harry.

Grief over his loss was expressed endless times throughout organized baseball and beyond. "Am terribly downcast over the sad news," wrote Garry Herrmann. "Mr. Pulliam was one of the grandest characters in baseball, and one of the most lovable men in every way I ever met. He was as honest as the day is long, and a loyal and unselfish friend."

In Scottsville, a reporter wrote, "The news that Harry C. Pulliam, the noted baseball magnate, had met his death by his own hands was received with profound sorrow here, his old home, where he was born and reared. He was popular with all classes, and was intimately known to everybody in Allen County. He was last here on a visit to relatives about a year ago, when he received an ovation from old friends."

In Pittsburgh, upon hearing the news, Harry's old friend Hans Wagner wept openly.

Harry's brother-in-law, George Cain, handled the funeral arrangements. As the train carrying his body passed through Pittsburgh, several of the old Pirates boarded to accompany him. The day of the funeral, both major Leagues canceled all games scheduled to honor his memory, as did several other leagues as well. Along with countless others, a reporter for the Cincinnati Enquirer attended:

"In the presence of sorrowing hundreds of his friends, including many of the most prominent men in the baseball world, the mortal remains of Harry Clay Pulliam, late President of the National League, were laid away for their final rest in beautiful Cave Hill Cemetery this bright summer afternoon.

"The funeral was attended by an enormous crowd. Many of the big baseball magnates came from great distances, while the local friends of Mr. Pulliam were present in large numbers. The mortuary chapel was filled to overflowing, and hundreds were forced to remain outside. The procession to the cemetery was a long one, and hundreds followed the carriages on foot. At the grave the sight showed the esteem in which the departed leader was held. The slopes on every side were occupied by the sorrowing friends of the dead chieftain, who stood with bowed heads and moist eyes while the last sad words were being spoken."

Meeting in Louisville after the funeral, the Board of Directors gave the remainder of Harry's salary for the year to his estate, and at the suggestion of Charlie Ebbets, formed a committee to arrange for a monument to Harry to be built for his grave site. They ordered all National League players to wear crepe for thirty days.

Many have speculated over the years why Harry Pulliam chose to end his own life. The easy answer has always been that he was depressed over the state of his health, and that almost assuredly was a factor. There was reportedly a history of mental illness in his family, and his sister Grace committed suicide herself eight years later. Most likely, though, there was more to it than that. Some suggest it was the vitriol he was subjected to for his decision in the Merkle game. It might have been the death of his father, or the loss of close personal friendships with Hart, Dreyfuss and Murphy. His good friend George Dovey had died as well. Or, perhaps he was indeed homosexual, and someone had threatened to expose him. Perhaps it was all of the above. Then again, maybe it was something else altogether.

"It always seemed to me," said Patrick Powers after the funeral, "that it was some deep personal trouble that bothered Harry, and Billy Murray and I used to go and get him, when he had one of those brooding moods on him, and take him to a matinee or something. He'd go along, hardly saying a word, and just listen."

His impact on organized baseball is largely forgotten today. That does not diminish its significance. He brought peace to the two Leagues, marginalized kicking and rowdy ball, and ushered in an era of unprecedented growth and popularity to the national game.

"He was an idealist, plunged into the thick of a fierce contest for money, where the prizes and the losses may be large," concluded a reporter for the Brooklyn Standard Union. "His fine and sensitive nature could not stand the strain. It would have been well if so admirable a character could have been preserved for usefulness in some field not so destructive to nervous force."

Meeting prior to the World Series of 1909, at the suggestion of Garry Herrmann, the National Commission expressed the following sentiments on an engraved card:

"In memoriam Harry C. Pulliam. Friday, October 8, 1909, is the day scheduled for the playing of the first game of the world's series for this year. This series is the fifth one played under the auspices of the National Commission. A year makes changes, indeed. Harry C. Pulliam, one of the originators of these series, has passed away. His counsel in this body will be heard no more. Organized baseball never had a more zealous and devoted sponsor. In order, therefore, that his memory may forever remain green it is directed by the National Commission that a memorial card be printed, and that on the day scheduled for the first game of the world's series in each year the same be distributed to all of the players of the contesting clubs, the official umpires, scorers and business representatives, as well as to the owners of the contending clubs and the press, and that on the same day in each year there shall be placed on the grave of Harry C. Pulliam at Louisville, Ky., a floral wreath as a token of the esteem in which he was held by everyone connected with organized baseball. By order of the National Commission."

In what must have felt like one last tribute to Harry, the Pittsburgh Pirates won the World Series of 1909. They were led by his old friends – Clarke, Wagner, Leach and Phillippe – from his days in Louisville.

On August 10, 1909, the following appeared on page twelve of the Pittsburgh Press:

"Eighteen or more years ago, a freckled-faced little lad was sitting on the bench of the Louisville baseball club day after day. His big blue eyes never missed anything. Finally, after days of waiting he was told to play; someone was hurt and they wanted him.

"They laughed at him. He was a cyclone of energy that did not get any one place. He was all over the field, a streak of fiery red, but he booted the ball, fumbled it and threw wild. But his ceaseless running got the crowd. They laughed, they thought he was so funny.

"And the green boy left the field that night with heavy heart. He had come up from the coal mines of Pennsylvania where they had told him he was a good ball player. And this heartsick boy of the mines wanted to go back to his home in Pennsylvania.

"But in the morning he read the papers. One alone spoke kindly of him. It was suggested that in him there was the making of a great ball player – that all he needed was coaching.

"It gave him fresh courage and he decided to stick. And later in the day he met the man who wrote it. The author was a young Kentuckian, of gentle bearing and courtly manner, with a quiet, happy smile and a warm handshake.

"He was used to the ways of the city, and he told the country youth of his chances as though he were much older. In a hundred ways he fed the imagination of the red-haired boy.

"And from that encouragement Hughey Jennings developed from the coal miner to the highest pinnacle of baseball. The world has never seen his equal in the shortstop position. And he gives all credit to the man who saved him from going back home disgusted with his baseball ability. That man was poor Harry Pulliam."

Chapter Notes

Chapter One

1. Louisville Courier-Journal, January 5, 1896, page 11, poem.
2. Bob Bailey, SABR article online, ballparks in Louisville.
3. Joe Williams, SABR biography online, Pete Browning.
4. Paul Rogers III, SABR biography online, Hugh Jennings.
5. Sam Bernstein, SABR biography online, Barney Dreyfuss.
6. Bill Lamberty, "Deadball Stars of the National League," SABR, 2004.
7. Louisville Courier-Journal, January 25, 1895, p. 5, meeting at City Brewery.
8. The Sporting Life, February 16, 1895, p. 7, description of uniforms.
9. The Sporting Life, March 9, 1895, p. 3, Louisville Colonels schedule.
10. Louisville Courier-Journal, March 10, 1895, p. 7, Fred Pfeffer notes.
11. Louisville Courier-Journal, March 11, 1895, p. 3, first spring game.
12. The Sporting Life, Louisville Courier-Journal, March 11, 1895, p. 3, Fred Pfeffer.
13. Louisville Courier-Journal, March 29, 1895, p. 8, Pulliam at game in Houston.
14. The Sporting Life, March 30, 1895, p. 6, notes on spring practice.
15. Louisville Courier-Journal, April 9, 1895, p. 6, opening an office in Louisville.
16. The Sporting Life, April 13, 1895, p. 7, plans for opening day.
17. Washington Evening Star, April 13, 1895, p. 14, mayor to throw first ball.
18. Louisville Courier-Journal, April 18, 1895, p. 5, coverage of opening day.
19. Louisville Courier-Journal, April 24, 1895, p. 5, pitching needs.
20. Louisville Courier-Journal, May 6, 1895, p. 2, Pfeffer leaves the team.
21. Louisville Courier-Journal, April 24, 1895, p. 5, Ladies' Day.
22. Louisville Courier-Journal, May 20, 1895, p. 2, acquisition of Collins.
23. Louisville Courier-Journal, May 31, 1895, p. 5, Decoration Day game.
24. Charles Alexander, "John McGraw," University of Nebraska Press, 1988.
25. Pittsburgh Dispatch, July 5, 1892, p. 12, McGraw thrown out of game.
26. Philadelphia Inquirer, July 6, 1892, p. 3, McGraw fined.
27. Baltimore Sun, July 27, 1893, p. 6, McGraw dances at the plate.
28. Baltimore Sun, July 11, 1894, p. 6, McGraw hits umpire with ball.
29. Louisville Courier-Journal, June 11, 1895, p. 2, decision to replace McCloskey.
30. Louisville Courier-Journal, July 1, 1895, p. 2, Harry addresses the press.
31. Louisville Courier-Journal, July 14, 1895, p. 22, winning streak.
32. Louisville Courier-Journal, July 15, 1895, p. 6, quote from Nick Young.
33. Louisville Courier-Journal, August 11, 1895, p. 2, facing good pitchers.
34. Louisville Courier-Journal, September 14, 1895, p. 5, injured Colonels.
35. Louisville Courier-Journal, September 6, 1895, p. 3, losing Collins.
36. Louisville Courier-Journal, September 8, 1895, p. 22, McCloskey lets off steam.
37. Louisville Courier-Journal, September 29, 1895, p. 13, last game of season.

38. Louisville Courier-Journal, September 30, 1895, p. 2, players disperse.
39. Louisville Courier-Journal, December 13, 1895, p. 4, players not Colonels.
40. Louisville Courier-Journal, December 27, 1895, p. 8, meeting of stockholders.
41. Louisville Courier-Journal, December 30, 1895, p. 6, trip to Chicago.
42. Harold Seymour, "Baseball: The Early Years," Oxford University Press, 1960.

Chapter Two

1. Louisville Courier-Journal, January 4, 1896, p. 4, meeting of directors.
2. Louisville Courier-Journal, January 12, 1896, p. 8, Collins wants to stay in Louisville.
3. Louisville Courier-Journal, January 13, 1896, p. 3, Collins returns to Boston.
4. Louisville Courier-Journal, January 7, 1896, p. 6, McCreery meets with Mack.
5. Louisville Courier-Journal, February 2, 1896 p. 9, Harry designs the scorecard.
6. Philadelphia Inquirer, January 5, 1896, p. concern about rowdyism.
7. Louisville Courier-Journal, February 2, 1896, p. 9, Stucky and Dreher at league meeting.
8. Louisville Courier-Journal, February 9, 1896, p. 9, Bancroft refuses to play Colonels.
9. Louisville Courier-Journal, February 27, 1896, p. 5, bets on the Colonels.
10. Louisville Courier-Journal, February 29, 1896, p. 4, Harry arrives in Louisville.
11. Louisville Courier-Journal, March 2, 1896, p. 5, scheduling exhibition games.
12. Louisville Courier-Journal, March 3, 1896, p. 5, Clarke arrives in Louisville.
13. Louisville Courier-Journal, March 6, 1896, p. 5, McCreery denies meeting with Mack.
14. Louisville Courier-Journal, March 7, 1896, p. 3, trip to Montgomery delayed.
15. Louisville Courier-Journal, March 21, 1896, p. 3, exhibition games planned.
16. Louisville Courier-Journal, March 12, 1896, p. 5, readying the stadium.
17. Louisville Courier-Journal, March 11, 1896, p. 5, rivalry with Cinncinnati.
18. Louisville Courier-Journal, April 2, 1896, p. 6, skepticism over praise of the Colonels.
19. Louisville Courier-Journal, April 5, 1896, p. 11, moustaches not allowed.
20. Louisville Courier-Journal, April 3, 1896, p. 5, Holmes injured.
21. Louisville Courier-Journal, April 6, 1896, p. 5, exhibition games canceled.
22. Louisville Courier-Journal, April 12, 1896, p. 30, fans want free tickets.
23. Louisville Courier-Journal, April 14, 1896, p. 6, selling season tickets.
24. Louisville Courier-Journal, April 16, 1896, p. 6, new uniforms arrive.
25. Louisville Courier-Journal, April 17, 1896, p. 6, crowd at the opener.
26. Louisville Courier-Journal, April 20, 1896, p. 6, charter to Cincinnati.
27. Louisville Courier-Journal, April 26, 1896, p. 9, chance at redemption.
28. Louisville Courier-Journal, May 2, 1896, p. 4, home game against the Reds.
29. Louisville Courier-Journal, May 3, 1896, p. 6, pummeled by the Pirates.
30. Louisville Courier-Journal, May 4, 1896, p. 6, disappointing attendance.
31. Louisville Courier-Journal, May 8, 1896, p. 7, rumors about McCloskey.

32. Louisville Courier-Journal, May 9, 1896, p. 4, fining players for errors.
33. Louisville Courier-Journal, May 11, 1896, p. 6, McGunnigle takes over.
34. Louisville Courier-Journal, May 12, 1896, p. 2, installing discipline
35. Louisville Courier-Journal, May 15, 1896, p. 5, long home runs.
36. Louisville Courier-Journal, May 17, 1896, p. 10, blue flag on game days.
37. Louisville Courier-Journal, May 24, 1896, p. 8, leaving on a road trip.
38. Louisville Courier-Journal, June 14, 1896, p. 8, losing road trip
39. Louisville Courier-Journal, June 22, 1896, p. 6, mocking the team.
40. Louisville Courier-Journal, July 1, 1896, p. 6, alone in last place.
41. Louisville Courier-Journal, July 20, 1896, p. 6, honoring Charlie Dexter.
42. Louisville Courier-Journal, August 10, 1896, p. 8, Clarke arrested for assaulting an umpire.
43. Louisville Courier-Journal, August 11, 1896, p. 6, cases dismissed in court.
44. Baltimore Sun, September 8, 1896, p. 6, losing a tripleheader.
45. Louisville Courier-Journal, September 27, 1896, p. 11, losing to Cy Young.
46. Louisville Courier-Journal, October 1, 1896, p. 6, someone borrowed Harry's coat.
47. Louisville Courier-Journal, November 18, 1896, p. 6, Harry in the hospital.
48. Louisville Courier-Journal, December 20, 1896, p. 19, the baseball cannon.
49. Louisville Courier-Journal, December 30, 1896, p. 6, support for Harry to be team president.

Chapter Three

1. Louisville Courier-Journal, January 7, 1897, p. 6, Harry takes control of the Colonels.
2. Louisville Courier-Journal, January 8, 1897, p. 6, congratulations from Brush.
3. Louisville Courier-Journal, January 11, 1897, p. 6, acquiring players.
4. Louisville Courier-Journal, January 15, 1897, p. 4, negotiations with McCreery.
5. Louisville Courier-Journal, January 27, 1897, p. 6, money to strengthen the team.
6. Louisville Courier-Journal, January 25, 1897, p. 4, negotiations with other teams.
7. Louisville Courier-Journal, January 28, 1897, p. 6, franchise rumors.
8. Louisville Courier-Journal, February 3, 1897, p. 6, recruiting McGann.
9. Louisville Courier-Journal, February 17, 1897, p. 6, Dolan joins the team.
10. Louisville Courier-Journal, February 14, 1897, p. 11, Clarke still unsigned.
11. Louisville Courier-Journal, February 26, 1897, p. 6, money owed to McGunnigle.
12. Louisville Courier-Journal, February 27, 1897, p. 3, Rogers the new manager.
13. Louisville Courier-Journal, February 28, 1897, p. 10, league meeting.
14. Louisville Courier-Journal, March 9, 1897, p. 6, condition of the field.
15. Louisville Courier-Journal, March 10, 1897, p. 2, players begin arriving
16. Louisville Courier-Journal, March 13, 1897, p. 3, letters to players

17. Louisville Courier-Journal, March 19, 1897, p. 6, efforts to sign Clarke.
18. Louisville Courier-Journal, March 24, 1897, p. 6, spring practice.
19. Louisville Courier-Journal, March 30, 1897, p. 6, Clarke arrives at the hotel.
20. Louisville Courier-Journal, April 4, 1897, p. 10, no more free tickets.
21. Louisville Courier-Journal, April 6, 1897, p. 6, salary advances.
22. Louisville Courier-Journal, April 12, 1897, p. 6, meeting of owners.
23. Louisville Courier-Journal, April 23, 1897, p. 6, season opener.
24. Louisville Courier-Journal, April 24, 1897, p. 3, 500 copies of the newspaper.
25. Louisville Courier-Journal, April 30, 1897, p. 6, recruiting McMahon.
26. Baltimore Sun, May 7, 1897, p. 6, billiards.
27. Louisville Courier-Journal, May 17, 1897, p. 5, McGraw thrown out of game.
28. Louisville Courier-Journal, May 30, 1897, p. 11, Clarke becomes manager.
29. Louisville Courier-Journal, June 30, 1897, p. 6, injured Colonels.
30. Louisville Courier-Journal, July 1, 1897, p. 6, quote about injuries.
31. Louisville Courier-Journal, July 9, 1897, p. 6, Harry goes scouting.
32. Louisville Courier-Journal, July 10, 1897, p. 3, fight between Colonels and Orioles.
33. Chicago Tribune, July 17, 1897, p. 7, more shenanigans.
34. Chicago Tribune, July 18, 1897, p. 4, McGraw hit by pitch.
35. William Hageman, "Honus: The Life and Times of a Baseball Hero," Sagamore Pub. 1996.
36. Louisville Courier-Journal, July 16, 1897, p. 6, McGraw starts riot.
37. Louisville Courier-Journal, July 20, 1897, p. 6, Wagner's debut.
38. Louisville Courier-Journal, July 26, 1897, p. 6, Clarke carries second base to third.
39. Louisville Courier-Journal, July 27, 1897, p. 6, Clarke takes blame.
40. Louisville Courier-Journal, August 1, 1897, p. 9, pennant race update.
41. Louisville Courier-Journal, August 2, 1897, p. 6, quote about Wagner.
42. Louisville Courier-Journal, August 10, 1897, p. 6, Lynch hands out fines.
43. Louisville Courier-Journal, August 14, 1897, p. 3, Colonels travel to Pittsburg.
44. Louisville Courier-Journal, September 9, 1897, p. 6, new battery.
45. Louisville Courier-Journal, October 4, 1897, p. 6, Clarke presented a ring.
46. Louisville Courier-Journal, September 15, 1897, p. 6, Harry runs for office.
47. Louisville Courier-Journal, September 29, 1897, p. 6, fines collected.
48. Louisville Courier-Journal, November 18, 1897, p. 6, failure to improve the team.

Chapter Four

1. Louisville Courier-Journal, January 1898, p. 2, Harry introduces a bill.
2. Wyandotte Herald (KS), September 16, 1898, p. 1, info on Harry's bill.
3. Lenoir Times (NC), September 29, 1898, p. 1, quote about catching birds.
4. Louisville Courier-Journal, January 2, 1898, p. 11, cost cutting measures.
5. Louisville Courier-Journal, January 1, 1898, p. 3, new catchers.

6. Louisville Courier-Journal, January 23, 1898, p. 13, no spring trip.
7. Louisville Courier-Journal, February 28, 1898, p. 6, quote about Brush rule.
8. Louisville Courier-Journal, March 2, 1898, page 6, vote on Brush resolution.
9. Louisville Courier-Journal, March 3, 1898, p. 6, Harry's outburst.
10. Louisville Courier-Journal, February 24, 1898, p. 6, league meeting.
11. Louisville Courier-Journal, February 22, 1898, p. 6, quote about rowdy ball.
12. Louisville Courier-Journal, March 13, 1898, p. 3, quote about red-bird bill.
13. Washington Times, March 4, 1898, p. 6, quote from John McGraw.
14. Louisville Courier-Journal, March 14, 1898, p. 6, Clarke arrives.
15. Louisville Courier-Journal, March 16, 1898, p. 6, hot water fixture.
16. Louisville Courier-Journal, March 8, 1898, p. 6, Hoy joins the team.
17. Louisville Courier-Journal, March 23, 1898, p. 6, Colonels team goes on excursion.
18. Louisville Courier-Journal, March 27, 1898, p. 10, bat factory.
19. Louisville Courier-Journal, March 31, 1898, p. 8, sign language class.
20. Louisville Courier-Journal, April 6, 1898, p. 6, Harry and Clarke discuss finances.
21. Louisville Courier-Journal, April 10, 1898, p. 10, season opener.
22. Louisville Courier-Journal, April 15, 1898, p. 6, Brush amendment,
23. Louisville Courier-Journal, April 16, 1898, p. 4, ceremonial first pitch.
24. Louisville Courier-Journal, April 17, 1898, p. 11, kicking by Gleason.
25. Louisville Courier-Journal, May 1, 1898, p. 7, quote about Orioles kicking.
26. Louisville Courier-Journal, April 28, 1898, p. 5, bad start.
27. Louisville Courier-Journal, May 16, 1898, p. 6, hard luck Colonels.
28. Louisville Courier-Journal, May 17, 1898, p. 4, quote from Baltimore Herald.
29. Louisville Courier-Journal, May 22, 1898, p. 15, new mascot.
30. Louisville Courier-Journal, May 26, 1898, p. 6, Rusie pitches against Colonels.
31. Louisville Courier-Journal, May 31, 1898, p. 8, losses on Decoration Day.
32. Louisville Courier-Journal, June 3, 1898, p. 6, loss to Senators.
33. Louisville Courier-Journal, June 5, 1898, p. 5, evaluating Brush rules.
34. Louisville Courier-Journal, May 28, 1898, p. 4, Quote about Orioles kicking.
35. Philadelphia Inquirer, May 16, 1898, p. 4, McGraw on Brush rule.
36. Louisville Courier-Journal, June 19, 1898, p. 19, interest level in baseball.
37. Pittsburgh Press, June 16, 1898, p. 5, Harry threatens to sue Boston paper.
38. Louisville Courier-Journal, July 4, 1898, p. 6, response from Boston Herald.
39. Louisville Courier-Journal, July 1, 1898, p. 1, McGraw thrown out of game.
40. Louisville Courier-Journal, July 6, 1898, p. 6, Clarke gets married.
41. Louisville Courier-Journal, July 16, 1898, p. 10, moving game venues.
42. Louisville Courier-Journal, July 18, 1898, p. 6, fate of franchises.
43. Louisville Courier-Journal, July 20, 1898, p. 6, fans in Cleveland.
44. Louisville Courier-Journal, July 21, 1898, p. 6, 400 fans in Brooklyn.
45. Louisville Courier-Journal, July 22, 1898, p. 6, Altrock joins Colonels.
46. Louisville Courier-Journal, July 24, 1898, p. 13 Harry blamed for team losses.
47. Louisville Courier-Journal, July 26, 1898, p. 6, Ducky Holmes incident.

48. Louisville Courier-Journal, July 28, 1898, p. 6, quote from Holmes.
49. Louisville Courier-Journal, July 30, 1898, p. 4, Freedman bans Holmes from Polo Grounds.
50. Louisville Courier-Journal, August 16, 1898, p. 6, Harry recruits Phillippe.
51. Louisville Courier-Journal, August 21, 1898, p. 14, quote supporting Holmes.
52. Louisville Courier-Journal, August 26, 1898, p. 6, suspension of Holmes.
53. Louisville Courier-Journal, July 29, 1898, p. 6, winning streak.
54. Louisville Courier-Journal, August 4, 1898, p. 6, too many mascots.
55. Louisville Courier-Journal, September 8, 1898, p. 6, twelve errors.
56. Louisville Courier-Journal, September 23, 1898, p. 6, quote about low attendance.
57. Louisville Courier-Journal, September 14, 1898, p. 6, winning continues.
58. Louisville Courier-Journal, September 19, 1898, p. 6, Harry acquires Leach.
59. Louisville Courier-Journal, September 29, 1898, p. 8, debut of Leach.
60. Louisville Courier-Journal, October 6, 1898, p. 6, benefit game.
61. Louisville Courier-Journal, October 7, 1898, p. 6, game against Pittsburg.
62. Louisville Courier-Journal, October 10, 1898, p. 6, game called due to darkness.
63. Louisville Courier-Journal, October 17, 1898, p. 6, banquet at Gait House.
64. Louisville Courier-Journal, October 27, 1898, p. 6, Hoy gets married.
65. Louisville Courier-Journal, December 10, 1898, p. 4, Colonels for sale.
65. Chicago Tribune, December 16, 1898, p. 6.
66. Louisville Courier-Journal, December 17, 1898, p. 4, Baltimore players transferred to Brooklyn.
67. Louisville Courier-Journal, December 20, 1898, p. 6, quote from Harry.
68. Louisville Courier-Journal, September 24, 1898, p. 6, poem.

Chapter Five

1. Louisville Courier-Journal, January 1, 1899, page 8
2. Louisville Courier-Journal, January 4, 1899, page 6.
3. Louisville Courier-Journal, January 5, 1899, page 6.
4. Louisville Courier-Journal, January 8, 1899, page 16.
5. Louisville Courier-Journal, January 11, 1899, page 6.
6. Louisville Courier-Journal, January 15, 1899, page 17.
7. Louisville Courier-Journal, March 10, 1899, page 4.
8. Louisville Courier-Journal, January 13, 1899, page 4.
9. Louisville Courier-Journal, February 17, 1899, page 6.
10. Louisville Courier-Journal, February 19, 1899, page 17.
11. Louisville Courier-Journal, February 25, 1899, page 10.
12. Washington Times, February 25, 1899, page 6.
13. Louisville Courier-Journal, February 28, 1899, page 6.

14. Louisville Courier-Journal, March 2, 1899, page 6.
15. Louisville Courier-Journal, March 7, 1899, page 6.
16. Louisville Courier-Journal, March 18, 1899, page 10.
17. Louisville Courier-Journal, March 19, 1899, page 9.
18. Louisville Courier-Journal, March 21, 1899, page 6.
19. Louisville Courier-Journal, March 24, 1899, page 6.
20. Louisville Courier-Journal, March 26, 1899, page 20.
21. Louisville Courier-Journal, March 27, 1899, page 6.
22. Louisville Courier-Journal, March 29, 1899, page 6.
23. Louisville Courier-Journal, March 30, 1899, page 6.
24. Louisville Courier-Journal, April 1, 1899, page 10.
25. Louisville Courier-Journal, April 13, 1899, page 13.
26. Louisville Courier-Journal, April 15, 1899, page 10.
27. Louisville Courier-Journal, April 29, 1899, page 10.
28. Louisville Courier-Journal, May 2, 1899, page 8.
29. Louisville Courier-Journal, May 20, 1899, page 4.
30. Louisville Courier-Journal, May 22, 1899, page 6.
31. St. Louis Post-Dispatch, June 14, 1899, page 6.
32. Chicago Tribune, June 6, 1899, page 4.
33. Louisville Courier-Journal, June 29, 1899, page 8.
34. Louisville Courier-Journal, July 1, 1899, page 10.
35. Louisville Courier-Journal, July 2, 1899, page 7.
36. Louisville Courier-Journal, July 13, 1899, page 6.
37. Louisville Courier-Journal, July 17, 1899, page 6.
38. Louisville Courier-Journal, July 21, 1899, page 6.
39. Louisville Courier-Journal, July 24, 1899, page 6.
40. Louisville Courier-Journal, August 2, 1899, page 6.
41. Louisville Courier-Journal, August 5, 1899, page 10.
42. Louisville Courier-Journal, August 13, 1899, page 7.
43. Louisville Courier-Journal, August 17, 1899, page 6.
44. Louisville Courier-Journal, August 21, 1899, page 6.
45. Louisville Courier-Journal, August 23, 1899, page 6.
46. Philadelphia Inquirer, August 30, 1899, page 4.
47. Louisville Courier-Journal, September 3, 1899, page 6.
48. Louisville Courier-Journal, September 23, 1899, page 10.
49. Louisville Courier-Journal, October 18, 1899, page 8.
50. Louisville Courier-Journal, November 3, 1899, page 3.
51. Louisville Courier-Journal, November 21, 1899, page 8.
52. Louisville Courier-Journal, December 5, 1899, page 6.
53. Louisville Courier-Journal, December 8, 1899, page 6.
54. Louisville Courier-Journal. December 9, 1899, page 6.
55. Louisville Courier-Journal, December 10, 1899, page 11.
56. Louisville Courier-Journal, December 12, 1899, page 6.
57. Louisville Courier-Journal, December 14, 1899, page 8.
58. Louisville Courier-Journal, September 24, 1898, page 3, poem.

Chapter Six

1. Louisville Courier-Journal, January 6, 1900, p. 10, Harry has malarial fever.
2. Pittsburgh Post-Gazette, January 9, 1900, p. 6, new office in Pittsburg.
3. Pittsburgh Press, January 17, 1900, p. 1, rumor about Harry managing the Colts.
4. Pittsburgh Post-Gazette, January 26, 1900, p. 6, Harry unsure about future.
5. Pittsburgh Post-Gazette, February 1, 1900, p. 6, resigns from legislature.
6. Louisville Courier-Journal, February 18, 1900, p. 9, become secretary of the Pirates.
7. Pittsburgh Post-Gazette, February 19, 1900, p. 4, wearing two hats.
8. Pittsburgh Press, February 26, 1900, p. 5, quote from Harry,
9. Pittsburgh Daily Post, March 1, 1900, p. 6, spring practice.
10. Pittsburgh Press, March 4, 1900, p. 12, league meeting.
11. Pittsburgh Daily Post, March 9, 1900, p. 6, reduction of National League.
12. Pittsburgh Post-Gazette, March 12, 1900, p. 6, Harry returns to Pittsburg.
13. Pittsburgh Daily Post, March 15, 1900, p. 6, Waddell on the train.
14. Pittsburgh Press, March 16, 1900, p. 5, quote about fans of Colonels.
15. Pittsburgh Post-Gazette, March 17, 1900, p. 6, no rooms at the hotel.
16. Pittsburgh Press, March 25, 1900, p. 13, games in Louisville.
17. Pittsburgh Post-Gazette, March 28, 1900, p. 6, leaving early.
18. Pittsburgh Press, April 3, 1900, p. 10, exhibition games.
19. Pittsburgh Press, April 12, 1900, p. 5, small gate in Louisville.
20. Pittsburgh Daily Post, April 18, 1900, p. 6, opening games.
21. Pittsburgh Press, April 20, 1900, p. 5, the "new Pirates."
22. Pittsburgh Daily Post, April 27, 1900, p. 6, home opener.
23. Pittsburgh Post-Gazette, April 27, 1900, p. 1, attendance at opener.
24. Pittsburgh Post-Gazette, May 1, 1900, p. 5, quote about counting money.
25. Pittsburgh Press, June 1, 1900, p. 5, quote about Waddell.
26. Pittsburgh Press, June 3, 1900, p. 14, game in the rain.
27. Pittsburgh Press, June 4, 1900, p. 5, Harry attends church.
28. Pittsburgh Press, June 8, 1900, p. 5, quote about Waddell.
29. Pittsburgh Press, June 18, 1900, p. 5, Clarke tries to return.
30. Pittsburgh Post-Gazette, June 23, 1900, p. 5, quote about finances of the Pittsburg team.
31. Pittsburgh Post-Gazette, June 28, 1900, p. 6, Waddell disappears.
32. Pittsburgh Press, July 7, 1900, p. 8, Waddell suspended.
33. Pittsburgh Post-Gazette, July 10, 1900, p. 6, Waddell leaves.
34. Pittsburgh Press, July 12, 1900, p. 5, quote about Waddell.
35. Pittsburgh Press, July 5, 1900, p. 5, Independence Day game.
36. Pittsburgh Press, May 15, 1900, p. 5, ball hits Wagner on top of head.
37. Pittsburgh Post-Gazette, July 13, 1900, p. 6, Clarke Returns.
38. Pittsburgh Post-Gazette, July 14, 1900, p. 6, Pirates outslug Quakers.
39. Pittsburgh Post-Gazette, July 26, 1900, p. 6, players repair field in the rain.

40. Pittsburgh Post-Gazette, August 11, 1900, p. 6, crate of dogs.
41. Pittsburgh Press, August 16, 1900, p. 5, series against Brooklyn.
42. Pittsburgh Post-Gazette, August 17, 1900, p. 6, pitching of McGinnity.
43. Pittsburgh Post-Gazette, August 18, 1900, p. 6, game against Brooklyn.
44. Pittsburgh Press, August 19, 1900, p. 14, rematch against McGinnity.
45. Pittsburgh Post-Gazette, August 22, 1900, p. 6, practice on an off day.
46. Pittsburgh Press, September 3, 1900, p. 5, Waddell returns.
47. Pittsburgh Post-Gazette, September 5, 1900, p. 6, Wagner steals home.
48. Pittsburgh Press, September 7, 1900, p. 6, games against Brooklyn.
49. Pittsburgh Press, September 20, 1900, p. 5, large crowd greets Pirates.
50. Pittsburgh Post-Gazette, September 25, 1900, p. 6, Waddell vs. Young.
51. Pittsburgh Press, September 26, 1900, p. 5, update on pennant race.
52. Chicago Journal, September 27, 1900, p. 6, poem.
53. Pittsburgh Press, September 28, 1900, p. 5, last Sunday game.
54. Pittsburgh Post-Gazette, September 29, 1900, p. 6, momentum gone.
55. Pittsburgh Post-Gazette, October 2, 1900, p. 6, treatment of Waddell.
56. Pittsburgh Post-Gazette, October 8, 1900, p. 6, fans attack Emslie.
57. Pittsburgh Press, October 15, 1900, p. 5, season ends.
58. Pittsburgh Daily Post, December 14, 1900, p. 6, league meeting.
59. Pittsburgh Press, November 21, 1900, p. 5, rumors about Harry leaving.
60. Pittsburgh Press, December 16, 1900, p. 14, attempts to replace Harry.
61. Pittsburgh Press, December 22, 1900, p. 5, Harry speaks to press.

Chapter Seven

1. Pittsburgh Post-Gazette, January 18, 1901, p. 6, American Assoc. formed.
2. Pittsburgh Post-Gazette, March 4, 1901, p. 6, fight for players.
3. Pittsburgh Post-Gazette, January 22, 1901, p. 6, Harry returns as secretary.
4. Pittsburgh Post-Gazette, February 5, 1901, p. 6, death of O'Brien.
5. Pittsburgh Post-Gazette, January 4, 1901, p. 6, reduction of rosters.
6. Pittsburgh Post-Gazette, March 7, 1901, p. 6, Wagner signs contract.
7. Pittsburgh Post-Gazette, March 9, 1901, p. 6, Tannehill and Ely sign.
8. Pittsburgh Post-Gazette, March 14, 1901, p. 6, bird shoot.
9. Pittsburgh Post-Gazette, March 28, 1901, p. 6, Mack approaches Waddell.
10. Pittsburgh Post-Gazette, March 16, 1901, p. 6, vampire as a mascot.
11. Pittsburgh Post-Gazette, April 1, 1901, p. 6, quote about McGraw.
12. Pittsburgh Post-Gazette, April 10, 1901, p. 6, Harry as an umpire.
13. Pittsburgh Post-Gazette, April 13, 1901, p. 6, description of legislature.
14. Pittsburgh Post-Gazette, May 6, 1901, p. 6, Pirates defeat Waddell.
15. Pittsburgh Press, May 10, 1901, p. 1, update on injury to Clarke.
16. Pittsburgh Press, May 23, 1901, p. 8, criticism of Mathewson.
17. Pittsburgh Post-Gazette, May 24, 1901, p. 6, Wagner hits ball into train car.
18. Pittsburgh Post-Gazette, May 30, 1901, p. 6, flooding in Pittsburg.
19. Pittsburgh Press, June 1, 1901, p. 8, attendance up.
20. Pittsburgh Press, June 2, 1901, p. 18, fans rush umpire.

21. Pittsburgh Post-Gazette, June 1, 1901, p. 6, Orioles forfeit game in Detroit.
22. Pittsburgh Press, June 2, 1901, p. 18, notes on game between Pirates and Reds.
23. Pittsburgh Press, June 12, 1901, p. 8, rain helps Pirates beat Mathewson.
24. Pittsburgh Post-Gazette, July 8, 1901, p. 6, ticket speculation.
25. Pittsburgh Press, July 28, 1901, p. 17, attendance remains strong.
26. Pittsburgh Press, July 31, 1901, p. 8, a week of vacation.
27. Pittsburgh Post-Gazette, August 2, 1901, p. 8, mystery player.
28. Pittsburgh Press, August 5, 1901, p. 1, Leever offers to forego pay.
29. Pittsburgh Press, August 18, 1901, p. 17, Harry on vacation.
30. Pittsburgh Post-Gazette, August 17, 1901, p. 8, Wagner in Atlantic City.
31. Pittsburgh Post-Gazette, August 30, 1901, p. 8, Waddell is a no-show.
32. Pittsburgh Press, September 1, 1901, p. 16, rumor about Waddell.
33. Pittsburgh Press, September 14, 1901, p. 8, update on pennant race.
34. Pittsburgh Press, September 28, 1901, p. 3, plans for season finale.
35. Pittsburgh Press, September 28, 1901, p. 8, fan wants fifty cents to see game.
36. Pittsburgh Press, October 3, 1901, p. 8, Pirates win celebration game.
37. Pittsburgh Post-Gazette, October 4, 1901, p. 4, exhibition series not played.
38. Pittsburgh Press, October 16, 1901, season ending banquet.
39. Pittsburgh Press, November 24, 1901, p. 5, quote about Harry.
40. Pittsburgh Press, December 8, 1901, p. 22, league meeting.
41. Pittsburgh Press, December 21, 1901, p. 1, Dreyfuss quote about Harry.
42. The Sporting News, December 28, 1901, support of Harry to be league president.

Chapter Eight

1. Pittsburgh Press, January 12, 1902, p. 18, Harry's winter travels.
2. Pittsburgh Press, January 28, 1902, p. 11, damage to diamond stud.
3. Cincinnati Enquirer, January 15, 1902, p. 12, quote about Spalding.
4. Pittsburgh Press, February 22, 1902, p. 12, meeting of magnates in Pittsburg.
5. Pittsburgh Press, April 3, 1902, p. 12, Spalding resigns.
6. Pittsburgh Weekly Gazette, April 6, 1902, p. 14, Harry not interested in presidency of National League.
7. Pittsburgh Press, April 7, 1902, p. 10, Harry as a storyteller.
8. Pittsburgh Weekly Gazette, April 7, 1902, p. 8, flag pole erected.
9. Pittsburgh Press, April 20, 1902, p. 21, pans for raising championship flag.
10. Pittsburgh Press, April 23, 1902, p. 12, opening day crowd.
11. Pittsburgh Press, April 28, 1902, p. 10, world trip for winning pennant.
12. Pittsburgh Press, May 19, 1902, p. 10, Cubs' star players.
13. Pittsburgh Press, June 3, 1902, p. 10, winning 30 of first 36 games.
14. Pittsburgh Press, June 12, 1902, p. 12, rumors of Wagner and O'Connor leaving.
15. Pittsburgh Press, June 24, 1902, p. 12, fight between Conroy and Tinker.

16. Pittsburgh Press, June 29, 1902, p. 22, quote about Harry's wardrobe.
17. Pittsburgh Press, July 24, 1902, p. 12, Ban Johnson interested in the Pirates.
18. Pittsburgh Press, July 28, 1902, p. 10, Cardinal fans assault Pirates.
19. The Sporting News, August 1902, details of the assault on the Pirates.
20. Pittsburgh Press, August 15, 1902, p. 1, quote from Harry on sale of the Reds.
21. Pittsburgh Weekly Gazette, August 17, 1902, p. 3, coal miners sing at Exposition Park.
22. Pittsburgh Weekly Gazette, August 21, 1902, p.1, Johnson and Somers try to steal players.
23. Pittsburgh Press, September 3, 1902, p. 10, quote from Harry about Ban Johnson.
24. Pittsburgh Press, September 30, 1902, p. 12, Harr signs Leach and Conroy.
25. Pittsburgh Weekly Gazette, August 26, 1902, p. 8, leads reaches 21 games.
26. Pittsburgh Press, October 5, 1902, p. 19, win #103 on last day of the season.
27. Pittsburgh Press, November 16, 1902, p. 21, Harry meets with Johnson.
28. Pittsburgh Press, November 16, 1902, p. 20, quote from Ben Shibe.
29. Pittsburgh Press, November 30, 1902, p. 20, Harry's plan to end contract jumping.
30. Pittsburgh Press, December 8, 1902, p. 10, Harry attends winter meetings.
31. Pittsburgh Press, December 9, 1902, p. 16, notes on the winter meeting.
32. Pittsburgh Press, December 10, 1902, p. 16, American League franchise in Pittsburg.
33. Pittsburgh Press, December 11, 1902, p. 16, rumor of Harry being considered for National League presidency.
34. Pittsburgh Press, December 13, 1902, p. 10, Harry becomes president of National League.
35. Pittsburgh Press, December 14, 1902, p. 20, quotes about Harry.
36. Pittsburgh Press, December 21, 1902, p. 18, Harry returns to Kentucky.
37. Pittsburgh Press, December 31, 1902, p. 10, quote from Harry about the baseball wars.

Chapter Nine

1. Pittsburgh Press, January 2, 1903, page 16.
2. Cincinnati Enquirer, January 1, 1903, page 4.
3. St. Louis Post-Dispatch, January 2, 1903, page 8.
4. Pittsburgh Press, January 4, 1903, page 6.
5. St. Louis Post-Dispatch, January 4, 1903, page 18.
6. Pittsburgh Press, January 5, 1903, page 1.
7. Chicago Tribune, January 6, 1903, page 6.
8. Chicago Tribune, January 8, 1903, page 10.
9. Philadelphia Inquirer, January 10, 1903, page 10.
10. Louisville Courier-Journal, January 11, 1903, page 26.
11. Pittsburgh Press, January 11, 1903, page 18.

12. Louisville Courier-Journal, January 12, 1903, page 6.
13. Philadelphia Inquirer, January 14, 1903, page 10.
14. Louisville Courier-Journal, January 17, 1903, page 8.
15. Cincinnati Enquirer, January 18, 1903, page 10.
16. Chicago Tribune, January 19, 1903, page 10.
17. Pittsburgh Press, January 21, 1903, page 12.
18. Louisville Courier-Journal, January 22, 1903, page 9.
19. Philadelphia Inquirer, January 22, 1903, page 10.
20. New York Times, January 27, 1903, page 10.
21. Cincinnati Enquirer, January 31, 1903, page 3.
22. Cincinnati Enquirer, February 1, 1903, page 3.
23. Pittsburgh Press, February 16, 1903, page 10.
24. Pittsburgh Press, February 17, 1903, page 12.
25. Chicago Tribune, February 24, 1903, page 7.
26. Chicago Tribune, March 5, 1903, page 6.
27. Pittsburgh Press, March 9, 1903, page 11.
28. Bill Lamb, SABR article online.
29. New York Times, March 14, 1903.
30. Harold Seymour, "Baseball: The Golden Age," Oxford Univ. Press, 1971.
31. Philadelphia Enquirer, March 21, 1903, page 10.
32. Chicago Tribune, March 22, 1903, page 13.
33. Pittsburgh Press, April 5, 1903, page 20.
34. Pittsburgh Press, March 29, 1903, page 20.
35. Pittsburgh Press, May 2, 1903, page 12.
36. St. Louis Post-Dispatch, April 10, 1903, page 15.
37. St. Louis Post-Dispatch, April 14, 1903, page 6.
38. Pittsburgh Press, April 15, 1903, page 14.
39. Pittsburgh Press, April 21, 1903, page 21.
40. Chicago Tribune, April 26, 1903, page 14.
41. Pittsburgh Press, April 19, 1903, page 18.
42. Pittsburgh Press, May 9, 1903, page 10.
43. Chicago Tribune, May 9, 1903, page 7.
44. Pittsburgh Press, May 14, 1903, page 18.
45. Pittsburgh Press, May 21, 1903, page 18.
46. Louisville Courier-Journal, May 26, 1903, page 9.
47. St. Louis Post-Dispatch, August 2, 1903, page 21.
48. Pittsburgh Press, May 17, 1903, page 1.
49. Pittsburgh Press, July 12, 1903, page 20.
50. New York Times, July 21, 1903, page 7.
51. Louisville Courier-Journal, July 23, 1903, page 9.
52. Pittsburgh Press, July 29, 1903, page 12.
53. Pittsburgh Press, August 3, 1903, page 10.
54. Louisville Courier-Journal, August 27, 1903, page 7.
55. Pittsburgh Press, September 3, 1903, page 4.
56. Philadelphia Inquirer, August 10, 1903, page 1.

57. Pittsburgh Press, October 1, 1903, page 12.
58. Pittsburgh Press, October 2, 1903, page 20.
59. Cincinnati Enquirer, November 22, 1903, page 34.
60. Louisville Courier-Journal, December 6, 1903, page 23.
61. Louisville Courier-Journal, December 9, 1903, page 6.

Chapter Ten

1. Cincinnati Enquirer, January 4, 1904, p. 3, quote from Harry about theater fire.
2. Louisville Courier-Journal, January 8, 1904, p. 7, salaries of baseball players.
3. Cincinnati Enquirer, January 7, 1904, p. 4, Highlanders' plan to move Sunday games.
4. Pittsburgh Press, January 7, 1904, p. 10, Brooklyn team files protest.
5. Cincinnati Enquirer, January 15, 1904, p. 4, Ridgewood Park dispute.
6. Louisville Courier-Journal, January 31, 1904, p. 20, Harry considers buying Boston team.
7. Philadelphia Inquirer, February 2, 1904, p. 6, Harry denies interest in buying Boston team.
8. Pittsburgh Press, February 8, 1904, p. 10, salary cuts for players.
9. Cincinnati Enquirer, February 12, 1904, p. 4, Baseball Commission meets.
10. Cincinnati Enquirer, February 14, 1904, p. 8, quote from Garry Herrmann.
11. New York Times, February 19, 1904, p. 6, resolution of Ridgewood Park dispute.
12. Philadelphia Inquirer, March 4, 1904, p. 10, Baseball Commission rules on Ridgewood Park dispute.
13. Philadelphia Inquirer, March 9, 1904, p. 10, dispute over schedule conflicts.
14. Philadelphia Inquirer, March 10, 1904, p. 10, quote from Harry about Ban Johnson.
15. Louisville Courier-Journal, March 10, 1904, p. 6, quote about schedule disputes.
16. Pittsburgh Press, May 4, 1904, p. 11, quote from Harry about drinking whiskey.
17. Pittsburgh Press, May 8, 1904, p. 20, Harry tours New Bedford, Mass.
18. Cincinnati Enquirer, May 16, 1904, p. 3, tour of the National League circuit.
19. Pittsburgh Press, May 18, 1904, p. 10, suspension of Joe Kelley.
20. St. Louis Post-Dispatch, May 22, 1904, p. 23, Harry's all-star team.
21. Pittsburgh Press, June 3, 1904, p. 20, broom for home plate.
22. Charles Alexander, "John McGraw," University of Nebraska Press, 1988.
23. Louisville Courier-Journal, September 28, 1904, page 7.
24. Philadelphia Inquirer, August 1, 1904, p. 10, quote about the prospects of a world series.
25. Pittsburgh Press, August 17, 1904, p. 8, Kelley suspended again.
26. Pittsburgh Press, August 22, 1904, p. 8, Harry on vacation at Saratoga.
27. Cincinnati Enquirer, August 5, 1904, p. 4, quote from Goldfish Dooin.

28. Pittsburgh Press, August 28, 1904, p. 20, mottoes on the wall of Harry's office.
29. Pittsburgh Press, September 22, 1904, p. 12, Harry travels to London without Hart.
30. Pittsburgh Press, September 25, 1904, p. 21, Harry on the verge of a breakdown.

Chapter Eleven

1. Cincinnati Enquirer, January 1, 1905, p. 33, attendance in both leagues.
2. Philadelphia Inquirer, January 8, 1905, p. 14, Harry optimistic about Pirates.
3. Philadelphia Inquirer, January 9, 1905, p. 10, Harry falls ill.
4. Cincinnati Enquirer, January 9, 1905, p. 6, details about illness.
5. Louisville Courier-Journal, January 9, 1905, p. 6, illness update.
6. Louisville Courier-Journal, January 10, 1905, p. 6, meeting of magnates.
7. Pittsburgh Press, January 15, 1905, p. 18, Dreyfuss cares for Harry.
8. Cincinnati Enquirer, January 11, 1905, p. 4, Harry recovers.
9. Louisville Courier-Journal, January 14, 1905, p. 9, no spring championship series.
10. Pittsburgh Press, April 2, 1905, p. 18, Harry targets rowdyism.
11. St. Louis Post-Dispatch, April 9, 1905, p. 23, millionaires in the bleachers.
12. St. Louis Post-Dispatch, May 21, 1905, p. 23, kicking on the rise.
13. St. Louis Post-Dispatch, April 24, 1905, p. 8, McGann attacks Abbott.
14. Cincinnati Enquirer, April 25, 1905, p. 4, Harry suspends McGann.
15. Chicago Tribune, April 25, 1905, p. 6, fans attack Giants.
16. Pittsburgh Press, May 22, 1905, p. 10, Clarke on McGraw.
17. Pittsburgh Press, May 23, 1905, p. 14, Clarke files protest.
18. Pittsburgh Press, May 24, 1905, p. 10, quote from McGraw.
19. St. Louis Post-Dispatch, May 24, 1905, p. 6, Dreyfuss on McGraw.
20. St. Louis Post-Dispatch, May 27, 1905, p. 1, McGraw suspended and fined.
21. Chicago Tribune, May 28, 1905, p. 2, Brush defends McGraw.
22. Philadelphia Inquirer, May 29, 1905, p. 10, New York press defends McGraw.
23. St. Louis Post-Dispatch, May 29, 1905, p. 8, quote from Harry.
24. St. Louis Post-Dispatch, June 2, 1905, p. 14, McGraw exonerated.
25. Philadelphia Inquirer, June 2, 1905, p. 10, McGraw speaks out.
26. Pittsburgh Press, June 3, 1905, p. 4, Harry reacts to McGraw.
27. St. Louis Post-Dispatch, June 5, 1905, p. 8, injunction against Harry.
28. Pittsburgh Press, June 7, 1905, p. 1, McGraw boasts.
29. St. Louis Post-Dispatch, June 13, 1905, p. 16, McGraw wins again.
30. Philadelphia Inquirer, June 12, 1905, p. 10, quote about Harry.
31. St. Louis Post-Dispatch, June 15, 1905, p. 16, rift between Harry and Dreyfuss.
32. Philadelphia Inquirer, June 15, 1905, p. 5, quote from Harry.

33. Louisville Courier-Journal, July 30, 1905, p. 32, Dreyfuss threatens to leave National League.
34. Pittsburgh Post, July 31, 1905, p. 10, criticisms of Harry.
35. Philadelphia Inquirer, August 6, 1905, p. 14, McGraw predicts Harry will not be re-elected.
36. St. Louis Post-Dispatch, August 2, 1905, p. 5, better record keeping.
37. Pittsburgh Press, August 6, 1905, p. 18, another incident with McGraw.
38. Pittsburgh Press, August 27, 1905, p. 20, forfeiture would stand.
39. Cincinnati Enquirer, September 17, 1905, p. 33, World Series gate receipts.
40. Philadelphia Inquirer, October 4, 1905, p. 15, rules for World Series.
41. Louisville Courier-Journal, October 11, 1905, p. 6, Dreyfuss skips World Series.
42. Chicago Tribune, November 7, 1905, p. 6, letters to Murphy and Hart.
43. Cincinnati Enquirer, December 12, 1905, p. 4, plan to replace Pulliam.
44. Louisville Courier-Journal, December 12, 1905, p. 6, quote about plan to replace Harry.
45. Pittsburgh Press, December 12, 1905, p. 18, notes about league meeting.
46. Cincinnati Enquirer, December 14, 1905, p. 4, Harry re-elected.
47. Pittsburgh Press, December 15, 1905, p. 28, Harry given power to set fines and suspensions.
48. Chicago Tribune, December 15, 1905, p. 10, quote from Hart.

Chapter Twelve

1. Chicago Tribune, October 9, 1906, page 2.
2. Pittsburgh Press, January 5, 1906, page 20.
3. Pittsburgh Press, January 7, 1906, page 19.
4. New York Times, January 6, 1906, page 7.
5. Pittsburgh Press, February 3, 1906, page 8.
6. New York Sun, January 10, 1906.
7. Chicago Tribune, January 19, 1906, page 10.
8. Cincinnati Enquirer, April 12, 1906, page 4.
9. Pittsburgh Press, May 12, 1906, page 10
10. Pittsburgh Press, June 2, 1906, page 10.
11. Cincinnati Enquirer, June 13, 1906, page 4.
12. Pittsburgh Press, June 14, 1906, page 4.
13. Pittsburgh Press, July 5, 1906, page 14.
14. Chicago Tribune, July 22, 1906, page 1.
15. Louisville Courier-Journal, July 31, 1906, page 2.
16. Pittsburgh Press, August 1, 1906, page 11.
17. Chicago Tribune, August 1, 1906, page 6.
18. Pittsburgh Press, August 3, 1906, page 16.
19. Charles Dryden, Pittsburgh Press, August 4, 1906, page 8.
20. Pittsburgh Press, August 7, 1906, page 12.
21. Pittsburgh Press, August 11, 1906, page 8.

22. Pittsburgh Press, August 8, 1906, page 10.
23. Chicago Tribune, August 12, 1906, page 2.
24. Pittsburgh Press, August 25, 1906, page 8.
25. Cincinnati Enquirer, October 15, 1906, page 3.
26. Pittsburgh Press, December 2, 1906, page 21.
27. Philadelphia Inquirer, December 10, 1906, page 10.
28. Pittsburgh Press, December 13, 1906, page 14.
29. Louisville Courier-Journal, December 23, 1906, page 29.

Chapter Thirteen

1. Cincinnati Enquirer, October 4, 1905, page 15.
2. Chicago Tribune, March 26, 1907, page 8.
3. Louisville Courier-Journal, March 27, 1907, page 2.
4. Ralph S. Davis, Pittsburgh Press, January 6, 1907, page 21.
5. Cincinnati Enquirer, January 30, 1907, page 4.
6. Pittsburgh Press, April 17, 1907, page 1.
7. Pittsburgh Press, May 16, 1907, page 18.
8. Pittsburgh Press, May 3, 1907, page 26.
9. Pittsburgh Press, April 22, 1907, page 24.
10. Pittsburgh Press, May 15, 1907, page 14.
11. St. Louis Post-Dispatch, May 28, 1907, page 14.
12. Pittsburgh Press, May 19, 1907, page 19.
13. Pittsburgh Press, May 24, 1907, page 26.
14. St. Louis Post-Dispatch, June 13, 1907, page 16.
15. Philadelphia Inquirer, May 22, 1907, page 9.
16. Pittsburgh Press, May 25, 1907, page 8.
17. Philadelphia Inquirer, July 12, 1907, page 10.
18. Chicago Tribune, July 15, 1907, page 8.
19. New York Times, September 17, 1907, page 9.
20. Philadelphia Inquirer, September 24, 1907, page 2.
21. Pittsburgh Press, September 26, 1907, page 14.
22. The Pittsburgh Press, September 29, 1907, page 20.
23. St. Louis Post-Dispatch, October 7, 1907, page 10.
24. Philadelphia Inquirer, October 7, 1907, page 10.
25. Chicago Tribune, October 8, 1907, page 8.
26. Pittsburgh Press, November 7, 1907, page 18.
27. St. Louis Post-Dispatch, November 8, 1907, page 16.
28. Cincinnati Enquirer, November 12, 1907, page 4.
29. St. Louis Post-Dispatch, November 13, 1907, page 7.
30. Pittsburgh Press, December 1, 1907, page 18.
31. Philadelphia Inquirer, December 11, 1907, page 10.
32. Pittsburgh Press, December 11, 1907, page 14.
33. St. Louis Post-Dispatch, December 12, 1907, page 16.
34. Pittsburgh Press, December 14, 1907, page 8.

35. Pittsburgh Press, December 23, 1907, page 12.

Chapter Fourteen

1. Pittsburgh Press, February 15, 1904, page 10.
2. Pittsburgh Press, February 18, 1908, page 8.
3. Cincinnati Enquirer, February 27, 1908, page 4.
4. Pittsburgh Press, February 27, 1908, page 8.
5. Cincinnati Enquirer, February 29, 1908, page 3.
6. New York Times, March 1, 1908, page 30.
7. St. Louis Post-Dispatch, March 7, 1908, page 6.
8. Pittsburgh Press, March 16, 1908, page 8.
9. Pittsburgh Press, March 21, 1908, page 5.
10. Pittsburgh Press, April 14, 1908, page 14.
11. Pittsburgh Press, April 26, 1908, page 21.
12. Pittsburgh Press, May 11, 1908, page 12.
13. Cincinnati Enquirer, June 16, 1908, page 4.
14. Cincinnati Enquirer, June 17, 1908, page 4.
15. Pittsburgh Press, June 20, 1908, page 8.
16. St. Louis Post-Dispatch, July 1, 1908, page 7.
17. Pittsburgh Press, August 16, 1908, page 17.
18. Cincinnati Enquirer, August 7, 1908, page 4.
19. Pittsburgh Press, September 5, 1908, page 7.
20. Chicago Tribune, September 6, 1908, page 1.
21. Pittsburgh Press, September 10, 1908, page 1.
22. Louisville Courier-Journal, September 24, 1908, page 7.
23 William A. Cook, "August 'Garry' Herrmann: A Baseball Biography," McFarland & Company, Inc., 2008.
24. St. Louis Post-Dispatch, September 24, 1908, page 14.
25. New York Times, September 25, 1908, page 8.
26. Louisville Courier-Journal, September 25, 1908, page 6.
27. St. Louis Post-Dispatch, October 2, 1908, page 16.
28. New York Times, October 3, 1908, page 7.
29. St. Louis Post-Dispatch, October 3, 1908, page 6.
30. Philadelphia Inquirer, October 5, 1908, page 1.
31. Peter Golenbock, "Wrigleyville: A Magical History Tour of the Chicago Cubs," St. Martin's Griffin, 1999.
32. Pittsburgh Press, October 6, 1908, page 1.
33. Charles Alexander, "John McGraw," University of Nebraska Press, 1988.
34. Philadelphia Inquirer, October 9, 1908, page 10.
35. Peter Golenbock, "Wrigleyville: A Magical History Tour of the Chicago Cubs," St. Martin's Griffin, 1999.
36. Charles Alexander, "John McGraw," University of Nebraska Press, 1988.
37. William A. Cook, "August 'Garry' Herrmann: A Baseball Biography," McFarland & Company, Inc. 2008.

38. Louisville Courier-Journal, October 10, 1908, page 10.
39. Cincinnati Enquirer, September 25, 1908, page 4.
40. Charles Alexander, "John McGraw," University of Nebraska Press, 1988.
41. Cincinnati Enquirer, December 9, 1908, page 8.
42. Philadelphia Inquirer, December 12, 1908, page 10.
43. Chicago Tribune, December 15, 1908, page 12.
44. Philadelphia Inquirer, December 15, 1908, page 10.
45. Cincinnati Enquirer, December 28, 1908, page 6.

Chapter Fifteen

1. Pittsburgh Press, October 18, 1906, p. 14, quote from Harry about the future of baseball.
2. Louisville Courier-Journal, January 6, 1909, p. 8, Harry visits Louisville.
3. Pittsburgh Press, January 8, 1909, p. 22, Harry visits family of Edward McLaughlin.
4. Pittsburgh Press, January 11, 1909, p. 12, quote from Harry about his job.
5. Louisville Courier-Journal, January 17, 1909, p. 31, notes on the committee on bribery.
6. Philadelphia Inquirer, January 25, 1909, p. 6, movement to assist Cap Anson.
7. Pittsburgh Press, February 3, 1909, p. 8, quote from Cap Anson.
8. Pittsburgh Press, February 9, 1909, p. 15, Charles Murphy accuses Harry.
9. Cincinnati Enquirer, February 13, 1909, p. 3, quote from Harry regarding Murphy.
10. Cincinnati Enquirer, February 15, 1909, p. 4, Harry refuses dinner with George Dovey.
11. St. Louis Post-Dispatch, February 15, 1909, p. 8, accusatory quotes from Harry regarding Murphy.
12. Cincinnati Enquirer, February 17, 1909, p. 4, Harry hosts a dinner for the Baseball Writers of American.
13. St. Louis Post-Dispatch, February 18, 1909, p. 14, Harry loses control at the dinner.
14. Philadelphia Inquirer, February 18, 1909, p. quote from Harry about his job.
15. St. Louis Post-Dispatch, February 19, 1909, p. 12, Harry granted leave of absence.
16. New York Times, February 19, 1909, p. 10, quote about Harry's health.
17. Cincinnati Enquirer, February 19, 1909, p. 4, Harry leaves for St. Louis.
18. Louisville Courier-Journal, February 20, 1909, p. 9, Harry claims he is going to get married.
19. Chicago Tribune, February 21, 1909, p. 2, denies he is getting married.
20. Cincinnati Enquirer, March 5, 1909, p. 8, Harry recuperates in Florida.
21. Philadelphia Inquirer, April 11, 1909, p. 8, operation on Harry's eye is a success.
22. Pittsburgh Press, April 17, 1909, p. 12, Harry attends game in Cincinnati.

23. Cincinnati Enquirer, May 23, 1909, Murphy promotes Anson for president of the National League.
24. St. Louis Post-Dispatch, May 26, 1909, p. 7, Herrmann supports Harry.
25. Cincinnati Enquirer, May 28, 1909, p. 4, meeting of magnates.
26. Chicago Tribune, June 5, 1909, p. 10, Harry's leave of absence.
27. New York Times, June 27, 1909, p. 29, Harry will return to his job.
28. Pittsburgh Press, June 19, 1909, p. 1, George Dovey dies.
29. Pittsburgh Press, June 30, 1909, p. 1, Harry attends dedication of Forbes Field.
30. Cincinnati Enquirer, July 17, 1909, p. 9, Harry issues a bulletin.
31. Louisville Courier-Journal, July 29, 1909, p. 1, details of Harry's suicide.
32. New York Times, July 29, 1909, p. 1, details of Harry's suicide.
33. New York Times, July 30, 1909, p. 14, quote about Harry's last day.
34. Louisville Courier-Journal, July 30, 1909, p. 1, letter from Harry's sister.
35. Cincinnati Enquirer, July 30, 1909, p. 4, Flags lowered to half-mast.
36. Louisville Courier-Journal, July 30, 1909, p. 1, notice of death.
38. Philadelphia Inquirer, July 30, 1909, p. 10, reaction to Harry's death.
37. Louisville Courier-Journal, July 31, 1909, p. 4, train carrying the body.
38. Cincinnati Enquirer, August 3, 1909, p. 4, coverage of the funeral.
39. New York Times, August 3, 1909, p. 8, monument for Harry.
40. Philadelphia Inquirer, July 30, 1909, page 10, funeral arrangements.
41. Louisville Courier-Journal, August 2, 1909, p. 4, quote about Harry's sensitive nature.
42. Cincinnati Enquirer, October 8, 1909, p. 8, statement from National Commission.
43. Pittsburgh Press, August 10, 1909, p. 12, article about Harry and Hugh Jennings.

Index

Abbott, Fred, 181
Abell, Ferdinand, 88
Alberta, Laura, 24
Altrock Nick, 71
Ames, Leon, 193
Angus, S.F., 143
Anson, Cap, 6, 7, 16, 18, 27, 37, 64, 228, 232
Auten, P.L., 117, 118, 120, 144
Baillet, Frank, 117, 118
Bancroft, Frank, 19
Bausewine, George, 188
Beaumont, Clarence, 128, 159, 166, 174
Beckley, Jake, 11, 115
Bowerman, Frank, 205
Boyle, Eddie, 23
Bradley, Gov., 15
Bransfield, Kitty, 126, 142
Bresnahan, Roger, 182, 202, 203, 205
Bridwell, Al, 215, 217, 218
Brodie, Walter, 67
Brown, Mordecai, 204, 222
Browning, Pete, 2
Bruce, John, 193
Brush, John, T., 37, 43, 56, 67, 88, 89, 102, 104, 133, 135, 137, 141-145, 148, 150, 152, 154, 157, 158, 163, 167, 175, 176, 184, 188-190, 198, 199, 207, 219, 223, 228, 232
Buckenberger, A.C., 103
Burke, Jimmy, 142
Burkett, Jesse, 159
Cain, George W., 231, 235
Camp, Jas. B., 115
Carey, Scoops, 55, 62

Cassidy, Pete, 25
Caylor, Miss, 233
Chadwick, Henry, 18
Chance, Frank, 136, 192, 204, 205, 211, 215, 217, 218, 219, 221, 222
Chase, Hal, 224
Chapman, (captain), 48
Chesbro, Jack, 110, 112, 113, 142
Clark, (unknown), 64
Clarke, Dad, 64
Clarke, Fred, 19, 20, 21, 23, 25, 30, 32, 33, 37-39, 41-43, 46, 47, 49-51, 54, 57, 58, 59, 61, 62-65, 69, 70, 76, 77, 79, 81, 82, 83, 85-88, 92, 94, 95, 96, 97, 100-103, 106-110, 112, 113, 115, 120-122, 124-126, 128-129, 131, 139, 166, 174, 182, 183, 188, 202, 203, 213, 214, 238
Clarke, Miss, 94
Clausen, Fred, 24
Clements, Jack, 37
Clingman, Billy, 47, 55, 62
Collins, James, 10, 13, 15, 17, 174
Connor, Jim, 37
Conrad, (groundskeeper), 22, 40
Conroy, Wid, 138, 142
Cooley, Dick, 107
Corbett, Joe, 50
Crawford, Sam, 170
Cross, Lave, 37
Cunningham, Bert, 63, 79, 97, 126, 127
Davis, George, 127, 157, 158, 159, 162, 163, 167

Davis, Henry, 115
Lefty, Davis, 142
Dahlen, Bill, 205
Davis, Ralph S., 201, 203
Deal, (unknown), 98
Delahanty, Ed, 65, 157, 158
Devlin, Art, 205
Dewey, (mascot), 64, 65
Dexter, Charlie, 25, 32, 46, 47, 79, 85
Dillard, Pat, 55, 62
Dinneen, Bill, 109
Dixon, Henry, 55
Doe, Fred, 173
Doheny, Ed, 161
Dolan, Joe, 37, 38, 39, 47
Donlin, Mike, 126
Dooin, Goldfish, 177
Douglass, Will W., 115
Dovey, George, 229, 230, 232, 236
Dowling, Pete, 77, 85
Doyle, Jack, 18, 48, 50, 51, 97
Dreher, Charles, 18, 20, 27, 38, 58, 63, 64, 78, 81, 93, 98
Dreyfuss, Barney, 3, 4, 5, 16, 27, 36, 38, 49, 78, 81-86, 88, 89, 90-98, 100-102, 108, 113-115, 117-119, 121, 124, 131, 132, 134, 136-139, 142-145, 149, 153, 172, 180, 183-187, 189, 190, 228, 230, 233, 236
Duffy, Hugh, 18, 121
Durham, Israel, 235
Ebbets, Charles, 172, 230, 236
Ehret, Phil, 55
Elberfeld, Kid, 157, 158, 163
Ely, Fred, 121, 122
Emslie, Bob, 116, 198, 204, 215, 220
Ernest, (unknown), 46
Eustace, Frank, 25, 28

Evans, Billy, 205
Evers, Johnny, 192, 212, 214, 216, 218
Farrell, Frank, 170
Fay, Johnny, 129, 200
Flaherty, Patsy, 97
Flick Elmer, 65, 106, 110, 158, 170
Flower, Roswell P., 172
Fox, (unknown), 98
Fraser, Chic, 24, 28, 37, 38, 40, 44, 65, 80
Freedman, Andrew, 20, 72-74, 80, 84, 102, 133, 135, 142, 157
Fuller, Shorty, 55, 62
Gans, Ed, 115
Gardner, Cuppy, 14
Gettinger, Tom, 14
Gibson, George, 203
Gilday, Walter Dr., 234
Gill, Warren, 213, 214
Gleason, Kid, 63
Goebel, William, 100, 101
Gould, (unknown), 98
Grant, Grace, 193
Griffith, Clark, 48
Gwilliam, Shad, 180
Halligan, Jocko, 11
Hammer, Casper, 27, 98
Hanlon, Ned, 40, 73, 80, 84, 88, 92, 111-113
Hart, James, 88, 96, 97, 117, 130, 134, 135, 144, 145, 150, 177, 189, 190, 197, 228, 236
Hassamaer, Bill, 14
Hemming, George, 45
Herman, Art, 40
Herrmann, Garry, 141, 144, 145, 149-151, 153, 154, 159, 165, 170-172, 174, 180, 190, 193, 194, 199, 210, 212, 231, 232,

235, 237
Herndon, Lamar, 115
Heydler, John, 11, 187, 197, 200, 230
Higgins, J.J., 233
Hill, Bill, 24, 40, 47, 55
Hinton, Professor, 34
Hofman, Solly, 216, 218
Holliday, James, 161
Holmes, Ducky, 20, 22, 25, 26, 37, 41, 42, 72-74, 102, 192
Holt, (Rev.), 77
Hoy, Billy, 55, 59, 61, 62, 65, 66, 76, 77, 87, 88, 92, 94, 95, 97, 101
Hurst, Tim, 116
Inks, Bert, 14
Jennings, Hugh, 3, 10, 11, 48, 60, 92, 116, 238
Johnson, Abbie, 40, 46
Johnson, Ban, 119, 122, 139, 140, 141-144, 146-150, 155-158, 159, 162-165, 170-173, 175, 189, 191, 192, 205, 210, 223
Johnstone, Jim, 184, 198, 211, 223
Joyce, Bill, 65
Keeler, Willie, 116, 174
Kelley, Joe, 11, 48, 65, 111, 112, 116, 160, 162, 174, 176, 177, 186
Kelley, Mike, 97
Kerr, W.W., 117, 112, 144
Kilfoyl, John, 143
Kililea, Henry, 149
King Louis XVI of France, 1
Kittredge, Malachi, 91
Klem, Bill, 205, 223
Kling, Johnny, 174
Knowles, Fred, 152, 171
Lajoie, Nap, 50, 65, 106, 110, 162, 174

Lally, Bud, 32, 33, 33
Latimer, Tacks, 97, 124
Lauder, Billy, 161
Leach, Tommy, 75-77, 86, 97, 120, 121, 126, 127, 142, 152, 238
Leever, Sam, 77, 104, 106, 110, 112, 113, 119, 129
Long, Herman, 13
Lowe, Bobby, 136
Lowery, Anna M., 77
Lush, Johnny, 193
Lynch, Mike, 182
Lynch, Tom, 12, 45, 46, 50, 65, 72, 73
Mack, Connie, 8, 18, 20, 62, 113, 119, 121, 122, 188
Madison, Art, 98
Magee, (Lieutenant), 165
Magee, Sherry 65, 77, 91, 92
Mahaffy, Lou, 55, 62
Mathewson, Christy, 110, 124, 127, 152, 190, 193, 204, 210, 215, 218, 222
Matthis, Robert W., 84
McCarthy, Jack, 175
McCloskey, Manager, 6, 7, 13, 14, 15, 19, 22-24, 26, 29
McCormick, Moose, 215, 218
McCreery, Tom, 14, 18, 20, 30, 37, 38, 39, 41, 49
McDermott, Mike, 15, 17, 48
McDonald, Jim, 48, 76
McFarlan, 49
McGann, Dan, 38, 39, 114, 181, 186, 205
McGinnity, Joe, 111, 112, 174, 194, 195, 204, 216
McGraw, John, 10, 11, 12, 33, 45, 46, 47, 48, 51, 58, 64, 67, 69, 70, 91, 116, 120, 122, 126, 158, 160, 162, 175, 182-188, 194,

198, 203-205, 207, 211, 212, 218-220, 222
McGunnigle, William, 29, 30, 33, 36, 39
McLaughlin, Edward, 227
McLaughlin, Tom, 11
McMahon, Sadie, 45
Meakin, George, 14
Mercer, Win, 110
Merkle, Fred, 207, 208, 215-220, 223, 230, 236
Miller, Fog Horn, 20
George, Miller, 29, 30
Miller, Will, 10, 24
Moran, Gus, 154
Morrison, Jack, 161
Muldoon, Professor, 210
Murphy, Charles W., 189, 194, 212, 213, 228, 229, 232, 236
Murphy, Morgan, 107
Murray, Billy, 236
Murray, umpire, 14
Nance, Doc, 55, 62, 63
Neal, William, 27
Nellis, James, 122
Newman, Harry, 131
Newton, (unknown), 62
Nichols, Kid, 113
Nichols, (Umpire), 64
O'Brien, John, 30
O'Brien, (senator), 108
O'Brien, Tom, 98, 120
Ochiltree, Tom, 146
O'Connor, Jack, 108, 121, 138, 141, 142
O'Day, Hank, 49, 69, 106, 127, 138, 154, 189, 192, 194-197, 202, 204, 205, 212, 213, 214, 215, 217-219
O'Rourke, Tim, 3
Orth, Al. 158
Pearson, (undertaker), 47

Peitz, Heinie, 116, 162, 194, 195
Pfeffer, Fred, 7, 9
Pfeister, Jack, 215, 222
Phelps, Zach, 89, 132
Phillippe, Deacon, 75, 77, 85, 90, 97, 113, 121, 124, 127, 166, 238
Phyle, Bill, 127
Pickering, Oliver, 37
Potter, James, 196, 197
Powers, Patrick, 163, 165, 236
Pulliam, Harry, 4, 5, 7, 9-20, 22, 23, 25-34, 36-47, 49, 51, 52, 54, 55, 57, 61, 64, 65, 68, 71, 74-78, 80, 82, 83, 85, 88, 91, 93-96, 98-109, 111-121, 123, 124, 125, 127-139, 141-150, 152-169, 171-213, 218-220, 223, 224, 227-239
Rhines, Billy, 14
Ritchey, Claude, 55, 62, 63, 97, 98, 126
Robinson, Wilbert, 11
Robison, Frank de Hass, 44, 56, 70, 71, 88, 140, 150
Rogers, James, 36, 39, 40, 41, 43, 46
Rusie, Amos, 65, 74
Russell, Harry, 200, 231
Ryder, Jack, 220
Schneier, Bill, 180
Schreckengost, Ossie, 51
Sheckard, Jimmy, 222
Sheldon, (Justice), 185, 186
Sheridan, Jack, 31, 125, 189
Shettsline, Bill, 197
Shibe, Ben, 143
Shrady, (coroner), 233
Shugart, Frank, 14
Slagle, Jimmy, 213
Smith, Heinie, 55
Snyder, Pop, 11, 12, 63

Sockalexis, Louis, 44
Soden, Arthur, 15, 135, 189
Somers, Charles, 141, 144, 149
Spalding, Albert, 133, 134
Spies, Harry, 14
Steinfeldt, Harry, 116, 192
Stenzel, Jake, 47, 48
Stuart, Bill, 206
Stucky, Dr., 15, 22, 29, 34, 39, 40, 58, 64
Swartwood, Ed, 91
Tannehill, Jesse, 108, 113, 121, 122, 124, 142
Taylor, Harry, 3
Taylor, Jack, 181
Taylor, Luther, 127
Taylor, O.P., 38
Tebeau, Oliver, 71
Tebeau, Patsy, 18, 122
Temple, W.C., 131, 134, 135, 144
Tenney, Fred, 174, 207, 215
Tinker, 136, 138, 192, 215, 216
Treadway, George, 31
Trost, Mike, 14
Twain, Mark, 225
Twineham, Arthur, 55
Tyler, Henry, S., mayor, 8
Van Derbeck, George, 78
Van Haltren, George, 161
Varden, (unknown), 109
Voorhees, Cy, 130
Waddell, Rube, 51, 54, 62, 77, 85, 87, 93, 94, 96, 97, 102-109, 111-114, 116, 122, 124, 130, 159
Wagner, Earl, 67
Wagner, Hans, 49-51, 54, 59, 62, 65, 75, 76, 77, 85, 87, 92, 95, 96, 97, 104, 109, 110, 113, 120, 121, 124, 125, 129, 130, 138, 161, 174, 186, 207, 210, 211, 235, 238

Wall, Berry, 139
Wallace, Roderick, 114
Ward, John Montgomery, 29, 158, 189
Watkins, W.H., 38
Watterson, Henry, 232
Weaver, (mayor), 63
Wehmhoff, Henry, 200
Werden, Perry, 40
Whiteside, I.F., 115
Wilson, Bill, 46, 62
Wilson, Owen, 212, 213, 214
Wiltse, Hooks, 124
Wolverton, Harry, 158
Woods, Walter, 82, 97
Young, Cy, 14, 44, 103, 104, 114, 166, 174, 175
Young, Nick, 14, 56, 94, 123, 133, 145-148, 191
Zimmer, Chief, 97, 113, 123

Made in the USA
Middletown, DE
21 July 2021